Essentials of Commercial Real Estate

DATE DUE

Joseph L. Petrole, CCIM, MAI

Dearborn
Real Estate Education

This publication is designed to provide accurate and authoritative information in regard to the subject matter covered. It is sold with the understanding that the publisher is not engaged in rendering legal, accounting, or other professional service. If legal advice or other expert assistance is required, the services of a competent professional should be sought.

President: Roy Lipner

Vice President of Product Development & Publishing: Evan Butterfield

Managing Editor: Kate DeVivo

Editorial Project Manager: Amanda Rahn

Director of Production: Daniel Frey

Production Editor: Caitlin Ostrow

Creative Director: Lucy Jenkins

Typesetter: Janet Schroeder

Published by Dearborn™ Real Estate Education

30 South Wacker Drive

Chicago, IL 60606-7481

(312) 836-4400

www.dearbornre.com

Printed in the United States of America

07 08 09 10 9 8 7 6 5 4 3 2

Library of Congress Cataloging-in-Publication Data

Petrole, Joseph L.

  Essentials of commercial real estate / Joseph L. Petrole.—1st ed.

    p. cm.

  Includes bibliographical references.

  ISBN-13: 978-1-4195-2208-6

  ISBN-10: 1-4195-2208-6

1. Commercial real estate—United States. I. Title.

  HD1393.58.U6P48 2006

  333.33068—dc22

2006018951

DEDICATION

This book is dedicated to those persons who really made a difference in my life—my entire family, who patiently demonstrated what is truly important, especially:

My mother, Rosemary, for providing a fabulous start in life;

My brother, Louis, for encouraging me to focus beyond my personal comfort zone;

My cousin, Louis, for inspiring me to view the world from mountain tops; and

My grandfather, Louis, who prophetically told me "Someday you will understand . . . ."

CONTENTS

NOTES TO THE READER

The author believes that at least as many women as men will read and benefit from this material. However, for the sake of simplicity, the terms *he* and *him* were employed throughout the text, as opposed to *he or she* and *him and her*. The terms describing the individuals in this text are referring to both women and men.

If you have any suggestions or comments, I would appreciate you contacting me.

You may e-mail me at

jpetrole@petrogroup.net

Visit our Web site at

www.petrogroup.net

PREFACE

"Before you begin to 'crunch numbers' for an investment decision about commercial property, you need to have a command of the facts that justify the real estate decision in the first place."

This reference material is custom designed for both those active in commercial real estate and those who need to know about the industry. This information-packed referenced material will provide an insightful overview of the essentials of the commercial real estate industry that will *immediately* benefit you and your clients. The caliber of the information and the presentation is "best quality" and draws upon experience and some of the most prestigious references available anywhere at any price.

The reference material presented herein is a high-quality ±175-page text plus a ±50-page addendum that is "reader friendly" with numerous tables, charts, and exhibits, along with a *useable* glossary of terms. The manual includes both technical definitions and the business jargon that is the "language of real estate." Each chapter is designed to build upon the previous chapter and is presented in a format that provides key terminology, an overview, learning objectives, chapter material, a summary, and review and application questions that will reinforce the readers' learning experience. Readers will obtain a clear understanding of both commercial real estate and sophisticated investment methodology employed by top institutional investors that they can *put into practice* immediately.

Following is a chapter preview highlighting how *the reader will benefit* from this material.

■ Chapter 1: Commercial Real Estate as a Business

Chapter 1 provides an overview of the core components of the real estate industry as they apply to commercial property. Commercial real estate brokerage is introduced first, along with agency and fiduciary relationships. The role of a real estate broker is discussed, and becomes the foundation for combining additional opportunities within the commercial real estate industry. The opportunities include those provided by the financing industry, the appraisal industry, the investment services industry, the counseling industry, and other related industries. Ultimately, the continued combination and integration of these services results in the creation of yet another core business—real estate investment banking.

A commercial real estate sale is introduced as a transaction involving a seller and buyer who are negotiating a deal. Because there are different perspectives in a transaction, a commercial real estate transaction is presented from a seller's perspective, a buyer's perspective, and a deal perspective.

■ Chapter 2: Commercial Property Types and Office Properties

Chapter 2 introduces commercial property types. This chapter then discusses in great detail office properties. Important trends impacting office buildings are discussed. The purpose and variation in office building classifications are presented. The evolution of building locations and office building design are evaluated. The need and methods of proper office building measurement are discussed. Office building rent and expense standards are calculated. Simply explaining these terms is both intricate and complex and the need for such explanations becomes obvious.

As new terms are introduced, the "language of real estate" begins to take shape. Calculations for determining the various types of rent and tenant pro rata allocations are presented. The unique qualities of each property type provide justification for commercial property specialization in brokerage and other real estate professions.

■ Chapter 3: Retail Properties

Chapter 3 discusses retail properties in great detail. Trends impacting retail buildings are discussed. The wide variety in classification of retailers is introduced. The demands of users of the retail space are presented. These concepts provide the foundation for a discussion of the different types of shopping centers, including how they draw power from clustering and key anchor tenants.

A retail property's location is presented not only in absolute physical terms, but in terms of an economic trade area as well. Trade areas are further refined into primary and secondary trade areas. Complementing a viable trade area is a viable building design. A building design's three main criteria—site characteristics, exterior building characteristics, and interior building characteristics—are considered. The need for accurate building measurement are presented from both the owner/landlord's and tenant's perspective. Calculations and examples for determining a building's size, rent, expenses, and pro rata allocations are provided.

■ Chapter 4: Commercial Real Estate as an Investment

Chapter 4 introduces real estate investment. Commencing from the basic answer to what real estate investors expect, the decision to invest in real estate is presented as a trade-off between its relative advantages and disadvantages. The good news is that these advantages and disadvantages are measurable. As such, the decision to invest in property can be set within a framework, which allows for a systematic and quantitative decision-making process that assists in removing guesswork, emotion, and unsupported conjecture. These measurable advantages and disadvantages are discussed in detail.

As we explore this decision-making process, numerous new terms are introduced. The language of real estate investment continues to take shape. The need for the application of practical business and financial mathematics comes to the forefront of the discussion. Multistep calculations for determining cash flow and taxable income are introduced. The ability to quantify monetarily the advantages and disadvantages of investing are seen as fundamental to the decision-making process.

Chapter 5: Market Analysis for Commercial Real Estate

Chapter 5 introduces market analysis as a core tool for both investors and decision makers in real estate. Market analysis provides fundamental answers to investors' questions and concerns about their established investment objectives and goals. The various steps in the preparation of a market analysis are presented in detail. The interdependence between economic principles and market forces that impact market analysis are emphasized.

Market analysis is presented as both a self-contained tool for investors and part of the foundation of other, more complex forms of analysis. It is important to complete one form of analysis as the foundation for the next, more complex form of analysis. These analyses form a continuum of analysis, which provides a great deal of insight into the historical, current, and projected market conditions for real estate.

It is the author's intent that this material open new vistas of opportunity for readers of this text. If readers are able to move closer to their goals, the author will have accomplished his objectives.

ABOUT THE AUTHOR

Joseph L. Petrole, CCIM, MAI, is a seasoned real estate professional with over 25 years of experience in the industry. He is principal of PetroGroup Realty Advisors, Inc. ("PetroGroup"). PetroGroup was established in 1997 to serve the commercial real estate industry. PetroGroup's primary objective is to provide the highest quality and results-oriented real estate services to investors and institutions in the areas of valuation advisory services (VAS), which include litigation support services, market analysis, and specialized services; transaction services, which include property sale, acquisition, and investment services; and capital market services, which include the identification and delivery of debt and equity to clients. These three areas of service constitute the core of what the industry has come to define as real estate investment banking services.

Since 2003, Joseph has served as director of Beacon Realty Advisors, Inc. ("Beacon"), a Coconut Grove, Florida–based real estate brokerage and mortgage brokerage services firm that specializes in real estate investments and capital markets services to investors, entrepreneurs, and institutions. Prior to joining Beacon as a director, Joseph was director of resources and a real estate investment banker with Aztec Group ("Aztec"), one of Florida's most successful and respected privately held real estate investment banking firms. During his more than four-year tenure with Aztec, Joseph participated in a wide range of investment banking services including the positioning and closing of investment-grade real estate transactions; analysis, underwriting, packaging, and marketing; and the identification, interpretation, and utilization of market information that directly influences transactions and capital market activities.

Joseph's career also included his role as a senior vice president and senior manager at Appraisal and Real Estate Economic Associates, Inc. ("AREEA"), one of Florida's most successful and respected privately held real estate valuation advisory services and consulting firms, where he spent over 12 years. During that time Joseph participated in a wide range of valuation advisory services including valuations, acquisition due diligence services, litigation support services, and appraisal review services. Joseph also has a formidable corporate financial and accounting background gained during 4 years as a senior financial analyst and cost accountant at Gang-Nail Systems, Inc., a wholly owned subsidiary of Redland Braas Corporation, a European-based multinational corporation providing vertically integrated real estate property solutions including design, engineering, truss fabrication, and building materials throughout the world.

Joseph has had the opportunity to participate in the marketing, sale, financing, consulting, and valuation of high-profile properties and developments in the United States and the Caribbean, and has provided litigation support services to some of the most prominent investors, entrepreneurs, and institutions.

Joseph earned a BBA in finance and real estate from the University of Miami, where he also received the William G. Heuson award for his academic achievements. He has also earned the prestigious MAI designation from the Appraisal Institute, and the prestigious CCIM designation from the CCIM Institute. Joseph is a practicing Florida-licensed real estate broker, a practicing Florida certified appraiser, a practicing Florida-licensed real estate instructor, and a graduate of the Dale Carnegie School for salesmanship.

ACKNOWLEDGMENTS

The author gratefully acknowledges all of the sources of information employed in the development of this material. The sources are specifically referenced within the narrative sections of this text. Special acknowledgment goes to those who reviewed early drafts of this book, including:

Herbert S. Fecker, Jr. CCIM, licensed real estate broker and instructor

George Grierson

James Howze, Advanced Career Training, Inc.

Jim McCloskey, American Real Estate College

chapter one

COMMERCIAL REAL ESTATE AS A BUSINESS

1

■ Key Terminology

agency relationships	components of capital	investment banker
appraisal	consulting	loan-to-value ratio
commercial real estate	debt-coverage ratio	negative leverage
commercial real estate business	fiduciary relationship	positive leverage

■ Overview

Chapter 1, Commercial Real Estate as a Business, provides an overview of the core components of the real estate industry as they apply to commercial property. Commercial real estate brokerage is introduced first, along with agency and fiduciary relationships. The role of a real estate broker is discussed and becomes the foundation for combining additional opportunities within the commercial real estate industry. The opportunities include those provided by the financing industry, the appraisal industry, the investment services industry, the counseling industry, and other related industries. Ultimately, the continued combination and integration of these services results in the creation of yet another core business—real estate investment banking.

A commercial real estate sale is introduced as a transaction involving a seller and buyer who are negotiating a deal. Because there are different perspectives in a transaction, a commercial real estate transaction is presented from a seller's perspective, a buyer's perspective, and a deal perspective.

■ Learning Objectives

After completing this chapter, the reader should be able to accomplish the following:

1. Explain what *commercial real estate* is
2. List the *four general service lines* within the commercial real estate business
3. Identify the role of a *commercial real estate broker*
4. Describe the advantages of *combining opportunities* in the commercial real estate industry
5. Discuss the reasons for *financing* real estate
6. Explain the difference between a *mortgage broker*, *mortgage banker*, and *correspondent lender*
7. Describe the concept of *financial leverage*
8. Explain the difference between *cost*, *price*, and *value*
9. Define what a *real estate investment banker* is
10. Describe a sales transaction from the perspective of the *seller*, *buyer*, and *deal*

■ The Commercial Real Estate Business

Commercial Real Estate

Commercial real estate is any real estate that is required for the operation of a business enterprise, or as a part of a business. For example, if a group of physicians decided to form a medical services business enterprise, they would require real estate, consisting of land and improvements, at a specific location to provide professional medical services to their patients. In this circumstance, the real estate is required for the operation of the business enterprise. Because the real estate is required for the operation of a business enterprise, it is considered a specific type of real estate—commercial real estate. There are as many types of commercial real estate as there are business enterprises that require such real estate for the operation of their business.

Commercial Real Estate as a Business

The concept of commercial real estate services as a business enterprise is not the same concept as commercial real estate. A **commercial real estate business** is any business enterprise that provides the professional commercial real estate services to the buyers, sellers, and others who interact within the commercial real estate marketplace. For example, consider the group of physicians who are going into business. One important decision the medical services business enterprise would have to make is whether to lease or own the medical office space it would occupy. If it were decided that the medical business enterprise should own the medical space it would occupy, the medical business enterprise would now have to interact with some of the commercial real estate professionals and enterprises found within the real estate industry; a listing or buyer's broker, for example.

Commercial Real Estate Industry

The commercial real estate business consists of the varied professions that have developed a specialization within the commercial real estate industry and possibly within a commercial property type as well. These real estate professionals are part of business enterprises themselves and include, but are not necessarily limited to, the specializations of:

- Commercial real estate brokerage firms
- Commercial real estate mortgage brokerage and mortgage banking firms
- Commercial real estate lenders, such as financial institutions
- Commercial real estate appraisal and valuation analysis firms
- Commercial real estate counseling and advisory firms
- Commercial real estate asset, property, and leasing management firms
- Commercial real estate investment firms
- Commercial real estate law firms, including contract, litigation, and tax law
- Commercial real estate accounting firms, including audit and tax accounting
- Commercial real estate–related businesses such as surveyors; planners, design, and architectural; environmental, structural, electrical, and mechanical engineers; and pest control, landscape design, and maintenance firms

One important characteristic of all of these business professions is that they are all in the same industry, the commercial real estate industry. Another important characteristic of these business professions is that they combine a significant amount of expertise with a specialized commercial real estate service. Perhaps the most important characteristic of these business professions is that they are all *interdependent*. Accordingly, the commercial real estate industry, which is comprised of all of these business professions, is very large indeed.

These specialized commercial real estate services also tend to cluster within larger groupings, or "service lines" (see Table 1.1). By grouping theses businesses, their larger service lines become clear, as follows:

1. Real estate *sales* and property brokerage
2. Real estate *advisory* and counseling
3. Real estate *financing* and mortgage brokerage
4. Real estate–*related* services

The interdependent nature of these service lines is evident when one attempts to "place the service into a box," because it is natural that one service line will seamlessly integrate into another. For example, part of transaction representation services may include counseling and advisory. Part of legal services may include counsel regarding how a purchase or sale should be structured for tax purposes. The valuation conclusion of a real estate appraisal may influence the type and amount of financing. The type and amount of financing available may influence how a purchase or sale is structured. Part of management services may include accounting services.

Table 1.1

Service Lines within the Commercial Real Estate Business

Sales	Advisory	Finance	Related
Transaction representation	Real estate counsel	Mortgage brokerage	Appraisal/valuation
Seller representation	Law and tax planning	Mortgage banking	Asset management and leasing
Buyer representation	Financial investments and strategies	Correspondent lenders	Accounting
	Property planning, expansion, and design	Financial institution	Surveyors and other contractors

Although these seemingly independent professions can be grouped into their larger service lines, it is also important to see these real estate businesses as part of a "network" where each profession is at least partially dependent upon the other for success. Real estate transactions are based upon a multitude of information required for the decision-making process. Due to the dynamic nature of real estate transactions, many decisions are made based on an iterative process, requiring a repetitive analysis of changing information creating the need for the rapid acquisition of accurate information, which can be correctly analyzed and interpreted for the decision-making process. As an asset increases in size, the transaction tends to become more complex and the information-gathering process more involved. This is illustrated in Figure 1.1.

A user of these services may call upon any of these businesses at any time. However, all of these businesses are normally utilized during a real estate transaction, which occurs within the real estate market. Because real estate markets are considered inefficient markets, real estate transactions, which

Figure 1.1

Service Lines within the Commercial Real Estate Business

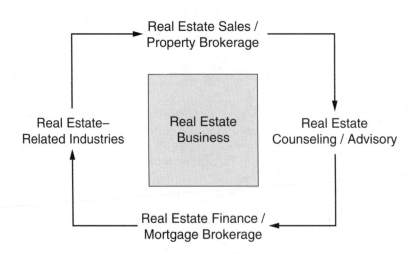

occur within those markets, by definition, are also inefficient. This is why the *coordination* of all the unique commercial real estate business services and specializations during a real estate transaction are so important. As a result, the varied professionals can be considered analogous to team players. But who is in control of the team players, the transaction, and the "deal"?

A Sports Analogy—Team Players, the Playing Field, and the Game

The purpose of assembling the real estate team is to execute a real estate transaction game plan. That transaction game plan is the strategy that is expected to result in a successfully executed *real estate transaction*. The purpose of the strategy is to have a framework to complete a transaction that fulfills the investment goals of the buyer or seller of commercial real estate. It is the buyer or seller of commercial real estate who *assembles the team* and pays the team bills. The playing field is the real estate market, where buyers and sellers gather to exchange real property rights for valuable consideration such as money. Accordingly, it is the buyer or seller who is in control of his team players. The team players provide guidance to the buyer or seller, and should execute their specific team function in a *coordinated* effort. The buyer or seller delegates some or all of his responsibilities to the team members qualified to accept those responsibilities. The delegation of these responsibilities creates a relationship with legal implications known as an **agency relationship.**

Agency Relationships

Agency is a relationship created when one person, the principal, delegates to another, the agent, the right to act on his behalf in business transactions and to exercise some degree of discretion while so acting. An agency gives rise to a fiduciary or statutory relationship and imposes on the agent, as a representative of the principal, certain duties, obligations, and a high standard of good faith and loyalty. An agency may be a *general agency*, as when a principal gives a property manager the power to manage a real estate project on behalf of the principal on a continuing basis, or it may be a *special agency*, such as the standard listing contract wherein the broker is employed only to find a ready, willing, and able buyer and is neither authorized to sell the property nor bind the principal to any contract for the sale of the property.

The Commercial Real Estate Brokerage Business

The commercial real estate brokerage business is that aspect of the real estate business that is concerned with bringing together buyers and sellers, and completing real estate transactions. Generally, brokers and their associates will represent a principal, who can be either someone who wants to sell a property or someone who wants to buy a property. For this service, the broker is usually compensated by commission based on a percentage of the gross sales price of the property. This commission is paid directly to the broker—or brokerage company—who then may compensate the participating sales associates according to a prearranged schedule.

A *broker* is a person who performs real estate services for another party for compensation. A broker is an intermediary between parties to a transaction. A real estate broker is a properly licensed individual, corporation, or partnership who for valuable consideration or a promise of valuable consideration serves as a special agent to others to facilitate a transaction involving real property. A broker can accept or reject agency relationships with principals. Brokers represent their principals and accept the fiduciary responsibility of exercising care, skill, and integrity in carrying out their instructions. Legal restrictions are imposed on brokers by legislative action, and federal, state, and local fair housing laws place new social obligations on them.

To qualify as a real estate broker, one must meet the requirements set forth in the real estate license law of the state in which one intends to practice. A broker is permitted by law to hire others to assist the brokerage in representing its clients. However a broker is the primary agent in any agency relationship with a buyer or a seller. This is true even though the salespeople, who are agents of the broker, have most of the direct contact with the buyer or the seller client.

A *broker associate* is a real estate classification used in some states to describe a person who is qualified to be issued a license as a broker but who still works for and is supervised by another broker and accordingly operates as a salesperson in the employ of another. Depending on the state, a broker associate may also be referred to as broker-salesperson, associate broker, or affiliate broker.

A *sales associate* is a person who performs real estate services for compensation, but who does so under the direction, control, or management of a licensed real estate broker. The sales associate is employed, either directly or indirectly, by a licensed broker. A sales associate cannot act as an agent for another person, nor can he list or advertise property under his own name. The sales associate can carry out only those responsibilities assigned to him by the supervising broker. Depending on the state, a sales associate may also be referred to as salesperson or associate licensee.

Agency Relationships and Commercial Real Estate Brokerage

As a matter of normal business practice, commercial real estate brokers may provide any of the broadly defined areas that constitute real estate services. During the course of providing these services, a legally based relationship with specified responsibilities is formed between a broker and his client. The type of legal relationship established between the broker and the broker's client is referred to as a type of agency or fiduciary relationship. Transactions usually cause legally based responsibilities to be formed between a broker and his client. This client, who actually employs the broker to perform some real estate–related service, may be referred to as the broker's *principal.*

A principal is the person who engages the broker to perform a service of real estate. The principal is the broker's employer. The broker is authorized by the principal to fulfill the services that the principal has requested. As such, the broker acts on behalf of the principal. This type of relationship is known as an agency relationship.

In the typical real estate transaction, a broker who represents the seller is called the *listing broker*. The listing broker is the agent of the seller. This also includes the associate licensees working for the listing broker. The broker who works with the buyer is called various terms including the *selling broker*, the *cooperating broker*, or the *buyer's broker*. The selling broker is either the agent of the buyer or the subagent of the seller. This also includes the associate licensees working for the selling broker.

In order to simplify and disclose agency relationships to the general public, many states have adopted agency disclosure laws requiring a licensee to disclose early in the transaction the party the licensee represents. The agency relationship must then be confirmed in writing on the contract between the buyer and seller. States have also created classifications of agency, such as *limited agent*, *designated agent*, *transaction coordinator*, and *facilitator*.

In some cases there is only one broker involved. Some states have adopted an agency relationship that has designated a category of service where the agent represents *both* the buyer and seller in the transaction as a *dual agent*. Other states have adopted a nonagency relationship known as a *transaction agent*, a designated category of service where the broker represents *neither* the buyer nor the seller in the transaction, treating both as customers.

Agency relationships create the need for trust and confidence between the principal and the broker. This need for trust and confidence increases during a transaction because more sensitive and privileged information tends to be disclosed as a transaction evolves. A moral obligation develops between the principal and the broker to honor this relationship of trust and confidence. A legal obligation also develops. The trust and confidence that results in a moral and legal obligation between the principal and the broker is called a **fiduciary relationship.**

Fiduciary Relationships and Commercial Real Estate Brokerage

A *fiduciary* relationship implies a position of trust and confidence. The term *fiduciary* describes the faithful relationship owed by a broker and the broker's associates to his principal, or an attorney to his client. The fiduciary owes a level of allegiance with commensurate obligations to the client that is influenced by the type of agency relationship. Among these obligations are the use of skill, care, and diligence; the duty to account for all money; loyalty and obedience; and full disclosure. When there is a breach of any of these fiduciary duties, the principal can usually bring civil action for damages.

Because of the close personal relationship between broker as an agent and seller as a principal, the broker often learns certain confidential information about the principal and his financial situation. The broker cannot disclose this information, even after the transaction is completed and the fiduciary relationship terminated. One reason it is so difficult to represent both parties in a real estate transaction is the conflict of interest that arises for the broker, who has a duty to keep confidential any information learned from the principal and also a duty to disclose all pertinent information to the principal.

Because the broker has an agency and fiduciary relationship with the principal, and is expected to close the deal, a proficient broker will strive to stay in control of the deal. The broker knows that the ultimate responsibility for the success of the transaction is his. Accordingly, it is the principal who strives to stay in control of the team players. The broker, at the principal's direction, strives to stay in control of the transaction.

Licensure Requirements and Commercial Real Estate Brokerage

License laws are enacted by all 50 states, the District of Columbia, and certain Canadian provinces that provide the United States with the authority to license and regulate the activities of real estate brokers, salespeople, and appraisers. Any person who has a valid real estate or appraiser license is considered a *licensee*. A real estate licensee can generally be a salesperson or broker, active or inactive, or an individual, corporation, or partnership. However, only individuals can be licensed appraisers. Details of the law vary from state to state, however, the main provision of each remains the same. Many states' license laws are based on the pattern law recommended by the National Association of REALTORS®. The general purposes of license law are to (1) protect the public from dishonest or incompetent real estate practitioners; (2) prescribe certain standards and qualifications for licensing; (3) raise the standards of the real estate profession; and (4) protect licensed real estate brokers and salespeople from unfair or improper competition.

All states require license applicants to pass an examination designed to test their real estate knowledge and competency. Sizable portions of such exams are based on the state license laws. Licenses or registration certificates are issued to qualified individuals and generally to partnerships and corporations. These licenses are legal permits to operate a real estate brokerage business as described and permitted by the state law. Each state law must be reviewed to determine whether a license is required for such activities as appraising, mortgaging, auctioning, or exchanging real estate.

Usually, anyone who performs any real estate services for another person for compensation of any type must be licensed, unless specifically exempted by law. Compensation may be defined as anything of value or a valuable *consideration* paid, promised, or expected to be paid or received. Valuable consideration distinguishes a contractual obligation from a gift and is negotiated and paid for a promise, including a return promise. The commercial real estate broker's compensation is usually contingent on a success performance basis, and is paid as a percentage of the sale amount, only "if, as, and when" a sale is accomplished.

Generally, within each state, the real estate license law is contained in the state statutes. It identifies the real estate services that require a state real estate license to perform as a broker, broker-salesperson, or salesperson. State statutes define brokers and others by their license category. One must be licensed in the state in order to perform the services of a real estate broker, broker-salesperson, or salesperson.

All commercial real estate brokers offer real estate services for their clients in expectation of compensation. These services may include, but are not necessarily limited to, (1) the preparation of a comparative market analysis (CMA), and unless other licensing is required by the state, appraisals for non–federally regulated transactions; (2) auctioning; (3) selling; (4) exchanging; (5) buying; (6) renting or providing rental information or rental lists; (7) leasing; and (8) advertising of real estate services.

The Role of a Commercial Real Estate Broker

A buyer or seller may employ the services of a real estate broker to fulfill his investment goals. If so, the broker is given authority so as to fulfill the investment goals of his employer. The broker can be viewed as a team leader, interacting and coordinating with the team members for the purpose of fulfilling the broker's employment obligation, which is to successfully implement a transaction. The broker is also uniquely motivated to ensure that a transaction occurs. With the exception of a mortgage broker or other financier, usually all of the other team members are paid a fee for their professional services and involvement in a transaction process regardless of whether a transaction occurs. However, a broker is compensated for his professional services and involvement in a transaction only if a transaction occurs (i.e., the service is performed).

As an agent for the seller or as a transaction broker, the role of a commercial real estate broker is to understand the seller's disposition objectives, then properly place, price, market, negotiate (as directed), and sell (close) income-producing investment property on behalf of his client, the seller. In other words, *the role of the seller's broker is to successfully sell the property and close the deal.*

As an agent for the buyer or as a transaction broker, the role of a commercial real estate broker is to understand the buyer's acquisition objectives, then locate, secure, negotiate (as directed), and acquire (close) income-producing investment property on behalf of his client, the buyer. In other words, *the role of the buyer's broker is to successfully acquire the property and close the deal.*

Real estate brokers who specialize in commercial property are called commercial brokers, income property brokers, commercial property specialists, and real estate investment bankers, among other terms. To a great extent the knowledge, experience, level of services provided, combination of "skill sets," professional affiliations, property specialization, and focus define what a broker does and, as a result, what that broker may be called. What really defines a commercial real estate broker is the level of services that he provides and the type of property with which he is involved. Commercial brokers usually have developed a specialty in some aspect of commercial real estate properties.

Many commercial brokers have additional licenses, designations, and capabilities. For example, a licensed real estate broker may also have a mortgage broker's license, be an MAI member of the Appraisal Institute, or be a CCIM member of the CCIM Institute, and accordingly also serve the financing, valuation, consulting, or investment advisory needs of his clients during a real estate sales transaction by providing such additional professional services. Most commercial brokers focus on bringing together a buyer and a seller for the purpose of a sale. Other commercial brokers elevate their role to a counselor by providing guidance as to structuring transactions, optimal capital structure (equity and debt financing), investment or joint venture partners, and structuring future transactions with "take out" buyers who contract to acquire a property at a future date and thereby facilitate an owner's future sale and "exit strategy."

Combining Opportunities in Commercial Real Estate

There are many rewarding career opportunities in the commercial real estate brokerage business. The decision to be a "general practitioner" or "specialist" is a personal one. Some commercial brokers have a general brokerage practice, which focuses on many types of income-producing properties. These commercial property types include office property, retail property, industrial property, lodging property, residential multifamily apartment property, mixed-use developments, and vacant land. These properties may be either existing or proposed for development.

Some commercial brokers develop a specialized practice within the business and deal with only one type of income-producing property, for example, office buildings. Other commercial brokers develop a focused practice within a type of income-producing property, for example, medical office buildings.

Usually, as a commercial real estate broker gains experience, his knowledge base of commercial real estate increases. Accordingly, it is almost natural that brokers will gradually gain knowledge about related services such as financing and mortgage brokerage, valuation and investments, counseling and advisory, property leasing and management, and education.

It is clear that commercial real estate brokers could literally customize the development of their business practice simply by adding related services to their core brokerage service. Equally clear is that individuals in related real estate industries such as financing and mortgage brokerage, valuation and investments, counseling and advisory, property leasing and management, education, and so on, can literally customize the development of their business practice simply by adding related services to their core real estate service, thereby "customizing" the development of their business practice.

Figure 1.2 is a graphic presentation of how a commercial real estate purchase and sales transaction necessitates the real estate services of real estate sales and property brokerage, counseling and advisory, finance and mortgage brokerage, valuation, and related services. Varied professions within the real

Figure 1.2

Service Lines Involved in a
Real Estate Transaction

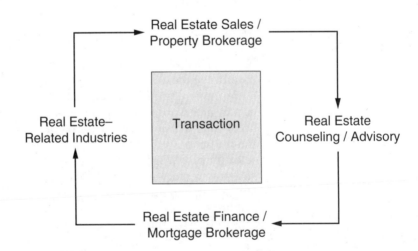

estate industry are available to provide these services. However, it is the combining of these services by talented professionals and firms into a seamless delivery of services that creates added value and economies of scale for all parties involved.

Commercial Real Estate and the Financing Industry

Reasons for Financing

Because approximately 90 percent of all U.S.-based real estate transactions involve some sort of financing, transaction-based financing services are most likely to be required. A commercial real estate broker may also serve the financing needs of his client's purchase in the same transaction by providing the professional services of a commercial mortgage broker. However, regardless of who actually provides the service, having a working knowledge of the essentials of real estate financing benefits all parties involved.

There are six compelling reasons for the use of financing in a real estate transaction:

1. Commercial real estate is capital intensive.
2. Financing increases the capital amount available for a purchase.
3. Financing a property acquisition affects investment returns and leverage.
4. Acquisition financing is repaid by the property's income.
5. The real estate broker is in the ideal position to provide this core service.
6. The real estate broker continues to "add value" to the transaction.

Commercial Real Estate Is Capital Intensive

From a transaction perspective, commercial real estate is "capital intensive" and requires a significant amount of money for purchase. Few investors have the financial capability to buy for cash. Even if the buyer has the capacity to purchase a property for cash, there are other considerations. For example, financing allows a purchaser to acquire and become the owner of real estate without actually owning the capital used to acquire that property. Essentially, he is borrowing someone else's money to acquire his property and achieve his goals.

Financing Increases the Capital Amount Available for a Purchase

Utilizing financing in a real estate purchase has the effect of increasing the capital amount available for the purchase, based on **loan-to-value ratios (LTVs).** A loan-to-value ratio is a basic yet important ratio that expresses the relationship of borrowed funds as a percentage of the value of the property. The term is also known as LTV. From a lender's perspective, the LTV is usually the lesser of the acquisition price or the appraised value of property. Accordingly, the LTV is an important risk measure for lenders because the property is usually pledged as security for the loan. The formula for determining the loan-to-value ratio is:

$$\text{Loan} \div \text{value} = \text{LTV ratio.}$$

Table 1.2

Components of Capital

	Capital Available	Lender Debt	Owner Equity
Acquisition Price	$550,000	$412,500	$137,500
Percent of Price	100%	75%	25%

For example, let's say an investor is considering the acquisition of a ten-unit rental apartment building for a negotiated purchase price of $550,000. The investor has cash equity of $137,500, which represents only 25 percent of the negotiated purchase price. One of the investor's concerns is where the balance of the money to purchase the property will come from. The investor considers employing a first (senior) loan. The property could be acquired with a combination of the investor's cash, which is called equity, and borrowed funds from a lender, which is called debt. If a lender will provide the debt based upon a 75 percent LTV, the lender could provide $412,500 of debt. This is illustrated in Table 1.2, which shows the **components of capital.**

Accordingly, the $550,000 property can be acquired with a combination of $137,500 of owner's equity and $412,500 of lender's debt, which together equal the $550,000 of capital available for the purchase. Capital is the total amount of money from all sources that is available for the acquisition. Utilizing financing in this purchase has the effect of increasing the capital amount available for the purchase from $137,500 to $550,000 based on a 75 percent loan-to-value ratio.

Financing a Property Acquisition Affects Investment Returns and Leverage

Borrowing money for the purpose of financing a property acquisition also has an effect on investment returns. Leverage is the effect that borrowed funds have on investment returns. Leverage may increase or decrease the investor's return that would otherwise be received on an all-cash basis. An investor borrows money for purchases with the expectation that the investment's financial returns will increase. When leverage increases the return to the investor, it is called **positive leverage.** Positive leverage occurs when the rate of return that an investment generates is greater than the interest rate charged by a lender for borrowed funds that are utilized to acquire that investment.

Positive leverage occurs when the rate of return that an investment generates is greater than the interest rate charged for borrowed funds utilized to acquire that investment.

Positive leverage.   For example, let's say that the investor acquired the ten-unit rental for $550,000. The investor anticipates a 10 percent rate of return on the investment, which would equate to $55,000. Furthermore, the $550,000 property was acquired with a combination of $137,500 of owner's equity and $412,500 of lender's debt. If we allocated the 10 percent return to its component parts, the pro-rata return on equity is also 10 percent, or $13,750; and the pro-rata return on debt is 10 percent, or $41,250, as shown in Table 1.3.

Table 1.3

Pro-rata Allocation of Property Investment Return to Debt and Equity

	Capital Available	Lender Debt	Owner Equity
Acquisition Price	$550,000	$412,500	$137,500
Percent of Price	100%	75%	25%
Return $	$55,000	$41,250	$13,750
Return %	10%	10%	10%

However, if a lender provides a loan commitment based on an interest rate of 7 percent and a loan amortization period of 25 years, then the total annual debt service required to service the loan is only $35,000, which would result in positive leverage as shown in Table 1.4.

Positive leverage occurs because the 10 percent rate of return that an investment generates is greater than the 7 percent interest rate charged by a lender for borrowed funds that are utilized to acquire that investment. In this case, the rate of return that the investment generates on an all-cash basis is 10 percent, which is greater than the 8.48 percent total return due the lender (i.e., 7 percent interest rate charged by a lender for borrowed funds plus return of principal) for the debt that is utilized to acquire that investment. Accordingly, the investor expects to make a $6,250 profit on the borrowed funds (i.e., $41,250 less $35,000 equals $6,250 profit). The profit of $6,250 is added to the investor's return of $13,750, which has the effect of increasing the return on the investor's cash portion of the investment from $13,750 to $20,000. It also has the effect of increasing the rate of return on the investor's cash portion of the investment from 10 percent to 14.55 percent.

From the lenders perspective, it receives a 7 percent rate of interest on the outstanding balance, in addition to a return of a portion of the original loan

Table 1.4

Leveraged Allocation of Property Investment Return to Debt and Equity

	Capital Available	Lender Debt	Owner Equity
Acquisition Price	$550,000	$412,500	$137,500
Percent of Price	100%	75%	25%
Return $	$55,000	$35,000	$20,000
Return %	10%	8.48%	14.55%

Table 1.5

Lender's Return of Interest and Principal from Amortizing 7 Percent Loan

Interest Paid	$28,675.09
Principal Reduction	$ 6,310.43
Total Annual Debt Service	$35,000.00 rounded
Original Principal Amount Borrowed	$412,500.00
Total Debt Service as Percent of Original Principal	8.48%

amount. For example, during the first year of this loan, the lender receives a total amount of interest of $28,675.09 plus a total amount of principal reduction of $6,310.43, resulting in total interest and principal payments of $34,985.52, rounded to $35,000, as shown in Table 1.5.

The rate of return to the owner's equity position of 14.55 percent and the rate of return to the lender's debt of 8.48 percent originate from the same rate of return that the investment generates on an all-cash basis of 10 percent. However, these rates of return to equity and debt must be adjusted by their relative percentage of capital to "tie back into" the 10 percent all-cash return, as shown in Table 1.6.

Negative leverage.   When leverage decreases the return to the investor it is called **negative leverage**. Negative leverage occurs when the interest rate

Table 1.6

Allocation of Available Capital to the Weighted Cost of Capital

	Capital Available	**Lender Debt**	**Owner Equity**
Acquisition Price	$550,000	$412,500	$137,500
Percent of Price	100%	75%	25%
Return $	$55,000	$41,250	$13,750
Return %	10%	10%	10%
multiplied by:			
Percent of Return	100% =	75% +	25%
equals:			
Weighted Return	10% =	6.36% +	3.64%

Table 1.7

Pro-rata Allocation of Property Investment Return to Debt and Equity

	Capital Available	Lender Debt	Owner Equity
Acquisition Price	$550,000	$412,500	$137,500
Percent of Price	100%	75%	25%
Return $	$55,000	$41,250	$13,750
Return %	10%	10%	10%

charged by a lender for borrowed funds is greater than the rate of return that an investment is capable of generating on those borrowed funds. Accordingly, investors are incurring a loss on the borrowed funds. This loss is deducted from the investor's return, which has the effect of reducing the rate of return on the investor's cash portion of the investment. For example, let's say that the investor acquired the ten-unit rental for $550,000. The investor anticipates a 10 percent rate of return on the investment, which would equate to $55,000. Furthermore, the $550,000 property was acquired with a combination of $137,500 of owner's equity and $412,500 of lender's debt. If we allocated the 10 percent return to its component parts, the pro-rata return on equity is also 10 percent, or $13,750; and the pro-rata return on debt is 10 percent, or $41,250, as shown in Table 1.7.

However, if a lender provides a preliminary loan commitment based on an interest rate of 12 percent and loan amortization period of 25 years, then the total annual debt service required to service the loan is $52,135, which would result in negative leverage, as shown in Table 1.8.

Negative leverage occurs because the 12 percent interest rate charged by a lender for borrowed funds utilized to acquire the investment is greater than then 10 percent rate of return that an investment generates. In this case, the rate of return that the investment generates on an all-cash basis is 10 percent,

Table 1.8

Leveraged Allocation of Property Investment Return to Debt and Equity

	Capital Available	Lender Debt	Owner Equity
Acquisition Price	$550,000	$412,500	$137,500
Percent of Price	100%	75%	25%
Return $	$55,000	$52,135	$2,865
Return %	10%	12.64%	2.08%

which is less than the 12.64 percent total return due the lender (i.e., 12 percent interest rate charged by a lender for borrowed funds plus return of principal) for the debt that is utilized to acquire that investment. Accordingly, the investor is incurring a loss of $10,885 on the borrowed funds (i.e., $41,250 less $52,135 equals $10,885 loss). This loss of $10,885 is deducted from the investor's return of $13,750, which has the effect of reducing the rate of return on the investor's cash portion of the investment to $2,865, or only 2.08 percent.

From the lender's perspective, it receives a 12 percent rate of interest on the outstanding balance, in addition to a return of a portion of the original loan amount. For example, during the first year of this loan the lender receives a total amount of interest of $49,350.16 plus a total amount of principal reduction of $2,784.44, resulting in total interest and principal payments of $52,134.60, rounded to $52,135, as shown in Table 1.9.

The rate of return to the owner's equity position of 2.08 percent and the rate of return to the lender's debt of 12.64 percent originate from the same rate of return that the investment generates on an all-cash basis of 10 percent. However, these rates of return to equity and debt must be adjusted by their relative percentage of capital to "tie back into" the 10 percent all-cash return as shown in Table 1.10.

Acquisition Financing Is Repaid by the Property's Income

While it is the investor who borrows money for the purpose of financing a property acquisition, the lender looks primarily to the property itself, and not the investor-borrower, for repayment of debt. The source of the repayment of debt is the property's operating income. From a lender's point of view, the greater the annual operating income available to pay back the annual debt service, the greater the probability the debt will actually be repaid.

The relationship between annual operating income and annual debt service is expressed by the use of a **debt-coverage ratio.** A debt-coverage ratio is a

Table 1.9

Lender's Return of Interest and Principal from Amortizing 12 Percent Loan

Interest Paid	$49,350.16
Principal Reduction	$2,784.44
Total Annual Debt Service	$52,135 rounded
Original Principal Amount Borrowed	$412,500.00
Total Debt Service as Percent of Original Principal	12.64%

Table 1.10

Allocation of Available Capital to the Weighted Cost of Capital

	Capital Available	**Lender Debt**	**Owner Equity**
Acquisition Price	$550,000	$412,500	$137,500
Percent of Price	100%	75%	25%
Return $	$55,000	$52,135	$2,865
Return %	10%	12.64%	2.08%
multiplied by:			
Percent of Return	100%	75%	25%
equals:			
Weighted Return	10%	9.48%	0.52%

basic yet important ratio that expresses the relationship of the annual net operating income (NOI) to the annual debt service of the property. The term is also known as DCR. From a lender's perspective, the larger the DCR, the more of the property's operating income that is available to pay annual debt service. Accordingly, the DCR is an important risk measure for lenders because the property is the primary source of income utilized for repayment of the loan. The formula for determining the debt-coverage ratio of a property is:

$$\text{Annual operating income} \div \text{Annual debt service} = \text{DCR}$$

For example, let's say an investor is considering the acquisition of a ten-unit rental apartment building for a negotiated purchase price of $550,000. The investor has cash equity of $137,500, which represents only 25 percent of the negotiated purchase price. The investor considers employing a first (senior) loan based on a 75 percent LTV, which would equate to $412,500 of debt. The investor finds a lender who provides a preliminary loan commitment based on an interest rate of 7 percent and loan amortization period of 25 years, contingent upon a DCR of at least 1.20. Based on initial underwriting, the lender calculates that the DCR for this loan would be 1.57, as shown in Table 1.11.

Because the DCR is greater than 1.20 the lender could continue with its underwriting for loan purposes.

The Real Estate Broker Is in the Ideal Position to Provide This Core Service

From a deal perspective, the commercial real estate broker should, at a minimum, know at least as much, and ideally more, about the historical, current,

Table 1.11

Ten-Unit Rental Apartment—First Year Projected NOI and DCR

Annual Effective Apartment Revenues	$95,000
less:	
Annual Operating Expenses	$40,000
equals:	
Annual Operating Income	$55,000
divided by:	
Annual Debt Service	$35,000
equals:	
Debt Coverage Ratio (DCR) =	1.57

and anticipated financial performance of the investment than just about anyone else. This knowledge places him in the ideal position to provide this core service.

The Real Estate Broker Continues to "Add Value" to the Transaction

From the buyer's perspective, the ability of a broker to provide a seamless delivery of brokerage and financing services will immediately "add value" to the broker's involvement in the transaction and increase his capabilities and credibility with his client. For these reasons, financing the acquisition is highly probable, creating a need for this service within the context of the transaction. However, if the broker desires to provide these services, the broker's "skill set" will have to increase to handle the complexities of financing.

Mortgage Brokers, Mortgage Bankers, and Correspondent Lenders

There are three primary ways that a commercial mortgage brokerage business can implement financing services on behalf of a client-borrower: as a mortgage broker, a mortgage banker, or a correspondent lender. These three sources of finance play an important role in providing mortgage funds to borrowers on a local, regional, and national level.

A *mortgage broker* brings a borrower of funds and a lender of funds together for the purpose of providing financing, so mortgage brokers are intermediaries. The mortgage broker's compensation is usually contingent upon "a success performance basis" and is paid as a percentage of the financing amount, if, as, and when a financing is accomplished. As part of his services, the broker might also negotiate with the lender to find the best possible financing deal for the borrower. However, the mortgage broker does not originate, close, or service the loan. The actual financing is accomplished through the lender's loan origination process.

Loans that are originated based on a mortgage broker's efforts are usually closed in the lender's name and are usually serviced by the lender. A mortgage broker may accept an application for a mortgage loan, solicit a mortgage loan on behalf of a borrower, negotiate the sale of an existing mortgage loan on behalf of a lender, or negotiate the sale of an existing mortgage loan to an investor in the secondary mortgage market.

A mortgage broker may expand his services further by acting in the capacity of a mortgage banker. A *mortgage banker* may originate, close, and service a loan. Mortgage bankers can provide short-term, interim, and long-term financing. Mortgage bankers utilize their own funds or they may borrow funds from other commercial sources for the mortgage financing. Accordingly, mortgage bankers are not the ultimate lender in the transaction. Usually, a mortgage banker will then sell the mortgage in the *secondary mortgage market,* which is a market in which existing mortgages and mortgage-backed securities are bought and sold.

The loans are sold in the secondary market based on specific criteria required by specific investors. These loans may be sold individually or as "bundles" or "pools" of like-kind loans. The real estate jargon for selling the loan in the secondary market is "selling the paper" or "turning the paper." However, the mortgage banker may service the underlying mortgage, which includes collecting monthly payments, disbursing the funds to pay taxes and property insurance, supervising the loan, preventing delinquencies, and taking appropriate action in the event of a default.

Some mortgage banking firms expand their services still further by acting in the capacity of a correspondent lender. A *correspondent lender* provides lending services on behalf of other lenders who desire to provide financing within a certain area but do not have a physical presence in that area. Also known as loan correspondents, they essentially negotiate a loan on behalf of another lender. Sources of financing for the correspondent lender include money center investment banking houses located in such markets as New York and Chicago, insurance companies, pension funds, and commercial banks. The correspondent lender originates loans on behalf of another lender through a process or system known as a correspondence system. Often, the correspondent will continue to service the loan for the lender and act as a collecting agent.

Table 1.12 summarizes the characteristics of these three financing sources.

Mortgage Brokerage Fees, Origination Fees, and Servicing Fees

A mortgage broker's compensation is generally computed as a percentage of the face value of the brokered loan. For example, let's say the mortgage broker was going to charge "a point," which is real estate jargon for a fee of 1 percent of the face value of the loan. If the loan amount were $412,500, then the compensation due to the mortgage broker would be $4,125. This 1 percent fee to the broker is the broker's compensation, not an origination fee.

Table 1.12

Mortgage Brokers, Mortgage Bankers, and Correspondent Lenders

Mortgage Brokers	Mortgage Bankers	Correspondent Lenders
Intermediary	Intermediary	Intermediary
Does not originate, close, or service loans	Can originate, close, or service loans	Can originate, close, or service loans
Financed through lender's loan origination process	Financed through mortgage banker's or lender's loan origination process	Financed through correspondent services on behalf of a lender
Loan closed in lender's name	Loan closed in lender's name	Loan closed in lender's name
Loan serviced by lender	Loan serviced by mortgage banker or lender	Loan serviced by correspondent lender or lender
Can sell mortgages in the secondary market	Can sell mortgages in the secondary market	Can sell mortgages in the secondary market

An *origination fee* is a fee charged by a lender for making a loan. Origination fees may be all inclusive or net of lender costs. An all-inclusive origination fee covers such costs as the lender's up-front costs, including general and administrative costs, preparation of documents, recordation costs, property inspections, environmental reports, and appraisals. For example, if the loan amount were $412,500 and the lender charged 2 points, which covered all fees and expenses, then the total origination fees due the lender would be $8,250. Alternatively, if the lender's origination fee was net of lender costs, and the lender charged 1 point plus costs associated with the preparation of documents, recordation costs, property inspections, environmental reports, and appraisals, then the total origination fees due the lender would be $4,125 and all other loan costs would be either prepaid or billed directly to the borrower. As a matter of business practice, mortgage brokerage fees, loan origination fees, and loan origination costs may be imposed on a borrower in the same financing transaction.

A mortgage banker or correspondent lender may have an agreement with a lender to service a loan. *Servicing a loan* includes the collection of payments that include principal, interest, insurance, and taxes on a note from a borrower in accordance with the terms of the note. Servicing also includes accounting, bookkeeping, preparation of insurance and tax records, loan payment follow-up, delinquency follow-up, and loan analysis. A servicing agreement is usually written, and includes the obligations of both parties. Servicing fees vary widely and range from one-quarter of 1 percent (0.025 percent) to one-half of 1 percent (0.50 percent) per year of the outstanding loan balance. Some lenders place a maximum on annual servicing income from one mortgage.

Those that service loans are interested in building a volume of loans to service because as the number of loans increases, so does the number of servicing fees. For example, if the loan amount were $412,500 and the service agreement called for a one-quarter of 1 percent (0.025 percent) servicing fee, then the total servicing fee would be approximately $1,031 for the year and average $86 per month. If, however, there were 1,000 such loans to service, then the total servicing fees would be approximately $1,031,000 for the year and average $85,917 per month. Because of the potential for a significant income stream from servicing loans, there are many loan servicing businesses that actively compete for such opportunities. As a matter of business practice, a mortgage banker or correspondent lender can earn mortgage brokerage fees and loan servicing fees in the same financing transaction.

Financial Intermediaries—the Traditional Lenders

A discussion pertaining to real estate financing would not be complete without at least a review of the traditional lenders in the real estate markets. Financial institutions have money to lend for real estate endeavors. A financial institution is an organization in the business of holding cash and other assets on behalf of others. Examples of financial institutions include commercial banks, savings associations, credit unions, insurance companies, pension funds, and investment companies. These financial institutions also act as fiduciaries of behalf of their depositors and investors. What makes these financial institutions unique is that they also act as financial intermediaries within the real estate markets.

Financial intermediaries are financial institutions that act as a "middleman" between depositors and borrowers. Intermediation is a process in which "middlemen" accumulate, combine, and consolidate a number of smaller, individual equity accounts for the purpose of either lending or investing in real estate properties. Due to their size and vast deposit base, these intermediaries can provide financing or investment funds for larger, more complex, and more management-and-capital-intensive real estate properties. However, if state or federal charter regulates these institutions, they operate with significantly less risk tolerance and are more conservative than mortgage brokers, mortgage bankers, and correspondent lenders.

If a financial institution is operating under a federal charter, it is considered a federally chartered financial institution. Any real estate transaction undertaken by such a financial institution is considered a federally related transaction. The Financial Institutions Reform, Recovery, and Enforcement Act (FIRREA) defines a federally related transaction as any real estate–related financial transaction in which any federal financial institution is involved. FIRREA restructured the savings and loan association (S&L) regulatory system and was enacted in response to the savings and loan crisis of the 1980s.

Market Niches

There is a link between traditional lenders and mortgage brokers, mortgage bankers, and correspondent lenders. All three provide lending opportunities for the traditional lenders that have money to lend but are located in other parts of the country. Other sources include insurance companies, pension funds, and private sources that actively seek out broker and correspondent relationships for the purpose of placing a portion of their loanable or investment funds. Accordingly, mortgage brokers, mortgage bankers, and correspondent lenders serve as a "virtual branch office" for these sources of equity and debt. As such, they bring additional vibrancy to the equity and debt markets, adding a new competitive element that encourages the creation of new capital and loan products for commercial real estate investments of all types.

Often mortgage brokers, mortgage bankers, and correspondent lenders create niche markets that serve a vital need in the financing arena. They can be more aggressive, more flexible, and more creative than traditional lenders that are closely regulated. For example, consider lending limits. As it pertains to property acquisition and refinancing, a traditional lender can generally provide an LTV of 70 percent to 75 percent. However, mortgage brokers can structure financing packages with LTVs of 80 percent. Moreover, utilizing sophisticated capital structuring techniques such as equity/"mezzanine" financing, they can provide even more capital for a transaction. *Mezzanine equity,* also referred to as a *mezzanine financing*, provides capital to "fill the gap" between the senior first mortgage loan and the owner's equity investment in a property acquisition. Because equity is not debt, the equity does not impact the loan-to-value ratio. For example, consider the lender who can provide both interest-only loans and mezzanine financing for a transaction. Indeed, very creative.

Because of their flexibility, mortgage brokers can also provide financing for a wider variety of real estate deals, which are differentiated within the industry as "prime" and "subprime" real estate. Based on a combination of a competitive environment and the growth of the commercial mortgage-backed securities (CMBs) market, their loan underwriting criteria for mortgages is often less stringent, making them more flexible lenders. CMBS loans are commercial real estate loans that are pooled together and transferred to a trust, which then issues securities based on the strength of the underlying mortgages. The results are more aggressive loans with higher loan-to-value ratios and lower debt-coverage ratios. At the more risky end of the lending spectrum, mortgage brokers can provide negative amortizing loans and other creative loan structures designed to "make a deal happen."

Historical Perspective

During the 1980s, there was a high-interest-rate environment, that led to creative and lax lending practices, ultimately resulting in a significant rate of loan default. These defaults, combined with the crisis and ultimate failure of the savings and loan industry, gave rise to the largest "bailout" of the U.S. banking system in history and the formation of the Resolution Trust Corporation (RTC). The RTC was a corporation formed by Congress in 1989 to replace the Federal Savings and Loan Insurance Corporation and respond to the insolvencies of about 750 savings and loan associations. As receiver, it sold assets of failed S&Ls and paid insured depositors. In 1995, its duties, including insurance of deposits in thrift institutions, were transferred to the Savings Association Insurance Fund. Today, lenders are more aggressive than they were in the 1980s. However, they are also subject to more stringent underwriting standards than they were in the 1980s.

Figure 1.3

Sources of
Financing a Transaction

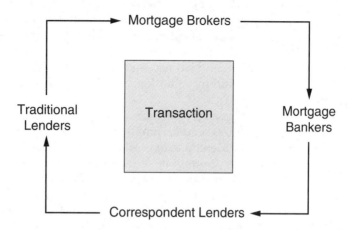

Figure 1.3 summarizes the predominant sources of financing a real estate transaction.

Commercial Real Estate and the Appraisal Industry

State-certified and Professionally Designated Appraisers

Much of the analytical and financial skills that are required in the commercial real estate and mortgage brokerage industries are utilized in the commercial appraisal industry. However, the appraisal industry places less emphasis on selling skills and more emphasis on unbiased and credible valuation methodology. One of the most coveted and respected professional commercial designations within the appraisal industry is the MAI designation (member of the Appraisal Institute), which is offered by the Appraisal Institute.

Real estate licensees may prepare a comparative market analysis to ascertain the best asking or list price for a property they are marketing. However, a comparative market analysis cannot be referred to as an appraisal. A CMA presents comparable properties that are listed for sale or that have sold. Accordingly, a CMA can be utilized as a pricing tool to assist in establishing a sales price for a listed property. A real estate licensee may appraise property for compensation, but is subject to the Uniform Standards of Professional Appraisal Practice, which is commonly referred to as USPAP. Even a casual review of USPAP reveals the financial, valuation, and technical acumen that is required by professional appraisers. For this reason, real estate appraisal has evolved into a separate profession within the real estate business.

The Appraisal Standards Board of the Appraisal Foundation developed USPAP. The Appraisal Foundation is authorized by the U.S. Congress as the source of appraisal standards and appraisal qualifications. The Appraisal Standards Board annually publishes, interprets, and amends USPAP on behalf of appraisers and users of appraisal services, which include state and federal regulatory agencies and others. It is considered important that individuals understand and adhere to changes in each annual edition of USPAP as state and federal regulatory authorities enforce the content of the current applicable edition of USPAP.

According to USPAP of the Appraisal Foundation, and the code of professional ethics of the Appraisal Institute, an **appraisal** is defined as the act or process of estimating value. It is an analysis, opinion, or conclusion relating to the nature, quality, value, or utility of specified interests in, or aspects of, identified real estate. As such, appraisal covers a variety of assignments, including valuation, consulting, and appraisal review.

Appraisers perform analyses and render opinions or conclusions relating to the nature, quality, value, or utility of specified interests in, or aspects of, identified real estate. Real estate appraisal involves selective research into appropriate market areas; the assemblage of pertinent data; the use of appropriate analytical techniques; and the application of knowledge, experience, and professional judgment to develop an appropriate solution to an appraisal problem. The appraisal process involves a significant amount of statistical, mathematical, financial, and other quantitative information. However, appraisal is considered an art and not a science because appraisers use professional reasoning and judgment to interpret this quantitative information and estimate value.

Each state regulates state-certified, licensed, and registered appraisers, who also must abide by the Uniform Standards of Professional Appraisal Practice. These regulated appraisers are allowed to prepare appraisals involving federally related transactions. The Financial Institutions Reform, Recovery, and Enforcement Act defines a federally related transaction as any real estate–related financial transaction in which any federal financial institution is involved. FIRREA restructured the savings and loan association regulatory system and was enacted in response to the savings and loan crisis of the 1980s.

The nature of the real estate problem will indicate whether the task is a valuation or a consulting assignment. The value estimate may be market value, insurable value, investment value, or some other properly defined value of an identified interest in real estate as of a given date. Valuation assignments may produce market value estimates of fee simple estates, leasehold estates, leased fee estates, air rights, and other clearly defined interests.

The Appraisal Foundation defines **consulting** as the act or process of providing information, analysis of real estate data, and recommendations or conclusions on diversified problems in real estate other than estimating value. Consulting assignments include land utilization studies, supply and demand studies, economic feasibility studies, highest and best use analyses, and marketability or investment considerations that relate to proposed or existing developments.

Cost, Price, and Value

In order to make sound investment decisions, buyers, sellers, investors, lenders, and financial institutions that participate within the real estate markets are very interested in the cost, the price, and the value of real estate. These concepts are at the very core of real estate appraisal and, as such, experienced real estate appraisers are actively sought to render unbiased and credible opinions as they pertain to these concepts. Because these three financial measures are constantly changing in relation to each other, astute real estate market observers will monitor the degree and direction of cost, price, and value. In fact, one of the most famous quotes in the real estate industry was stated by Paul Reichmann, one of the most famous developers, and addresses these very measures:

"You build on cost and you borrow on value . . . . "

Cost is the amount of capital required to develop, build, or essentially create real estate. Cost concerns itself with land and improvements. Cost includes the expenditure for the four factors of production: land, labor, coordination, and capital. For example, let's say a real estate investor-developer believes there is demand for a multifamily rental apartment and decides to construct such a building. The investor would have to pay for the land that is permitted to accommodate such a building. The investor would have to pay for all necessary plans, permits, and approvals to construct the building. These would include the services of professional land surveyors, engineers, architects, planners, contractors, landscape architects, marketing and leasing agents, and legal, tax, and accounting counsel. Additionally, the investor-developer is entitled to compensation for the coordination of land, labor, and capital and the entrepreneurial risks associated with such an endeavor. All of these expenses relate to the cost of development. Ideally, at completion the investor-developer will have an apartment building with a cost basis less than the price at which it may be sold.

Price is the amount of money that the real estate will sell for in the marketplace. It is the amount of money a purchaser of real estate is willing to pay for the property. A developer-seller of property wants the cost to be less than the price for which he receives it. After all, only if the developer-seller can sell the real estate for more than all of its development costs will the seller make a profit from the sale. A buyer of property wants the value of the property to be more than its price. The buyer and seller negotiate a price that reflects self-interests and the desire to make the best deal. A buyer will pay the negotiated price based on his perception that the value of the property is more than its price. However, the negotiated price is not necessarily the same as the property value. In fact, buyers seek to pay a price for real estate that is less than its value.

Value is the worth of real estate, as measured by its monetary equivalent within the real estate market. To a real estate investor, the value today represents the present worth of the anticipated future benefits associated with that real estate. Different potential purchasers may have different opinions about what will happen in the future and accordingly may arrive at different opinions of present value of a property. These varying opinions of the present value influence their offering price for property. That is why property available for sale in the real estate market will usually generate a variation of offers for purchase.

The value of real estate is impacted by its utility, scarcity, demand, and transferability. However, the estimation of what the present value of those anticipated future benefits are can become a very complex task. One reason is that there are many types of value, such as insurable value, assessed value, going concern value, and investment value. An appraisal is defined as the act or process of estimating value and most often appraisers estimate market value.

Estimating market value is important to lenders for their underwriting purposes as it pertains to loan-to-value ratios and debt-coverage ratios.

Consider the following two scenarios involving cost, price, and value, contained within Table 1.13.

Scenario A. The developer of a ten-unit rental apartment building incurs a total development cost of $400,000. After completion, when the property is fully leased and occupied, the developer becomes a seller and obtains a sales price of $500,000. The seller made a profit of $100,000 on the sale, which equates to about a 25 percent gross profit on cost. So from the seller's perspective, this is a good deal. What about the buyer? The buyer acquired the property for a sales price of $500,000. However, the appraised market value of the property is $550,000. The buyer acquired the property at a $50,000 discount to value, which equates to about a 9.09 percent discount to value. So from the buyer's perspective, this is a good deal.

Scenario B. The developer of a ten-unit rental apartment building incurs a total development cost of $550,000. After completion, when the property is fully leased and occupied, the developer becomes a seller and obtains a sales price of $500,000. The seller incurs a loss of $50,000 on the sale, which equates to about a 9.09 percent gross loss on cost. So from the seller's perspective, this is a bad deal. What about the buyer? The buyer acquired the property for a sales price of $500,000. However, the appraised market value of the property is only $400,000. The buyer acquired the property at a $100,000 premium over its value, which equates to about a 25 percent premium over its value. So from the buyer's perspective, this is a bad deal.

■ Commercial Real Estate and the Investment Services Industry

Ideally, a buyer, seller, owner, or investor of commercial real estate should have a working knowledge of the core concepts of what commercial real estate is, as well as a working knowledge of the core concepts of what its investment characteristics are. If a buyer, seller, owner, or investor of commercial real estate requires additional expertise, a broker is usually the first

Table 1.13

Effects of Cost, Price, and Value

Scenario	A	B
Market Perception	A Good Deal	A Bad Deal
Cost	$400,000	$550,000
Price	500,000	500,000
Value	550,000	400,000
Seller's Profit on Sale	100,000	(50,000)
Buyer's Discount to Value	50,000	(100,000)

person to come to mind for assistance. If a broker is going to develop a commercial brokerage practice, having a working knowledge of the core concepts of commercial real estate and its investment characteristics is both expected and required for success.

State licensing requirements are simply a starting point. While there is no doubt that credible experience is a valuable resource that increases in worth and marketability over time, experience based solely on trial and error is time consuming. However, experience combined with education equates to knowledge. As the saying goes, knowledge is power. One of the most influential, prestigious, and largest organizations offering commercial and investment education is the National Association of REALTORS® (NAR).

NAR is America's largest trade association, representing approximately 1 million members, including NAR's institutes, societies, and councils involved in all aspects of the residential and commercial real estate industries. NAR's membership is composed of residential and commercial REALTORS® who are brokers, salespeople, property managers, appraisers, counselors, and others engaged in all aspects of the real estate industry. Members belong to one or more of some 1,600 local associations/boards and 54 state and territory associations of REALTORS®. They are pledged to a strict code of ethics and standards of practice. NAR provides a facility for professional development, research, and exchange of information among its members and to the public and government for the purpose of preserving the free enterprise system and the right to own real property.

Equally prestigious are the many NAR-affiliated institutes, societies, and councils, which read like a who's who in the commercial real estate industry and include the following:

- *CCIM Institute.* Practitioners holding the CCIM designation are recognized as experts in commercial investment real estate and live up to their distinguished reputation as model business partners for commercial real estate users, owners, and investors. Only 7,500 commercial real estate practitioners nationwide hold the CCIM designation. This statistic reflects the caliber of the program and why it is the most coveted and respected designation in commercial investment real estate.

- *Counselors of Real Estate.* The Counselors of Real Estate (CRE) is a professional membership organization established exclusively for leading real property advisors. The purpose of the organization is to advance, enhance, and support these leaders by serving as a resource for information, by creating opportunities for professional development, by facilitating networking, and by providing the benefits of camaraderie. Members are awarded the CRE designation, bestowed by invitation only, in recognition of their achievements in real estate counseling.

- *Institute of Real Estate Management.* The Institute of Real Estate Management (IREM) is an association of property and asset managers who have met strict criteria in the areas of education, experience, and ethics. IREM offers the only comprehensive program exclusively developed for property and asset managers working with large portfolios of all property types. IREM confers the coveted Certified Property Manager (CPM) designation, which is considered to be the industry's premier real estate management credential. There are only 8,600 professional real estate managers who hold this distinguished designation worldwide.

■ *Real Estate Buyer's Agent Council.* The Real Estate Buyer's Agent Council (REBAC) is the world's largest association of real estate professionals focusing specifically on representing the real estate buyer. There are more than 42,000 active members of the organization worldwide. REBAC awards the Accredited Buyer's Representative (ABR) and the Accredited Buyer's Representative Manager (ABRM) designations.

■ *Society of Industrial and Office REALTORS®.* The society certifies its members with the prestigious SIOR (specialist, industrial and office real estate) designation, a professional symbol of the highest level of knowledge, production, and ethics in the commercial real estate industry. Designees specialize in industrial, office, sales manager, or advisory services categories.

■ *REALTORS® Land Institute.* The REALTORS® Land Institute is the only branch of the REALTOR® family focused on land brokerage transactions of five specialized types: farms and ranches; undeveloped tracts of land; transitional and development land; subdivision and wholesaling of lots; and site selection and assemblage of land parcels.

■ *Council of Real Estate Broker Managers.* The council confers the Certified Real Estate Brokerage Manager (CRB) designation, while continuously providing members with the educational, informational, and networking resources necessary to compete and succeed in the real estate marketplace.

■ *Council of Residential Specialists.* The Certified Residential Specialist (CRS) is the highest designation awarded to sales associates in the residential sales field. The CRS designation recognizes professional accomplishments in both experience and education. Since 1977, the Council of Residential Specialists has been conferring the CRS designation on agents who meet its stringent requirements. Currently, there are more than 34,000 active CRS designees.

As mentioned, to a great extent the knowledge, experience, level of services provided, combination of skill sets, professional affiliations, property specialization, and focus define what a broker does and, as a result, what they may be called. The affiliated institutes, societies, and councils of NAR offer the ability to literally customize the development of a real estate business practice within the areas of investment, counseling, asset management, buyer representation, commercial property specialist, land specialist, residential specialist, or brokerage management.

■ Commercial Real Estate and the Counseling Industry

Real estate counseling is a growing area of specialization within the real estate industry. Professional counseling involves giving others relevant and credible advice pertaining to real estate for a fee. The term *counselor*, or *real estate counselor*, is often misused and misinterpreted by those both inside and outside the industry. According to the Counselors of Real Estate, a leading organization in the field, and its predecessor, the American Society of Real Estate Counselors, real estate counseling is defined as providing competent, disinterested, and unbiased advice, professional guidance, and sound judgment on diversified problems in the broad field of real estate involving any and all segments of the business, such as merchandising, leasing, management, planning, financing, appraising, court testimony, and other similar services. Counseling may involve the utilization of any or all of these services.

To be considered a competent real estate counselor, one should have acquired, through both experience and education, a broad base of knowledge pertaining to the many facets of real estate. Many overlapping disciplines (skill sets) are necessary to be a successful counselor, including valuation analysis and appraising, real estate brokerage, property construction, property development and design, economics, financing of commercial real estate, leasing, an understanding of law, and an understanding of investments including investment analysis and property management. This knowledge must then be combined with an understanding of local, regional, national, and international market activities, and a command of the subject matter relating to the property type in question. To be a competent and sought-after real estate counselor, one must provide clients with supportable advice, which ultimately translates into a sustained track record of real estate successes.

■ Commercial Real Estate and Related Industries

Property Management

Property managers are responsible for the comprehensive management of residential, commercial, and industrial properties. They supervise every aspect of a property's operation so as to produce the greatest achievable financial return for the greatest period of time. They also may be asset managers or real estate executives because businesses that own their real estate also require these services. Property managers must have professional competence in a number of interrelated areas (skill sets), including property maintenance and operations, human resources management, marketing and leasing, financial operations, asset management, and legal and risk management. They are responsible for preparing detailed plans for the management of property. Successful property managers also have excellent communication skills and are public relations experts.

Investors

Many individuals are full-time investors for their own accounts. Although many are involved by choice, others have become investors by circumstance. Usually investors who buy, develop, lease, manage, or sell their own properties do not need to be licensed. Successful real estate investors anticipate financial rewards from the real estate assets and markets in which they invest. However, should a mistake be made, those same real estate assets and markets may also financially penalize real estate investors. *Caveat emptor!* ("Let the buyer beware!")

Some of the world's largest and most successful real estate firms were started by a single individual that happened upon the industry by accident or by good fortune. Among the most famous of these individuals is Paul Reichmann, a founding principal of Olympia and York Developments Limited (O&Y). The business grew out of Mr. Reichmann's frustration with the high cost of having a modest warehouse built for his tile and construction business. He decided to build it himself and in the process saved about 50 percent of the development cost. From his initial successful experience in building construction, the O&Y empire evolved. During its prime, Olympia and York Developments Limited was the world's largest private real estate developer, owning approximately 43,000,000 rentable square feet of prime office space contained in more than 40 buildings located throughout the United States. O&Y was also the developer of world-class real estate, including Canary Wharf in London, England, and the World Financial Center in New York City.

One resource available to the individual investor is the National Real Estate Investors Association (NREIA), which is a federation made up of local associations or investment clubs throughout the United States. The NREIA is an association of real estate professionals who know firsthand the unique problems and challenges of real estate investing. It represents local investor associations, property owner associations, apartment associations, and landlord associations on a national scale. Together the NREIA represents the interests of over 20,000 members across the United States and is the largest broad-based organization dedicated to the individual investor. The mission of the NREIA is to educate and support the leaders of real estate associations through training, networking, motivation, and provision of benefits to their associations. The NREIA promotes a high standard of business ethics and professionalism.

Syndications

Syndications are business entities, such as limited liability corporations (LLCs) and limited partnerships (LPs) that combine the equity and investment capital of a number of private and public individual investors, including other businesses, for the purpose of buying, developing, leasing, managing, and, perhaps, selling properties. These properties are usually larger, more complex, and more management-and-capital intensive than could be acquired by the syndication participants individually. Syndications function as intermediaries. Intermediation is a process in which "middlemen" accumulate, combine, and consolidate a number of smaller, individual equity investment capital accounts for the purpose of investing in larger, more complex, and more management-and-capital-intensive real estate properties.

Educators

There are a number of opportunities in real estate education. Because of this, individuals with experience in the industry who possess excellent communication and interpersonal skills and who can develop a rapport with students are sought after as instructors. Some states require educators to complete specified real estate and related courses before a real estate instructor's license can be issued. Other states also require continuing education for license renewal.

Commercial Real Estate and Investment Banking

Real estate investment banking is a specialized and sophisticated business within the commercial real estate industry, which has evolved from the commercial investment bank industry. Real estate investment bankers are talented individuals and entities that have combined multiple skill sets that

Table 1.14

Investment Banking Comprehensive Transaction Services

Sales	Real Estate Markets	Capital Finance Markets	Support Related
Buyer, seller, or transaction representation	International, national, regional, and local real estate market supply and demand research	International, national, regional, and local capital market information	Market, investment or other valuation; opinions of value and price
Transaction structuring and strategy including sale, joint venture, and sale-leaseback	Transaction structuring and strategy including sale, joint venture, and sale-leaseback	Capital structuring or restructuring, including amount, percent, and sources of equity and debt	Sales, marketing, negotiation, and closing skills as related to deals and business development
Sales analysis and underwriting, including preparation of a sales offering memorandum	Implement sophisticated market research for the evaluation of real estate and determination of use for value optimization	Financial analysis and underwriting, including preparation of a financing underwriting memorandum	Law and tax planning, including tax-deferred exchanges and estate planning
Financial analysis of property economics to NOI; preparation	Strategic planning, counseling, and advisory; property enhancements for value maximization	Financial analysis of property economics to CTO; preparation of DCF analysis	Asset management and leasing; risk analysis and mitigation

allow a seamless delivery of selected real estate services to clients. The result is that investment bankers can offer *comprehensive transaction services* to clients, saving valuable time and eliminating the need for assembling many of the appropriate team players required to implement real estate transactions. Real estate investment bankers combine sales and marketing acumen, real estate market expertise, and capital market savvy in the implementation of a property transaction (either a sale or purchase) or the delivery of capital (in the form of either equity or debt) on behalf of a client. Table 1.14 provides a summary of the core services that real estate investment bankers provide to clients.

From a business operating perspective, real estate investment banking firms are vertically integrated operating entities offering a "one stop shop" for most, if not all, of the real estate transaction services resulting in a seamless delivery of service. (See Figure 1.4.)

Money and Capital Markets Defined

A *capital market transaction* refers to a distinction made between the short-term and long-term equity (cash) and debt (including mortgage financing) markets. The main distinction is made between short-term markets for equity, debt, and financing that occur within "money markets," and long-term financing that occurs within "capital markets." Money markets are those markets that deal in financial instruments with a maturity (those that come due or are within a time frame) of less than one year, while capital markets deal in longer-term (greater than one year) mortgage obligations and equities.

Figure 1.4

Investment Banking —
Seamless Delivery of Services

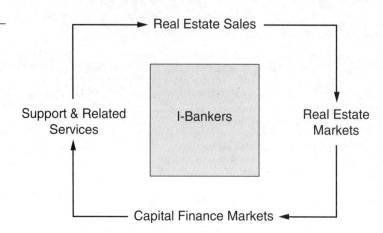

Real Estate Investment Banker Defined

A real estate **investment banker** is an individual or business that can provide the services of a loan underwriter, provide sources of capital, and act as a real estate broker for individual clients or businesses. Known within the industry as "I-bankers," they may act as an intermediary between a lender and a borrower, with similarities to the mortgage brokerage business. They may act as a real estate broker, with similarities to the real estate brokerage business. They may provide valuation services, with similarities to the appraisal business. They may provide advisory services to clients, with similarities to real estate counseling business. Ideally, investment bankers will strive to provide most, if not all, of these services during the same transaction or engagement thereby offering comprehensive transaction services. I-bankers can provide real estate sales, real estate markets, capital markets, and related support services, and are subject to appropriate state laws, including license law.

Real estate investment bankers underwrite or analyze commercial real estate from two potential points of view. First they may underwrite, or analyze, commercial real estate from a sales or transaction perspective and prepare a summary or detailed report, called an *offering memorandum,* relating to the prospective sale of the property. They also may underwrite, or analyze, commercial real estate from a financing perspective and prepare a report, called an *underwriting memorandum,* relating to such uses as the prospective financing of the property in connection with a proposed loan, an infusion of equity capital, or a capital restructuring.

Requirements

Investment banking combines the professional skills of a commercial real estate broker, mortgage broker and banker, real estate appraiser, and real estate counselor. Accordingly, those interested in investment banking should have a strong academic background at the undergraduate- and graduate-level programs in such areas as real estate, finance, economics, accounting, sales and marketing, law, and business administration. Additionally, investment bankers possess strong written and oral communication skills, strong analytical modeling and quantitative skills, and self-confidence. Generally, there are two primary levels of associates within a real estate investment banking firm: analyst and associate.

Real Estate Investment Banking Analyst

Responsibilities of an investment banking analyst include, but are not limited to, the following:

- Perform detailed property, market, and industry market research and analysis in support of potential property (real estate) or capital market (equity and debt financing, capital restructuring) transactions
- Identify potential risks and opportunities associated with these transactions
- Prepare offering or underwriting memorandums
- Prepare financial analysis, financial statements, income and expense projections, discounted cash flow (DCF) analysis, and performance projections
- Prepare detailed economic, financial, and investment models, including DCF analysis of pro-forma projections, analysis and risk of debt, and sensitivity analysis that compares the impact on value and risk when one or more model assumptions are changed

Real Estate Investment Banking Associate

An investment banking associate has mastered the responsibilities of an analyst and plays a key role within a real estate transactions group or a capital market transactions group. Responsibilities of an investment banking associate include, but are not limited to, the following:

- Advanced financial modeling skills
- Comprehensive understanding of, and ability to implement, sophisticated property, market, and industry research
- Advanced level of proficiency in the preparation of comparable transaction analysis and prospective property valuations
- Preparation of marketing materials and offering and underwriting memorandums
- Comprehensive understanding of a broad spectrum of capital market "products"; generally speaking, these products refer to capital market equity and debt sources and alternatives, also known as "vehicles" and "facilities"
- Sales, marketing, negotiating, and closing skills as they relate to client development, relationship management, business development, and transactions
- Client and employee management skills

Real estate investment bankers provide creative solutions, sound advice, and financial counsel to clients who have concerns, objectives, and goals pertaining to their real estate assets. Viewed from this perspective, real estate investment bankers take on many of the characteristics of real estate counselors. Additionally, they also combine real estate expertise, capital market savvy, and marketing acumen for superior sales transactions results. Accordingly, real estate investment bankers take on many of the characteristics of real estate brokers. Moreover, they specialize in individual structuring and tailor-made placement of financing transactions, utilizing equity and debt markets. Therefore, real estate investment bankers take on many of the characteristics of professional real estate mortgage brokers.

The assets, talents, and capabilities of investment bankers allow them to deliver a sophisticated level of service that is generally directed to larger real estate transactions. Larger real estate transactions tend to not only be more capital intensive, but more complex as well. These complexities involve the physical real estate itself; the current and forecasted market environment in which it exists; the financial structure and capital requirements of the assets; and legal issues, including form of ownership, zoning and future development and use limitations, and the rights and obligations of the investors and tenants. For these reasons, investment banking firms are usually involved with "institutional" real estate.

There is a clear distinction made between so-called institutional grade and noninstitutional grade real estate. *Institutional grade* or *institutional quality real estate* is usually the best in class, quality, location, and income within any given market. Institutional investors include large national pension funds, insurance companies, or private real estate entities, as well as the advisors who provide acquisition services to those investors. They invest and manage the most "pristine" of real estate, which is usually the most marketable and demanded within any given market. Individual transaction sizes can range in the hundreds of millions of dollars and total portfolio assets managed can reach into the billions of dollars. Because institutional real estate is considered best in class, quality, location, and income, it is also considered to possess less risk than noninstitutional real estate. *Noninstitutional real estate* is all real estate assets other than institutional real estate assets. Accordingly, there is more risk associated with noninstitutional real estate.

■ Introduction to Commercial Brokerage Transactions

Commercial real estate brokerage is a challenging and exciting business. It is also multifaceted and requires expertise in a number of interrelated disciplines. To be a successful professional in the commercial real estate brokerage business today requires mastery of a combination of skill sets. These skill sets include: (1) a legally imposed code of ethics, (2) licensure requirements, (3) the practical application of business principles, (4) sales and marketing skills, (5) research skills, (6) competency in mathematics, (7) a solid understanding of finance and investments, (8) an understanding of taxes and depreciation as they apply to real estate, (9) an advanced level of computer proficiency with word processing and financial and database management software programs, and (10) time management and self-discipline skills. Then there is the ever-expanding body of knowledge and options available within the real estate industry itself!

You have probably heard the cliché that experience is the best teacher. However, experience based solely on trial and error is extremely time-consuming. To be successful, there are two unique sets of circumstances that have to be acknowledged by today's real estate professionals. First, there are the sheer complexities, specialization, and competitiveness of the real estate industry. Second, within the past few years, computer- and Internet-based technologies have accelerated the efficient transmission of relevant information within an inherently inefficient real estate market and created "market transparency." With all the compelling reasons to be prepared, a far more realistic approach is to continue to acquire a solid foundation of knowledge that, when combined with practical experience, will indeed increase your worth as a professional over time. Credible experience can and should be converted to a valuable resource that increases real estate professionals worth and marketability over time.

> Credible experience can and should be converted to a valuable resource that increases real estate professionals worth and marketability over time.

Overview of Commercial Brokerage Transactions

Below are two separate outlines of a generic commercial real estate transaction. Because there are different motivations and objectives for a transaction, in some instances, there are multiple options and different approaches to consider. Although there must be a buyer and seller in a real estate sales transaction, their individual perspectives and goals of the transaction are not the same. A buyer and a seller who participate in a sale real estate transaction have different motivations and seek to accomplish differing objectives by participating in that transaction. Accordingly, if success is measured by a completed transaction, the accomplishment of that goal is more important than the importance to the seller, the seller's broker, the buyer, the buyer's broker, or the lender.

These overviews are outlines and are useful as universal tools for guidelines and structuring a conceptual plan for a successful commercial transaction, or understanding one that has been presented to us. A review of the various steps and procedures involved also highlights the need for a sophisticated skill set.

Figure 1.5 provides a presentation of a commercial real estate transaction from the seller (the seller is the broker's employer and principal) and selling broker's perspective.

Figure 1.5

Commercial Transaction Overview—Seller's Perspective

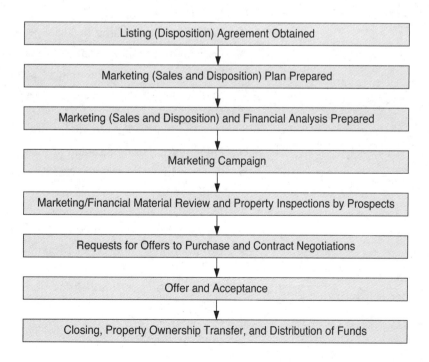

Listing (Disposition) Agreement Obtained

↓

Marketing (Sales and Disposition) Plan Prepared

↓

Marketing (Sales and Disposition) and Financial Analysis Prepared

↓

Marketing Campaign

↓

Marketing/Financial Material Review and Property Inspections by Prospects

↓

Requests for Offers to Purchase and Contract Negotiations

↓

Offer and Acceptance

↓

Closing, Property Ownership Transfer, and Distribution of Funds

The transaction overview from the seller's (principal's) and selling broker's perspective consists of eight major components. These eight components can be further detailed into their subcomponent categories as follows:

1. Listing agreement obtained
   - Listing agreement options defined and/or discussed with principal
   - Open listing agreement: broker duties and compensation structure defined
   - Exclusive listing agreement: broker duties and compensation structure defined
   - Exclusive-right-of-sale listing agreement: broker duties and compensation structure defined

2. Marketing plan prepared and presented to client
   - Principal's objectives, including price, terms, and contingencies, determined
   - Marketing/offering procedure alternatives determined
   - Marketing/offering criteria prepared
   - Multiple listing services considered as a market tool to achieve objectives
   - Web-based broadcast services considered as a market tool to achieve objectives
   - Web-based listing services considered as a market tool to achieve objectives
   - Marketing/offering plan outline prepared and presented to principal
   - Prospective purchaser list developed by broker for target marketing

3. Marketing and financial analysis material prepared by broker
   - Market analysis prepared
   - Financial analysis prepared
   - Investment analysis prepared
   - Preliminary marketing material presented to principal for approval
   - Preliminary financial analysis presented to principal for approval
   - Preliminary investment analysis presented to principal for approval
   - Marketing/offering memorandum presented to principal for approval
   - Confidentiality agreement presented to principal for approval
   - Noncircumvention agreement presented to principal for approval
   - Cooperating brokerage agreement presented to principal for approval

4. Marketing campaign
   - "Teaser letter" distributed by broker to prospects via mail or e-mail
   - Confidentiality and noncircumvention agreements distributed by broker to prospects
   - Confidentiality and noncircumvention agreements signed and returned by prospects to broker
   - Cooperating brokerage and noncircumvention agreement distributed by broker

- Cooperating brokerage and noncircumvention agreements signed and returned by cooperating brokers
- Preliminary marketing materials are forwarded to prospects and cooperating brokers
- Offering memorandums are forwarded to prospects and cooperating brokers

5. Property and marketing material review

- Property tours coordinated by broker
- Broker addresses questions regarding all aspects of the property, the marketing and financial materials, and responds to additional information requests
- Broker confers regularly with the principal and adjusts strategy as appropriate

6. Request for offers and negotiations

- Broker requests initial "call for offers" from prospects and/or prospects' agents
- Letters of intent (LOI) submitted by prospects or prospects' agents to principal through the principal's broker
- Principal accepts, counteroffers, or rejects LOI
- Principal's broker requests "best and final offers" from prospects and prospects' agents
- Revised LOIs submitted by prospects to principal through the principal's broker
- The principal accepts a revised LOI and requests a purchase and sales contract

7. Offer and acceptance

- Purchase and sales contract prepared and executed by buyer and seller
- Buyer deposits earnest money into escrow account ("soft money up")
- Due diligence and investigation period commences for buyer
- Buyer's financing considerations and other contingencies are resolved
- Due diligence and investigation period concludes for buyer
- Buyer commits to purchase with closing date
- Buyer's earnest money deposit becomes nonrefundable ("hard money up")
- Buyer deposits additional nonrefundable earnest money into escrow account

8. Closing

- Closing date arrives
- Closing statement prepared
- Title to property is delivered to buyer; title transfers
- Sales proceeds disbursed to seller
- Brokerage fees distributed from seller's sales proceeds to broker

Real estate transactions require an understanding of the "transaction process" to be implemented correctly and concluded efficiently. Most sellers understand that a property is usually listed for sale, and those properties available for sale usually close. The remainder of this highly intricate process is less obvious. This highlights why for the sale of a property, *the principal's broker is considered an expert and, accordingly, is responsible for the successful implementation of the transaction and its completion.*

What if a buyer seeks counsel, advice, and representation from a broker in a transaction? What would change and what would be the same? Figure 1.6 is a presentation of a commercial real estate transaction from the buyer's and buying broker's perspective.

The transaction overview from the buyer's (principal's) and buying broker's perspective consists of eight major components. These components can be further detailed into their subcomponent categories as follows:

1. Representation agreement obtained
   - Representation agreement options defined and/or discussed with principal
   - Nonexclusive right of representation agreement, broker duties, and compensation structure defined
   - Exclusive right of representation agreement, broker duties, and compensation structure defined
2. Acquisition plan prepared and presented to client
   - Principal's objectives, including price, terms, and contingencies determined
   - Acquisition/solicitation procedure alternatives determined.
   - Acquisition/solicitation criteria prepared

Figure 1.6

Commercial Transaction
Overview—Buyer's Perspective

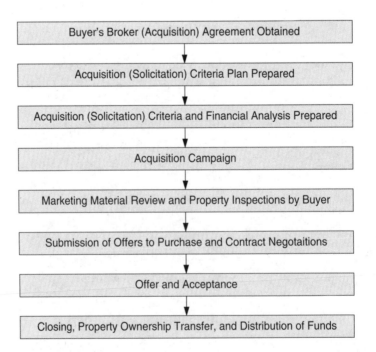

Buyer's Broker (Acquisition) Agreement Obtained

Acquisition (Solicitation) Criteria Plan Prepared

Acquisition (Solicitation) Criteria and Financial Analysis Prepared

Acquisition Campaign

Marketing Material Review and Property Inspections by Buyer

Submission of Offers to Purchase and Contract Negotaitions

Offer and Acceptance

Closing, Property Ownership Transfer, and Distribution of Funds

- Multiple listing services considered as an acquisition tool to achieve objectives
- Web-based broadcast services considered as an acquisition tool to achieve objectives
- Web-based listing services considered as an acquisition tool to achieve objectives

3. Acquisition and analysis material prepared by broker
   - Market analysis criteria prepared
   - Financial analysis criteria prepared
   - Investment analysis criteria prepared

4. Acquisition campaign
   - "Teaser solicitation letter" distributed by broker to prospective sellers via mail or e-mail
   - Confidentiality and noncircumvention agreements signed and returned by principal to prospective sellers
   - Cooperating brokerage agreement and noncircumvention agreements signed and returned by the buyer's broker to seller's broker
   - Preliminary marketing materials are received by the principal or buyer's broker
   - Offering memorandums received by the principal or buyer's broker

5. Property and marketing material review
   - Principal and buyer's broker tour property
   - Buyer's broker assists the principal regarding all aspects of the property, the marketing and financial materials, and responds to additional information requests
   - Buyer's broker confers regularly with the principal and adjusts strategy as appropriate

6. Submission of offers and negotiations
   - Letter of intent (LOI) submitted by principal to seller through buyer's broker
   - Seller accepts, counteroffers, or rejects LOI
   - Seller requests "best and final offer" from principal and buyer's broker
   - Revised LOIs submitted by principal to seller through buyer's broker
   - The seller accepts a revised LOI and requests a purchase and sales contract

7. Offer and acceptance
   - Purchase and sales contract prepared and executed by buyer and seller
   - Buyer deposits earnest money into escrow account ("soft money up")
   - Due diligence and investigation period commences for buyer
   - Buyer financing considerations and other contingencies resolved
   - Due diligence and investigation period concludes for buyer
   - Buyer commits to purchase with closing date

- Buyer's earnest money deposit becomes nonrefundable ("hard money up")
- Buyer deposits additional nonrefundable earnest money into escrow account

8. Closing
   - Closing date arrives
   - Closing statement prepared
   - Title to property is delivered to buyer; title transfers
   - Sales proceeds disbursed to seller
   - Buyer's broker fees distributed from seller's sales proceeds to buyer's broker as a cooperating broker and/or directly from the buyer as the principal of the buyer's broker

Most buyers understand that a property must become available for sale for a closing to occur. The remainder of this highly intricate process is less obvious. This highlights why for the sale of a property, *the principal's broker is considered an expert and, accordingly, is responsible for the successful implementation of the transaction and its completion.* Figure 1.7 is a presentation of the different buyer and seller perspectives of a property and a transaction. If the seller's both have representation, then the buyer's broker and the seller's broker, who are agents of their principals, are really facilitators of the property transaction.

The brokers are considered the experts and are responsible for the successful implementation of the transaction and its completion. It naturally follows that there is a macroperspective in a property transaction, which can be referred to as the deal perspective (see Figure 1.8).

Figure 1.7

Different Perspectives of the Buyer, Seller, and Broker in a Transaction

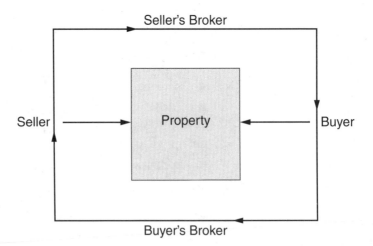

Figure 1.8

Commercial Transaction
Overview—Deal Perspective

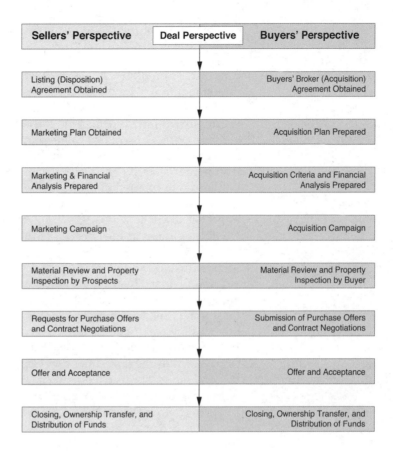

Viewing a transaction from such a perspective will give the seller, the buyer, and the principals' brokers a strategic advantage because they view the transaction globally and will be able to anticipate the next appropriate step as well as be proactive in their business dealings.

■ Summary

Commercial real estate is any real estate that is required for the operation of a business enterprise or as a part of a business. The concept of commercial real estate services as a business enterprise is not the same concept as commercial real estate. A commercial real estate business is any business enterprise that provides the professional commercial real estate services to the buyers, sellers, and others who interact within the commercial real estate marketplace.

The commercial real estate business consists of the varied professions that have developed a specialization within the commercial real estate industry and possibly within a commercial property type as well. When these businesses are grouped their larger service lines become clear. These four service lines—real estate sales and property brokerage, real estate advisory and counseling, real estate financing and mortgage brokerage, and real estate–related services—provide a basis for many opportunities. The opportunities include those provided by the property sales/brokerage industry, the financing industry, the appraisal industry, the investment services industry, the counseling industry, and other related industries. Ultimately, the continued combination and integration of these services results in the creation of yet another core business—real estate investment banking.

Any discussion of investment real estate will lead to a discussion about the capital required for those investments. That is why obtaining a basic understanding of the sources of real estate finance, leverage, and the use of basic yet important ratios such as the loan-to-value ratio and debt-coverage ratio are so important. Most real estate purchases require lending financing. Most real estate lender financings require an unbiased appraisal to support the lending decision. As such, any discussion of lender financing of real estate will lead to a discussion about the appraisals required for those financings. These concepts are at the very core of real estate appraisal and, as such, experienced real estate appraisers are actively sought to render unbiased and credible opinions as they pertain to these concepts.

In order to make sound investment decisions, buyers, sellers, investors, lenders, and financial institutions that participate within the real estate markets are very interested in the cost, the price, and the value of real estate. Because these three financial measures are constantly changing in relation to each other, astute real estate market observers will monitor the degree and direction of cost, price, and value. Real estate counselors, along with other professionals within the investment services industry, can provide advice about this and other aspects of commercial real estate. The National Association of REALTORS® offers many NAR-affiliated institutes, societies, and councils that can provide expertise in these and other related areas.

Real estate investment banking evolved from the commercial investment banking industry. Real estate investment bankers are talented individuals and entities that have combined multiple skill sets that allow a seamless delivery of selected real estate services to clients. The result is that investment bankers can offer comprehensive transaction services to clients, saving valuable time and eliminating the need of assembling many of the appropriate team players required to implement real estate transactions. Real estate investment bankers combine sales and marketing acumen, real estate market expertise, and capital market savvy in the implementation of a property transaction (either a sale or purchase) or the delivery of capital (in the form of either equity or debt) on behalf of a client.

Buyers, sellers, investors, lenders, and financial institutions that participate within the real estate markets are involved with either institutional real estate or noninstitutional real estate. Institutional real estate is usually the best in class, quality, location, and income within any given market. Institutional investors include large national pension funds, insurance companies, or private real estate entities, as well as the advisors who provide acquisition services to those investors. They invest and manage the most pristine of real estate, which is usually the most marketable and demanded within any given market. Individual transaction sizes can range in the hundreds of millions of dollars and total portfolio assets managed can reach into the billions of dollars. Because institutional real estate is considered best in class, quality, location, and income, it is also considered to possess less risk than noninstitutional real estate. Noninstitutional real estate is all real estate assets other than institutional real estate assets. Accordingly, there is more risk associated with noninstitutional real estate.

A commercial real estate sale is a transaction involving a seller and buyer who are negotiating a deal. Because there are different perspectives in a transaction, a commercial real estate transaction can be perceived from a seller's perspective, a buyer's perspective, and a deal perspective. Having an outline of a potential transaction is useful as a universal tool for guidelines and structuring a conceptual plan for a successful commercial transaction, or understanding one that has been presented to you. A review of the various steps and procedures involved also highlights the need for a sophisticated skill set.

■ **Review Questions**

1. Commercial real estate
   a. is any real estate required for the operation of a business enterprise.
   b. may be real estate that is owned.
   c. may be real estate that is leased.
   d. All of the above (A, B, and C)

2. The four general service lines within the commercial real estate business may be summarized as
   a. brokerage, banking, appraisal, and valuation.
   b. sales, advisory, finance, and related industries.
   c. counseling, advisory, management, and investment.
   d. law, accounting, planning, and maintenance.

3. The role of a commercial real estate broker
   a. should be consistent with the broker's agency relationship with the seller or buyer.
   b. when acting as an agent for the seller is to successfully sell the property and close the deal.
   c. when acting as an agent for the buyer is to successfully acquire the property and close the deal.
   d. All of the above (A, B, and C)

4. Reason(s) for combining services in the commercial real estate industry include which of the following?
   a. As a matter of business practice, brokers naturally gain knowledge about related commercial services as their professional experience increases.
   b. The broker is in the ideal position to provide these additional core services.
   c. Combining services allows the broker to add value to the transaction.
   d. All of the above (A, B, and C)

5. Advantages of financing real estate include the
   a. ability for positive leverage.
   b. ability for negative leverage.
   c. ability for repayment by borrower.
   d. All of the above (A, B, and C)

6. The primary difference between a mortgage broker, mortgage banker, and correspondent lender is
   a. mortgage brokers may originate, close, and service a loan.
   b. mortgage brokers and mortgage bankers may originate, close, and service a loan.
   c. mortgage bankers and correspondent lenders may originate, close, and service a loan.
   d. mortgage brokers and correspondent lenders may originate, close, and service a loan.

7. Financial leverage
   a. considers the effect that borrowed money for financing a property acquisition has on investment returns.
   b. occurs when the interest rate charged by a lender for borrowed funds is greater than the rate of return that an investment is capable of generating on those borrowed funds.
   c. occurs when the interest rate charged by a lender for borrowed funds is less than the rate of return that an investment is capable of generating on those borrowed funds.
   d. occurs when the interest rate charged by a lender for borrowed funds is equal to the rate of return that an investment is capable of generating on those borrowed funds.

8. Cost is
   a. the amount of money that real estate will sell for in the marketplace.
   b. usually more than value.
   c. the amount of money that is required to create real estate in the marketplace.
   d. usually more than price.

9. An advantage of working with a real estate investment banking firm is
   a. their ability to deliver comprehensive transaction services to clients.
   b. their ability to save clients valuable time.
   c. their advanced level of expertise in real estate transactions.
   d. All of the above (A, B, and C)

10. Sales transactions may be viewed from the
    a. buyer's perspective, the seller's perspective, and the deal perspective.
    b. broker's perspective, the lender's perspective, and the appraiser's perspective.
    c. buyer's perspective, the attorney's perspective, and the deal perspective.
    d. buyer's perspective, the seller's perspective, and the attorney's perspective.

11. An investor is considering the acquisition of a 25-unit rental apartment building for a negotiated price of $75,000 per unit. The investor wants to finance the purchase with debt and has cash equity of $500,000. A lender will underwrite a senior loan on a basis of 75 percent LTV. If the investor meets all of the other requirements of the lender, will he have enough capital to purchase this property?

    a.   No. The investor does not have enough equity.

    b.   No. The lender cannot provide enough debt.

    c.   Yes, but only if the investor can obtain additional gap financing.

    d.   Yes. The lender debt plus owner equity is enough for the capital required for the deal.

12. Using your answer from question 11, if this investment generates a return of 10 percent, what would the total return for this acquisition be?

    a. $187,500

    b. $140,625

    c. $46,875

    d.   There is not enough information to determine what the total return would be.

13. The lender from question 11 will provide a loan commitment based on an interest rate of 7.5 percent and a loan amortization period of 25 years. The annual debt service required to service this loan is $124,705. What is the lender's return and the investor's return, and what type of leverage does this financing create?

    a.   The lender's return is 13.40 percent and the investor's return is 8.87 percent, resulting in positive leverage.

    b.   The lender's return is 7.5 percent and the investor's return is 8.87 percent, resulting in negative leverage.

    c.   The lender's return is 8.87 percent and the investor's return is 13.40 percent, resulting in positive leverage.

    d.   The lender's return is 8.87 percent and the investor's return is 7.5 percent, resulting in negative leverage.

14. The lender requires a debt-coverage ratio of at least 1.25. Using the information and answers from questions 11, 12, and 13, what is the DCR for this loan and does it meet or exceed the lender's minimum DCR?

    a.   The DCR is 1.51 and it exceeds the lender's minimum DCR of 1.25.

    b.   The DCR is 1.41 and it exceeds the lender's minimum DCR of 1.25.

    c.   The DCR is 1.31 and it exceeds the lender's minimum DCR of 1.25.

    d.   The DCR is 1.21 and it does not meet the lender's minimum DCR of 1.25.

15. The seller of the 25-unit rental apartment building in question 11 is also the developer. The seller is making a 20 percent profit on his total development costs. How much profit did the seller/developer make on this deal?

    a. $375,000

    b. $312,500

    c. $300,750

    d. $250,000

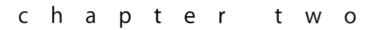

c h a p t e r   t w o

COMMERCIAL PROPERTY TYPES AND OFFICE PROPERTIES

■ Key Terminology

CBD	functional obsolescence	office node
cost-of-living adjustment (COLA)	gross construction area	rentable area
	loss factor	smart building
economic obsolescence	office building	step-up rent
flat rent	office building class	useable area

■ Overview

In this chapter, commercial property types are introduced. This chapter then discusses in great detail office properties. Important trends impacting office buildings are discussed. The purpose and variation in office building classifications are presented. The evolution of building locations and office building design is evaluated. The need and methods of proper office building measurement are discussed. The need and methods of proper office building measurement are analyzed. Office building rent and expense standards are calculated. Simply explaining these terms is both intricate and complex, and the need for such explanations becomes obvious.

As new terms are introduced, the language of real estate begins to take shape. Calculations for determining the various types of rent and tenant pro-rata allocations are presented. The unique qualities of each property type provide justification for commercial property specialization in brokerage and other real estate professions.

■ Learning Objectives

After completing this chapter, the reader should be able to accomplish the following:

1. List *six types of commercial properties*
2. Define *office building*
3. Discuss *trends* impacting office buildings

4. Differentiate between the *four classes* of office buildings

5. List the *five primary locations* of office buildings

6. Explain the differences between the *five types* of office buildings

7. State the *five design categories* of office buildings

8. Describe the *three factors of office building measurement*

9. Differentiate between the *five types of office building rent and expenses*

10. Explain what an office building *stopped expense* is

The Nature of Commercial Real Estate

The Real Estate Developer's Point of View

From a developer's perspective, commercial real estate is all about the ability to make a profit over and above all the costs of that development. Because of the long-term nature and significant capital requirements of building improvements, a commercial real estate developer seeks to incorporate desirable building features, as well as flexibility of use, into the building itself, to accommodate future market and tenant preferences. However, the decision to construct the most desirable building should also be based on an analysis of the costs of that development versus the profit over and above that cost. A successful real estate development must address all these issues. As any developer will tell you, this is easier to say than to accomplish.

The Real Estate Buyer's Point of View

From a buyer's perspective, commercial real estate is all about the ability to make a profit over and above the purchase price of the investment. Because of the long-term nature and significant capital requirements of buying the building improvements, an owner has the responsibility of maintaining the desirability of the improvements to ensure the greatest achievable financial returns for the longest period of time. However, the decision of maintaining the improvements should also be based on an analysis of the costs versus the profit over and above that cost. For a real estate investment to be successful, the buyer must address all these issues. As any buyer will tell you, this is easier to say than to accomplish.

The Real Estate Market's Point of View

Both developers and buyers of real estate are investors in real estate.

Let's consider the Chrysler Building. Located in midtown Manhattan, this highrise building had a groundbreaking ceremony on September 19, 1928, and was officially opened to the public on May 28, 1930. *It is no longer a "new" building yet has been maintained in excellent condition.* It was the tallest building in the world until 1931 when the Empire State Building overtook it. *It is no longer the world's tallest building yet has a rooftop observation deck with breathtaking views and a prestigious private sky lounge.* Built at the request of automotive businessman Walter P. Chrysler, the exterior of the building is clad with symbols of the Chrysler automobile including hood ornaments, radiator caps, and car fenders. It also has a lobby clad with exotic marble and onyx. *It has unusual building features yet is considered a stunning example of the art deco style.* At its completion in 1930, the building was only 10 percent leased. It enjoyed periods of 100 percent occupancy yet sank to a 17 percent occupancy rate during the recession of 1970. It cost the developer $20 million to build in 1930 and 71 years later was bought by GVP, a Dusseldorf, Germany–based company, for $395 million in 2001. *It is still considered valuable as a real estate investment.*

■ Commercial Property Types

Following are the six *primary* types of commercial properties:

1. Office properties
2. Retail properties
3. Multifamily apartment properties
4. Lodging properties
5. Industrial properties
6. Commercial land

Although commercial real estate can be described in generalities, each property type is unique. Commercial real estate can be described as any real estate used as part of a business. However, commercial property differs in such areas as how it is classified, the characteristics of its market, its physical design, how the property areas are measured, how rent is determined, what expenses are to be considered, and what the property's investment requirements and expectations are. These differences require an understanding of at least the basics about types of commercial property.

Consider an investor who wants to acquire a commercial property. He wants to pay cash for the property, but not more than $550,000. He requires a 10 percent rate of return on invested capital, which would equate to $55,000. The investor is presented with the six investment opportunities shown in Table 2.1.

Table 2.1

Alternative Investment Opportunities

Commerical Property	Office	Retail	Apartment	Lodging	Industrial	Land
All-cash Purchase Price	$550,000	$550,000	$550,000	$550,000	$550,000	$550,000
All-cash Return/Dollars	$ 55,000	$ 55,000	$ 55,000	$ 55,000	$ 55,000	$ 55,000
All-cash Return/% Price	10%	10%	10%	10%	10%	10%

The investor can choose only one of these possible investments from the six that have been presented. However, the choice can no longer simply be based on a $550,000 cash investment, nor can it be based on a 10 percent return, because all six investments meet both conditions.

The investor will have to look closely at other investment considerations that will influence his decision. Some basis questions that will arise include:

- What does the real estate look like, what condition is it in, and how old is it?
- How is the rent determined and how long will it last?
- Is the income stream expected to remain stable, increase, or decrease?
- What are the operating expenses for this property and who pays them?
- What is the location and market for this property?
- What are the economic, market, and property risks of this investment?
- Who will manage this property?

■ Office Properties

Definition of an Office Building

An **office building** is a building that contains office space. The purpose of having the office space is to provide a place where a specific type of work activity can occur, such as professional- or business-related work activity.

Trends Impacting Office Buildings

Evolving technology. Today, people all over the world are connected to each other and to businesses, information, and government agencies through a rapidly evolving network of telecommunication systems. This network has come to be known as the information superhighway. For businesses to remain competitive and viable, they must be able to capitalize on the information superhighway and existing and evolving technologies. Because office buildings serve businesses, they must provide these technologies as amenities.

Smart buildings. In addition to accelerating the regional and suburban growth of office buildings, the advent of various technologies, computers, the Internet, fiber optics, and the information superhighway has led to both the need for and creation of technologically advanced office buildings, which are also known as **smart buildings.**

Smart buildings offer the very latest systems available for fully integrated broadband communications service, high-speed Internet access, and data network service. These buildings also offer state-of-the-art security systems. Office building entrances, elevators, and parking garages are access-controlled with a card key or fingerprint reader. Security cameras monitor property entrances, common areas, elevators, garages, and restricted areas. The buildings' heating, ventilation, and air-conditioning (HVAC) systems employ the latest technologies and are geared to ensure complete tenant comfort and reliability. Smart buildings offer flexibility of use to accommodate future market and tenant preferences.

Suburban office development. The information superhighway and most new technologies are dependent upon fiber optics, broadband, cable, electric, and telecommunication utilities. These utilities are normally located along easement corridors that lie adjacent and parallel to major highways, freeways, heavily traveled main commercial arterials, and along major mass transit routes. In addition to the natural demand-based development for office buildings along these corridors, new and evolving technology has also played a significant role in where a building is located. As a result, suburban office buildings have developed along these easement corridors.

Office nodes and business parks. Suburban office development and growth can be found along the easement corridors within mature suburban communities that tend to grow in circular rings around the older urban core area. This growth has created suburban office "nodes." **Office nodes** are clusters of suburban office buildings forming a separate and distinct suburban-downtown central business district **(CBD)** within the particular suburb. These office nodes offer high-quality office space at a lower rental rate than comparable space within the historical CBD. Suburban office buildings tend to be developed in clusters or nodes, and this clustering has further evolved into the development of planned suburban business parks.

Office Building Classifications

An office building is the sum total of its age, location, building material, building systems, amenities, lease rates and terms, occupancy, tenant profile, and management. Office buildings are "classified" according to their unique combination of these characteristics. These characteristics are simply summed up to provide an opinion of a building's class.

There are four primary **office building classes:** A, B, C, and D. These classes were established by the Urban Land Institute and have become an internationally recognized "benchmark" for describing a building. The purpose of establishing the benchmark is to differentiate one building from another. Benchmarking office buildings is useful to developers, buyers, sellers, investors, lenders, and insurers in their consideration of office buildings. It also provides support and justifies decisions involving the concepts of cost, price, and value.

1. *Class A.* This class of office building is the most desirable building in its market area and offers excellent location and access. These buildings are distinguished by their excellent architectural design, superior construction and finish, building materials, systems, features, and amenities. They are usually the newest buildings in the market in which they are located. If they are not the newest, they are maintained to be competitive with new buildings by professional on-site management. Class A office buildings tend to draw the most prominent, financially stable, and creditworthy tenants who can afford to pay the market's highest rents. Because of the overall characteristics of Class A office buildings, they are highly sought after by investors. The very best Class A office buildings are comprised of unique and so-called "signature" or "trophy" buildings.

2. *Class B.* This class of office building has good location, management, construction, and tenancy. These buildings usually have some functional obsolescence or other form of depreciation due primarily to age.

Good quality Class B or Class B+ buildings can compete with certain segments of Class A office buildings.

3. *Class C.* This class of office building is generally older compared to a Class A or Class B building, with a reduced functional use and/or value due to the market in which the building is located.

4. *Class D.* This class of office building is older and in need of extensive renovation because it is no longer functional or has significant deterioration. Class D office buildings are often acquired for their redevelopment potential. In real estate jargon, these buildings are known as "teardowns" or "site scrapers," which implies demolition of the existing improvements for a new alternative use.

The Chrysler Building

Consider the historic Chrysler Building, a desirable "landmark" highrise office building located within midtown Manhattan. In addition to its excellent location on Lexington Avenue, it offers a stunning art deco architectural design, exceptional building materials, systems, smart building features, amenities, and on-site management. Because of the overall characteristics of the Chrysler Building, it can draw financially stable and creditworthy tenants who can afford to pay among the market's highest rents. The Chrysler Building is a unique investment-grade "signature" and "trophy" building. Clearly, the Chrysler Building is Class A. That is why a Germany-based company paid $395 million for it in 2001.

When the Chrysler Building was completed in 1930 it did not have Internet access for computers or smart building features because those technologies did not exist at the time. However, today it offers both. As these technologies became available in competitive buildings, the Chrysler Building began to suffer a loss in comparable use and value due to the aging building improvements, which were not considered *functional*. **Functional obsolescence** is a loss in value that results from deficiencies or needed improvements. These negative influences are caused by the property itself and not the market in which the property is located. Functional obsolescence may or may not be economically correctable or "curable." In the case of the Chrysler Building, it was economically correctable. And once cured, the building had an increase in use, desirability by tenants, and value in the market.

During the economic recession in 1970, the Chrysler Building's occupancy rate sank to 17 percent. With such low tenant occupancy, tenant lease income and property value also sank. This problem was widespread throughout the entire New York office market, so the problem was not the building but the *economic market*. **Economic obsolescence** is a loss in value that results from negative influences outside the site on which the property is located. These negative influences are caused by the market where the property is located and not the property itself. Economic obsolescence is usually beyond the control of the property owner and is usually not correctable. In the case of the Chrysler Building, it corrected itself as the recession ended and the market recovered. Once the market recovered, the building had an increase in value.

A reduction in building usefulness eventually leads to a reduction in building value.

A reduction in building value may not lead to a reduction in building usefulness.

The type and number of tenants that occupy an office building further define the use of an office building. The five types office buildings are the following:

1. *Office building.* A building in which most of the space is used or marketed for office-type activities
2. *Medical office building.* A building in which most of the office space is used or marketed for medical office–type activities
3. *Government office building.* A building in which most of the office space is used or marketed for use by government
4. *Single-tenanted building.* A building in which the space is occupied by one tenant
5. *Multiple-tenanted building.* A building in which the space is occupied by more than one tenant

Location of Office Buildings

A primary benefit provided by an office building to its tenants is the building's location as it relates to other surrounding buildings, businesses, industries, and all the supporting services that are required by the tenant. For example, law firms favor locations near courthouses or major clients. Medical doctors tend to locate near major hospitals and other medical facilities. The central business district, or CBD, has been the most desirable and sought after office building location. The CBD is generally identifiable as the historical core area of a city, which also may be referred to as "downtown." Office buildings in the CBD generally command the highest rents within the immediate and surrounding market area.

However, the continued development of office buildings has shifted away from the CBD for a number of reasons, including the advancement of highways and efficient mass transit into the growing suburban areas, information superhighway utilities located along easement corridors that lie adjacent and parallel to these highways, and the declining amount of prime commercial land itself. As a result, office buildings can now be found

■ within the historical downtown CBD district;

■ along major highways, freeways, and heavily traveled main commercial arterials;

■ along major mass transit routes;

■ within close proximity to major airports; and

■ within suburban areas, including planned office business parks.

Office Building Design Standards

Office buildings may be classified as *urban design* or *suburban design*. Office buildings of an *urban design* are structures that are designed to *vertically maximize* the use of the available site area by building a midrise, highrise, or skyscraper structure. Due in part to limitations of available land, urban-designed buildings usually combine office space with structured parking and other complementary commercial uses. From the market's perspective, these components are perceived as building amenities that increase the building's desirability by tenants, which generates marketing and leasing activities and raises the stature of the building within its market. From the investor's perspective, these components increase the income stream and thus the value of the property.

Office buildings of *a suburban design* are structures that are designed to *horizontally maximize* the use of the available site area by building a lowrise or midrise structure. Because there is usually land available for development, suburban-designed buildings do not necessarily have to combine other complementary commercial uses into the structure. These complementary uses are normally located in close proximity to the building, and, if so, would be minimized within the building itself. Suburban office buildings are usually part of a cluster, a node, or a suburban office park. From the market's perspective, the complementary uses within the office node or suburban office park are perceived as building amenities that increase the building's desirability by tenants, which generates marketing and leasing activities and raises the stature of the building within its market. From the investor's perspective, these components increase the income stream and thus the value of the property.

The size and shape of the building's floor area are also an important design consideration. In major market areas the availability of contiguous "blocks" of office space is an important marketing tool for the successful leasing of a building. Therefore, it is important for property managers to know the typical square footage "block" of office space demanded. For example, a tenant who requires 10,000 square feet of office space for a business would prefer that space to be a contiguous block and on the same floor because it is a more *functional* space. Occupying one office on the same floor containing 10,000 square feet of contiguous office space is much more conducive to a business enterprise than occupying four offices on four different floors containing 2,500 square each feet of noncontiguous office space. From the market's perspective, functional floor plans of typical size are perceived as building amenities that increase the building's desirability by tenants, which generates marketing and leasing activities and raises the stature of the building within its market. From the investor's perspective, these components increase the income stream and thus the value of the property.

> As a space becomes more functional, it becomes more useful to a tenant.

Generally, there are five design categories of office buildings: (1) skyscraper, (2) highrise, (3) midrise, (4) lowrise, and (5) subterranean. Any attempt to begin to quantify these five categories by such basis benchmarks as height, size, and scope, becomes difficult because regional, national, international, and trade organization standards are not the same. Each has different standards for gathering, interpreting, and presenting information, so it is important to understand what the information contains.

For example, in the United States, the Chrysler Building is considered to contain 77 floors including the ground floor. However, in Germany, the floor count usually begins on the second floor and completely ignores the ground floor, so by that standard the Chrysler Building is considered to contain 76 floors. In order for floor count statistics to be comparable in an international database, the standard for counting floors used one by country or another must be utilized. The standard you used would be at odds with the traditions of the other country.

Office Building Measurement Standards

The proper measurement of an office building is an important consideration for owners, tenants, investors, appraisers, and lenders. If an office building is to be properly measured, three factors must be considered:

1. An accurate measure of the space
2. The identification of areas that cause a loss of usable space, known as a **"loss factor"**
3. The determination of whether the floor area configuration is functional

The Building Owners and Managers Association (BOMA) has established a set of standards for office building measurement that are used in most areas nationally. Known as standards of floor measurement, office buildings are measured in terms of **gross construction area,** usable area, and **rentable area**.

Measurement factor 1: the accurate measurement of the space. Gross construction area is determined by computing the entire square footage within the floor's perimeter, excluding the building envelope. The gross construction area must be determined even though it is not used in leasing because it affects the cost of tenant installations. This area is also referred to as *gross building area,* or GBA.

> GBA equals the total of all space within the building, excluding the exterior walls.

Usable area on a multilevel floor is gross construction area minus core space. *Core space* includes the square footage used for such areas as lobbies, public corridors, stairways, bathrooms, elevators, electrical and janitorial closets, fan rooms, and mechanical system rooms for generators and HVAC. On a floor occupied by a single tenant, corridors and bathrooms are considered part of the usable area. GBA less core space equals usable area.

> Useable area equals GBA less the core area.

It is a generally accepted formula that a proportionate share of core space is added to the usable space of each tenant on the floor. The public elevators and stair space are usually excluded in making these calculations. In buildings where the heating, ventilating, and air-conditioning system is located in the basement or on the roof, the **rentable area** is identical to the usable area. However, in some office buildings, the HVAC may occupy one or more floors between the basement and the roof. This space is not rentable, but its gross construction area is apportioned to the rentable office floors serviced by the HVAC equipment and is considered part of their rentable space.

> Rentable area equals the useable area plus pro-rata allocation of the core area.

Rentable area must be calculated for two reasons:

1. The base rent is dependent upon the rentable area calculation.
2. The rent escalation and expense pass-through items such as real estate taxes and operating expenses are determined for each tenant on the basis of the relative rentable square footage attributable to each tenant.

Measurement factor 2: identification of a "loss factor." The difference between rentable and usable area is referred to as the loss factor. The rentable area less the usable area is equal to the loss factor in square feet. The usable area divided by the rentable area is equal to the loss factor percentage.

> Loss factor equals the rentable area less the useable area.

Measurement factor 3: configuration of the floor area.   Floor area configurations are important to the property manager in determining how marketable the space is, as well as the types of tenants who might be attracted to it. The practical uses to which various floor layouts can be put are important. Certain floor configurations allow better use of the space by tenants than others. As a practical matter, the more unusual a floor configuration is, the less desirable it is to prospective tenants, and therefore the greater the difficulty a property manager will have in leasing it.

Example of Building Measurement

Let's consider a rectangular-shaped floor area in a multistory office building. All of the square footage within this floor's perimeter, excluding the building envelope, is 25,000 square feet. This particular floor area contains a gross construction area of 25,000 square feet.

This particular multiple-tenanted floor area has an elevator landing, public corridors, bathrooms, electrical and janitorial closets, an HVAC room, and emergency exit stairways. Although these areas are used for their named purpose, it is not area that a tenant could use and occupy as office space (i.e., a desk cannot be placed in these areas). This nonusable space is called core space. The core space is measured and it contains a total area of 3,750 square feet.

Because the landlord now knows the gross building area and the core area, the usable area is determined to be 21,250 square feet, as shown in Table 2.2.

The landlord is quoting rent as $25 per square foot of rentable space. However, neither gross construction area nor usable area can be used as rentable space. In order to determine rentable space, the landlord first has to add back all of the core space, with the exception of the areas for elevators and stairs. The areas for elevators and stairs are determined to be 750 square feet, so the adjusted core area is 3,000 square feet, as shown in Table 2.3.

Now that the landlord knows the adjusted core area, he determines that the rentable area is 24,250 square feet, as shown in Table 2.4.

Table 2.2

Determining Usable Area

Measurement	Square Feet	% Square Feet
Gross Construction Area	25,000	100%
less:		
Total Core Space	3,750	15
equals:		
Usable Area	21,250	85

Table 2.3

Determining
Adjusted Core Area

Measurement	Square Feet	% Square Feet
Total Core Space	3,750	100%
less:		
Excluded Core Space	750	20
equals:		
Adjusted Core Space	3,000	80

Table 2.4

Determining
Rentable Area

Measurement	Square Feet	% Square Feet
Usable Area	21,250	88%
add:		
Adjusted Core Space	3,000	12
equals:		
Rentable Area	24,250	100

Office Building Leasing Rental and Expense Standards

To an office building owner and property manager, rent and recovery of expenses represent a return on the real estate investment. To a tenant, rent and expense payments represent a cost of business operations. Most office building leases are based on a form of payment of rent and recovery of expenses that falls into one of the following five categories:

1. *Flat rent.* Rental leases provide for fixed rental payments during the term of the lease. **Flat rent** is considered the traditional and least complex method of setting the rent. It calls for the rent to be a fixed dollar amount per annum, payable monthly in advance. Tenants prefer this type of lease provision because they know exactly what the rent obligation is during the term of the lease. Owners and property managers take the opposite view and avoid fixed rent because it subjects the owner to inflation risk. The primary disadvantage of a flat lease is that it does not have an adjustment mechanism for inflation and, accordingly, represents an income stream with a decreasing purchasing power over time.

2. *Step-up rent.* A **step-up rent** calls for an additional increment of rent to be paid at specific dates during the lease. This lease provision has the benefit of its simplicity. Because the amount and the timing of the step up are known, tenants usually accept step-up leases.

   For example, assume a lease term is ten years. In the first year, the rent starts at $50,000 per year and then steps up $2,500 per year for each of the nine years remaining in the base term of the lease. The

Table 2.5

Step-Up Rent Payments

Lease Year	Base Rent	Step Up	Total Rent
1	$ 50,000	$ —	$ 50,000
2	50,000	2,500	52,500
3	50,000	5,000	55,000
4	50,000	7,500	57,500
5	50,000	10,000	60,000
6	50,000	12,500	62,500
7	50,000	15,000	65,000
8	50,000	17,500	67,500
9	50,000	20,000	70,000
10	50,000	22,500	72,500
Total	$500,000	$112,500	$612,500

total rent during the term of the lease is $612,500, allocated to $500,000 in base rent and $112,500 in step-up rent. Table 2.5 presents an income stream from this step-up rent scenario.

3. *Flat rent with stopped expense recovery.* A popular form of lease rental arrangement is a fixed or flat rental component with a provision for the tenant to pay a fair share of increases in some or all of the building operating expenses. Operating expenses include fixed expenses, variable expenses, and capital expenses, such as reserves for replacement. *Operating expenses are established, fixed, and "stopped" by a "stop clause" in the base year of tenant occupancy.* In subsequent years to the base year, any increases in operating expenses are allocated in proportion or pro rata to the tenants on the basis of their rentable space.

For existing office buildings, the *base year* is the year during which the tenant takes occupancy of the office space. For proposed office buildings, the base year is usually the first year of income, expense, and occupancy stabilization. Other considerations include stopping the expenses at the beginning or end of the year and whether the expenses are to be based on a calendar year or fiscal year. Tenants are allocated their pro-rata share of additional operating expenses above the stop by the relationship of their occupied rentable space to the total rentable space in the office building.

For example, assume a tenant occupies 10,000 square feet of rentable space in an office building that contains 100,000 square feet of total rentable space. The formula, used in the calculation shown below, determines that the tenant's pro-rata share of additional expenses would be 10 percent.

Tenant's occupied rentable space ÷ total rentable space = pro-rata percent.

In our example:

10,000 square feet ÷ 100,000 square feet = 10 percent.

Now assume that the total building operating expenses are stopped in the base year of the tenant's occupancy, during which operating expenses are $600,000. If total operating expenses the following year increase by 3 percent to $618,000, then total operating expenses have increased by $18,000 over the stop. The formula, used in the calculation shown below, determines the increase in stopped total operating expenses between the base year and current year.

Current year operating expenses – base year operating expenses = increase.

In our example:

$$\$618,000 - \$600,000 = \$18,000.$$

Once increases above the stopped operating expenses and the tenant's pro-rata percent have been determined, calculating the tenant's pro-rata increase in operating expenses can be accomplished. The formula, used in the calculation shown below, determines the tenant's share of increased expenses.

Increases in operating expenses × tenant's percent =
Tenant's pro-rata expense.

In our example:

$$\$18,000 \times 10\% = \$1,800.$$

Table 2.6 illustrates a lease with a both a flat rent and stopped expense recovery component.

Base rent. In this lease scenario, the tenant occupies 10,000 square feet of rentable area in a building of 100,000 rentable square feet. This equates to a 10 percent pro-rata percent of the building's rentable space. The lease term is ten years. In the base year of the lease, the tenant pays $25 per square foot of rentable area, equating to $25,000. The rent remains the same (stays "flat") during the remaining nine years of the lease, also at $25,000.

Table 2.6

Stopped Expense Recovery

Lease Year	Base Rent	Expense Stop	Actual Expense	Increase in Expense	Tenant % Expense
1	$ 25,000	$600,000	$600,000	$ —	10%
2	25,000	600,000	618,000	18,000	10
3	25,000	600,000	636,540	36,540	10
4	25,000	600,000	655,636	55,636	10
5	25,000	600,000	675,305	75,305	10
6	25,000	600,000	695,564	95,564	10
7	25,000	600,000	716,431	116,431	10
8	25,000	600,000	737,924	137,924	10
9	25,000	600,000	760,062	160,062	10
10	25,000	600,000	782,864	182,864	10
Total	$250,000	N/A	N/A	N/A	N/A

Expense stop. The lease contains a stopped expense recovery over the base year during which the building's total operating expenses are $600,000, equating to $6.00 per square foot of total rentable area.

Actual expenses. The building's operating expenses grow at approximately 3 percent per year during the ten-year lease period.

Increase in expense. Each year the building's total operating expenses are increasing. The difference between the base year operating expenses and the current year operating expenses is measured by the increase in operating expenses. The building's operating expenses increase at approximately 3 percent per year during the ten-year lease period.

Tenant's % expense. The tenant's fair share of the building's increasing operating expense is 10 percent allocation. The 10 percent allocation is based on the tenant's pro-rata percentage as figured above.

Tenant's $ expense. The tenant's fair share of the building's increasing operating expense is calculated and presented in dollars. The dollars represent 10 percent of the increase in the building's operating expenses for each lease year.

Total rent. The tenant's total rent each year is equal to the base rent and the expense recovery for the year.

Total. The tenant's rent during the lease is equal to $250,000 for base rent, $87,833 for expense recoveries, and $337,833 in total rent.

To recap, although the rent remains flat and totals $250,000 during the ten-year lease period, the expense recovery amounts to an additional $87,833, equating to an additional 35.13 percent cost of occupancy to the tenant and source of expense recovery to the property owner.

4. *Cost-of-living rent increases.* In this popular method, rent escalation is tied to changes in the consumer price index (CPI) or other specified index. Rent changes are tied to an outside price index and do not require internal justification.

The building owner may require a minimum rent increase to be factored into a **cost-of-living adjustment (COLA).** For example, a lease provision may call for a cost-of-living increase based on the CPI or 3 percent per annum, whichever is greater. The tenant may respond by requesting that a ceiling or cap be placed on the potential rent increases during the term of the lease. The tenant may request a lease provision that calls for a cost-of-living increase based on the CPI or 3 percent per annum, whichever is less. Alternatively, a tenant may ask that the CPI consider both increases and decreases to the rent.

Table 2.7 illustrates a lease combining a flat rent component with a cost-of-living rent increase based on 3 percent per annum, compounded annually.

Base rent: In this lease scenario, the tenant occupies 10,000 square feet of rentable area in a building of 100,000 rentable square feet. This equates to a 10 percent pro-rata percent of the building's rentable space.

The lease term is ten years. In the base year of the lease, the tenant pays $25 per square foot of rentable area, equating to $25,000. The rent remains the same (stays "flat") during the remaining nine years of the lease.

Table 2.7

Flat Rent with Cost-of-Living
Adjustment

Lease Year	Base Rent	COLA	COLA Rent	Total Rent
1	$ 25,000	0%	$ —	$ 25,000
2	25,000	3.00	750	25,750
3	25,000	6.09	1,523	26,523
4	25,000	9.27	2,318	27,318
5	25,000	12.55	3,138	28,138
6	25,000	15.93	3,982	28,982
7	25,000	19.41	4,851	29,851
8	25,000	22.99	5,747	30,747
9	25,000	26.68	6,669	31,669
10	25,000	30.48	7,619	32,619
Total	$250,000		$36,597	$286,597

Cost-of-living adjustment (COLA): The tenant's base rent is subject to a cost-of-living adjustment of 3 percent per year during the ten-year lease period.

COLA rent: The tenant's rental cost-of-living adjustment is calculated and presented in dollars. The dollars represent a 3 percent increase in base rent for each lease year, growing at a compounded rate.

Total rent: The tenant's total rent each year is equal to the base rent plus the COLA rent for the year.

Total: The tenant's rent during the lease is equal to $250,000 for base rent, $36,597 for COLA rent, and $286,597 in total rent.

To recap, although the rent remains flat and totals $250,000 during the ten-year lease period, the COLA rent amounts to an additional $36,597, equating to an additional 14.64 percent cost of occupancy to the tenant and source of expense recovery to the property owner.

5. *Cost-of-living rent increase with stopped expense recovery.* This is a similar arrangement to the flat rent with stopped expense recovery previously discussed. There is a provision for the tenant to pay a fair share of increases in some or all of the building operating expenses. However, in this hybrid method, the rent is also tied to a cost-of-living index established in the base year of the lease.

Rent is adjusted annually by CPI changes or some other specified index. Operating expenses are determined annually by increases or decreases in the current year expenses as compared to the base year operating expenses. This method is gaining in popularity with owners

Table 2.8

Cost-of-Living Rent Increase
with Stopped Expense
Recovery

Lease Year	Base Rent	Expense Stop	Actual Expense	Increase in Expense	Tenant % Expense	Tenant $ Expense	COLA	COLA Rent	Total Rent
1	$25,000	$600,000	$600,000	$ —	10%	$ —	0%	$ —	$25,000
2	25,000	600,000	618,000	18,000	10	$1,800	3.00	750	27,550
3	25,000	600,000	636,540	36,540	10	3,654	6.09	223	28,877
4	25,000	600,000	655,636	55,636	10	5,564	9.27	516	31,080
5	25,000	600,000	675,305	75,305	10	7,531	12.55	945	33,476
6	25,000	600,000	695,564	95,564	10	9,556	15.93	1,522	36,079
7	25,000	600,000	716,431	116,431	10	11,643	19.41	2,259	38,903
8	25,000	600,000	737,924	137,924	10	13,792	22.99	3,171	41,963
9	25,000	600,000	760,062	160,062	10	16,006	26.68	4,270	45,276

and property managers because rent increases will offset inflation risk and expense recovery will offset any expense increases.

Table 2.8 illustrates a lease combining COLA increase recovery with stopped expense recovery.

Base rent: In this lease scenario, the tenant occupies 10,000 square feet of rentable area in a building of 100,000 rentable square feet. This equates to a 10 percent pro-rata percent of the building's rentable space. The lease term is ten years. In the base year of the lease, the tenant pays $25 per square foot of rentable area, equating to $25,000. The rent remains the same (stays "flat") during the remaining nine years of the lease.

Expense stop: The lease contains a stopped expense recovery over the base year during which the building's total operating expenses are $600,000, equating to $6 per square foot of total rentable area.

Actual expense: The building's operating expenses grow at approximately 3 percent per year during the ten-year lease period.

Increase in expense: Each year the building's total operating expenses are increasing. The difference between the base year operating expenses and the current year operating expenses is measured by the increase in operating expenses. The building's operating expenses increase at approximately 3 percent per year during the ten-year lease period.

Tenant's % expense: The tenant's fair share of the building's increasing operating expenses is 10 percent allocation. The 10 percent allocation is based on the tenant's pro-rata percentage that was calculated previously.

Tenant's $ expense: The tenant's fair share of the building's increasing operating expenses is calculated and presented in dollars. The dollars represent 10 percent of the increase in the building's operating expenses for each lease year.

COLA rent: The tenant's rental cost-of-living adjustment is calculated and presented in dollars. The dollars represent a 3 percent increase in base rent for each lease year, growing at a compounded rate.

Total rent: The tenant's total rent each year is equal to the base rent plus the COLA rent for the year.

Total: The tenant's rent during the lease is equal to $250,000 for base rent, $36,597 for COLA rent, and $286,597 in total rent.

To recap, although the rent remains flat and totals $250,000 during the ten-year lease period, the expense recovery amounts to an additional $87,833 and the COLA rent amounts to an additional $36,597, equating to an additional 49.77 percent cost of occupancy to the tenant and source of additional rent and expense recovery to the property owner.

■ Summary

Commercial property is any real estate used for business purposes or as part of a business. Although commercial real estate can be described in generalities, each property type is unique. There are five generally recognized types of commercial property: office, retail, apartments, lodging, and commercial land. The difference in commercial property types necessitates an understanding of at least the basics about types of commercial property.

The nature of commercial real estate creates different perspectives about commercial real estate. A developer will have a different perspective of commercial real estate than a buyer of commercial real estate. However, both are considered real estate investors. Each of the various types of real estate has its own unique development, design, market, and investment criteria. Because of the long-term nature and intense capital requirements of building improvements, developers seek to incorporate the most competitive building features possible as well as incorporate flexibility into the building itself to accommodate future upgrades and improvements. The decision of maximizing the efficiency of the improvements is based on a review of costs versus profits, as measured by financial projections, analysis, and investor-derived investment criteria.

An office building is a building that contains office space. The purpose of having the office space is to provide a place where a specific type of work activity can occur—professional- or business-related work activity. Trends impacting office buildings include evolving technology, the development of smart buildings, the development of office buildings within the suburbs, and the creation of office nodes and business parks.

Office buildings can be categorized by their building class. The "class" of a building consists of a combination of a number of characteristics including age, location, building material, building systems, amenities, lease rates and terms, occupancy, management, and tenant profile. There are four primary classes of office buildings: A, B, C, and D. Office buildings are also defined by the predominant user of the space and include office buildings, medical office buildings, government office buildings, single-tenanted buildings, and multiple-tenanted buildings. The class, type, and tenants in an office building affect the risk, return, and value of an office building as an investment.

A locational benefit provided by office buildings is proximity to additional supporting services. Historically, the downtown area, also known as the central business district or CBD, of a city or region has been the most desirable location for office buildings. However, a diminishing supply of land and the development of vehicular highways and efficient mass transit have shifted development away from the CBDs to the suburbs where office nodes have formed. Suburban office nodes are clusters of suburban office buildings forming a separate and distinct suburban-downtown CBD within a particular suburb.

Office buildings may be classified as urban design or suburban design. Office buildings of an urban design are structures that are designed to vertically maximize the use of the available site area by building a midrise, highrise, or skyscraper structure. Due in part to limitations of available land, urban-designed buildings usually combine office space with structured parking and other complementary commercial uses. Office buildings of a suburban design are structures that are designed to horizontally maximize the use of the available site area by building a lowrise or midrise structure. Because there is usually land available for development, suburban designed buildings do not necessarily have to combine other complementary commercial uses into the structure. These complementary uses are normally located in close proximity to the building, and, if so, would be minimized within the building itself. Suburban office buildings are usually part of a cluster, a node, or suburban office park.

Generally, there are five design categories of office buildings: (1) skyscrapers, (2) highrise, (3) midrise, (4) lowrise, and (5) subterranean. Any attempt to begin to quantify these five categories by such basis benchmarks as height, size, and scope becomes difficult because regional, national, international, and trade organization standards are not the same. Each has different standards for gathering, interpreting, and presenting information, so it is important to understand what the information contains.

The proper measurement of an office building is an important consideration for owners, tenants, investors, appraisers, and lenders. If an office building is to be properly measured, three factors must be considered. They are the accurate measurement of all of the space; the identification of areas that cause a loss of usable space, known as a "loss factor"; and the determination if the floor area configuration is functional. The Building Owners and Managers Association has established a set of standards for office building measurement that is used in most areas nationally. Known as standards of floor measurement, office buildings are measured in terms of gross construction area, usable area, and rentable area.

To an office building owner and property manager, rent and recovery of expenses represent a return on the real estate investment. To a tenant, rent and expense payments represent a cost of business operations. Most office building leases are based on a payment of rent that falls into one of five categories: (1) flat rent, (2) step-up rent, (3) flat rent with stopped expense recovery, (4) cost-of-living rent increases, and (5) cost-of-living rent increases with stopped expense recovery.

■ **Review Questions**

1. Commercial property
    a. includes vacant land.
    b. may be either existing or proposed.
    c. is used for business purposes.
    d. All of the above (A, B, and C)

2. Office buildings are categorized according to
    a. location, quality of tenants, and quality of construction.
    b. degree of on-site management.
    c. property size and amenities.
    d. All of the above (A, B, and C)

3. An office building's "class" refers to its
    a. trophy status.
    b. smart building technology.
    c. quality.
    d. sophistication.

4. Class A office buildings are considered investment grade because
    a. they are the most desirable buildings in the market.
    b. they draw financially stable and creditworthy tenants.
    c. they achieve the highest market rents.
    d. All of the above (A, B, and C).

5. In defining an office building, the predominant tenant type occupies
    a. none of the office space.
    b. some of the office space.
    c. most of the office space.
    d. all of the office space.

6. Due to a diminishing supply of land, office building development has shifted away from the central business district (CDB) to
    a. along major highways, freeways, and heavily traveled main commercial arterials.
    b. along major mass transit routes.
    c. within close proximity to major airports.
    d. All of the above (A, B, and C)

7. The information superhighway is a term used to describe
   a. a network of integrated highway systems with informative billboard and other signage connecting people to businesses, government, and each other.
   b. a network of interstate highway systems with informative billboard and other signage connecting people to businesses, government, and each other.
   c. a network of integrated highway systems built over buried fiber optics, providing informative billboard and other signage connecting people to businesses, government, and each other.
   d. a network of integrated telecommunication systems connecting people around the world to information businesses, government, and each other.

8. Office nodes
   a. are suburban office buildings forming a separate and distinct suburban-downtown CBD within a particular suburb.
   b. consist of high-quality office space at lower rental rates than comparable space within a CBD.
   c. are cluster developments of suburban office buildings.
   d. All of the above (A, B, and C)

9. Smart buildings
   a. are parts of the information superhighway.
   b. usually form office nodes.
   c. are technologically advanced office buildings.
   d. All of the above (A, B, and C).

10. The three factors in the proper measurement of an office building are
    a. the accurate measurement of the floor area ratio, the supportable identification of a "loss factor," and the configuration of the space.
    b. the accurate measurement of the space, the supportable identification of a "loss factor," and the configuration of the floor areas.
    c. the accurate measurement of the "loss factor," the supportable identification of the floor areas, and the configuration of the space.
    d. the accurate measurement of the space, the supportable identification of a "floor area factor," and the configuration of the floor areas.

11. A floor area in a multistory office building has a gross construction area of 20,000 square feet. Core space represents 15 percent of the gross construction area. Determine the gross building area (GBA), the total core space, and the usable areas of this floor area.

    a. The GBA equals 20,000 square feet, the total core space equals 3,000 square feet, and the usable area equals 17,000 square feet.

    b. The GBA equals 23,000 square feet, the total core space equals 3,000 square feet, and the usable area equals 20,000 square feet.

    c. The GBA equals 20,000 square feet, the total core space equals 3,000 square feet, and the usable area equals 23,000 square feet.

    d. The GBA equals 17,000 square feet, the total core space equals 3,000 square feet, and the usable area equals 14,000 square feet.

12. Twenty percent of the total gross building areas' core space for the floor area in question 11 consists of areas for elevators and stairs. Determine the adjusted core space and the rentable area of this floor area.

    a. The adjusted core space equals 4,000 square feet and the total rentable area equals 16,000 square feet.

    b. The adjusted core space equals 2,400 square feet and the total rentable area equals 17,600 square feet.

    c. The adjusted core space equals 3,000 square feet and the total rentable area equals 23,000 square feet.

    d. The adjusted core space equals 2,400 square feet and the total rentable area equals 19,400 square feet.

13. Rents are quoted as $20 per square foot, full service, base year stop for the floor area in question 11. What would the potential annual first-year rent be for this floor area if fully leased?

    a. $400,000

    b. $388,000

    c. $340,000

    d. $300,000

14. Base year operating expenses represent 25 percent of the full-service rent quoted in question 13. If operating expenses are stopped in the base year and second year operating expenses increase by 8 percent per square foot, what is the amount of the second-year operating expenses that can be charged back to the tenants on this floor?

    a. $0.45 per square foot and $7,900 in total

    b. $0.40 per square foot and $7,760 in total

    c. $0.35 per square foot and $7,560 in total

    d. $0.30 per square foot and $7,250 in total

15. Rents quoted in question 13 are subject to an annual cost-of-living adjustment (COLA). The index is the CPI, which in the second year of the lease has risen by 3 percent. What would the COLA rent be for the second year?

    a. $0.60 per square foot per annum

    b. $970 per month

    c. $11,640 per annum

    d.   All of the above (A, B, and C)

chapter   three

RETAIL PROPERTIES

■ Key Terminology

anchor tenant	net lease	retail building
breakpoint	parking index	shop tenants
common area factor	percentage rent	specialty shopping center
common area maintenance	power center	trade area

■ Overview

In this chapter, retail property is presented in detail. Trends impacting retail buildings are discussed. The wide variety in classification of retailers is introduced. The demands of users of the retail space are presented. These concepts provide the foundation for a discussion of the different types of shopping centers, including how they draw power from clustering and key anchor tenants.

A retail property's location is presented not only in absolute physical terms, but in terms of an economic trade area as well. Trade areas are further refined into primary and secondary trade areas. Complementing a viable trade area is a viable building design. A building design's three main criteria—site characteristics, exterior building characteristics, and interior building characteristics—are considered.

The need for accurate building measurement is presented from the perspectives of both the owner/landlord and tenants. Calculations and examples for determining a building's size, rent, expenses, and pro-rata allocations are provided.

■ Learning Objectives

After completing this chapter, the reader should be able to accomplish the following:

1. Explain what a *retail property* is
2. Discuss the *six trends impacting retail buildings*

3. List the *19 classifications of retailers*

4. Describe the concepts of *clustering* and *cumulative attraction*

5. List the *five primary types of traditional shopping centers*

6. List the *five primary types of specialty shopping centers*

7. Define what *primary* and *secondary trade areas* are

8. Describe what *three factors influence a retail building design*

9. Differentiate between *gross building area, gross leasable area, total floor area,* and *common area*

10. Differentiate between *base rent, escalation rent,* and *percentage rent*

11. Explain what a *net lease* is

■ Retail Properties

Definition of a Retail Building

A **retail building** is a building that contains retail space. The purpose of having the retail space is to provide a place where a specific type of business activity can occur—retail sales and related business activities. *Retailing* is any business involving the sale of goods, commodities, and products in small quantities directly to consumers.

A retail building's size and design is determined by its use.

In a free market economy, such as that of the United States, the types of goods, commodities, and products sold on a retail basis are almost endless. For example, consider the basic retail needs related to food, fuel, clothing, and shelter. Each of these retailers requires a specific type of space, including the size and design of that space. Accordingly, the design and configuration of retail buildings are as varied as the retail uses of those buildings.

Trends Impacting Retail Buildings

Changing consumer tastes and preferences.   Tastes and preferences in retail merchandising change regularly and rapidly. Trends in the design of retail buildings have also come under pressure to evolve at an increasingly rapid rate. The changing size and scope of local, regional, and national tenants dictate the physical configuration of the space and the property amenities.

Today, consumers expect more of an entertainment experience at their retail destination. Consumers tend to become tired of the same retail experience even if the service and product is desirable. Retailers must be able to change the décor or layout of their space to maintain the sense of an experience. Similarly, developers of retail property must incorporate flexibility of use into their buildings to accommodate these anticipated changes in consumer and tenant preferences.

Changing building sizes and locations.   Retail properties are constantly reinventing themselves to address changing market conditions. During the 1940s and 1950s, the dominant property for retail sales was an unanchored freestanding strip retail center containing approximately 50,000 square feet of leaseable area. These properties were developed along primary commercial arterials to serve the demand generated by the surrounding population base.

Many of these strip centers have evolved into super-regional shopping centers anchored by up to five or more national tenants, with space requirements of 100,000 to 200,000 square feet each, along with in-line "shop tenants" and freestanding outparcels. Today, super-regional shopping centers may contain over 1,250,000 square feet of anchor and shop tenant space, in addition to 75,000 square feet of outparcel tenant space. The land areas for these properties may exceed 100 acres. Super-regional shopping centers have the ability to draw customers from over a 20-mile radius in each direction.

Physical sales markets and virtual sales markets. Retailers operate in a fiercely competitive market. The advent of Internet-based merchandising, known as e-commerce, has created additional competitive pressures. Prior to Internet-based marketing, retailers were primarily concerned with their physical real estate assets, known in real estate jargon as *"sticks and bricks."* However, with the advent of the Internet, retailers today have two markets in which to compete for sales and merchandising: in-store sales and online sales. Accordingly, retailers are now concerned with both virtual and physical assets, referred to in real estate jargon as *"clicks and bricks."*

Changing tenant business strategies. Trends in tenant business strategies have impacted the tenant mix in occupancy of a retail property. For example, consider the neighborhood shopping center. This type of shopping center traditionally consisted of a regional grocery chain, a regional or national drugstore chain, and local area tenants, which are referred to as **shop tenants.** Today, however, it is common to see both the grocery chain and the drugstore chain located on their own individual sites in close proximity to other complementary demand generators. With the traditional grocer and drugstore tenants gone, today's neighborhood centers resemble the unanchored freestanding strip retail centers popular during the 1950s.

The shopping and entertainment experience. Retailers are constantly tinkering with creating, maintaining, and delivering the perfect "retail experience." This retail experience is based on a retailer's development concept, which is expressed in the building design. Today, this retail experience consists of the successful combination of various amounts of shopping *and* entertainment. Signature restaurants, upscale coffee houses, boutique and gourmet shops, theaters, and nightclubs increasingly tenant retail properties. Newer retail properties are pedestrian friendly and incorporate plazas, public spaces, and open-air seating that are designed to encourage socializing, meeting, and intermingling.

The entertainment aspects of the retailing experience continue to evolve. Today, in many retail properties, the entertainment *is* the experience. This trend has led to the evolution of the urban entertainment center or UEC. UECs combine a shopping experience as part of a larger entertainment experience. This retail experience consists of the successful combination of a limited amount of shopping with a significant amount of entertainment options. Signature restaurants, upscale coffee houses, boutique and gourmet shops, theaters, and nightclubs are the primary tenants at UEC retail properties.

Competition and market saturation. As cities mature, they expand from their historical core areas, pushing new residential and retail development out into the emerging suburbs. New retail development can create overlapping market areas, which leads to reduced market share for older retail properties located within urban core areas. When combined with the residential population migration into the suburbs, it can result in an urban residential economic base decline, which leads to a retail economic decline.

Depletion of suitable land and mixed-use properties.   The ongoing depletion of suitable land and competition for urban infill sites has led to the integration of retail property uses with other uses. Today it is common to find a significantly sized retail component as part of a residential property that also has office and health club space.

Classification of Retailers

A retail building's size and design are determined by its intended use. Therefore, a predominant factor in classifying a retail building is the intended user of the space. Different retail products sold require different retail building sizes and design. So a retail building size and design are tenant-specific.

> A retail building's size and design are tenant-specific.

Because a retail building's size and design are tenant-specific, a discussion of retail building classifications should include the discussion of the retailers that occupy those buildings. The Urban Land Institute has established 19 generally recognized classifications of retailers. The following summary of retailer classifications provides insight as to the reason for the wide variety and differences in the design, assemblage, and configuration requirements of retail space:

1. *General merchandise*—including department stores, showroom/catalog stores, discount department stores, and warehouse clubs
2. *Food*—including supermarkets, gourmet markets, delicatessens, and bakeries
3. *Food service*—including restaurants, lounges, pizzerias, and fast-food/carry-out restaurants
4. *Clothing and accessories*—including men's wear stores, women's wear stores, family wear stores, children's wear stores, and bridal shops
5. *Shoes*—including men's shoe stores, women's shoes stores, family shoe stores, children's shoe stores, and athletic footwear stores
6. *Home furnishings*—including kitchen stores, bath shops, furniture stores, and china and glassware stores
7. *Home appliances*—including audio/video stores, computer/software stores, appliance stores, and gourmet cookware shops
8. *Building materials/hardware*—including home improvement centers, paint and wallpaper stores, and hardware and specialty hardware stores
9. *Automotive*—including auto showrooms; service stations; and automotive tire, battery, and accessory stores
10. *Hobby/special interest*—including general sporting goods stores, art galleries, arts and crafts stores, and camera shops
11. *Gift and specialty*—including import stores, candle shops, newspaper and magazine shops, and aromatherapy stores
12. *Jewelry*—including various types of jewelry stores

13. *Liquor*—including liquor and wine stores

14. *Drugs*—including drugstores and pharmacies

15. *Other retail*—including tobacco shops, flower/plant stores, telephone stores/telecom services, and opticians

16. *Personal services*—including massage/day spas, shoe repair shops, and weight loss centers

17. *Entertainment/community*—including post offices, health clubs, general and special format cinemas, and armed forces recruiting centers

18. *Financial*—including banks, brokerage firms, real estate companies, and insurance companies

19. *Other*—including law firms, accounting firms, medical offices, and government offices

Retail Building Classifications

The mix of tenants that will occupy a retail building classifies the retail building. This tenant mix can be existing or proposed. The tenant mix represents the development and marketing concept of the property. It is this marketing concept that directs all other development aspects of the retail building, which in turn will determine the eventual success or failure of the property. The sum total of the retail property development concept is its building classification. A retail building classification is the sum total of its location, delineated market area, size and physical configuration of space, property amenities, quality of construction, and degree of on-site management.

> The predominant factor in classifying a retail building is the user of the space.

Retailers are in business to make a profit. A retailer will enter a market area to provide goods and services that are demanded by consumers within that market area. Retailers anticipate a profit for providing the goods and services that consumers demand. Each retailer enters a market area individually. Some retailers, such as larger regional grocers and national drug store chains, are located within their own individual freestanding buildings. Other retailers such as local or national merchants requiring a smaller amount of space tend to cluster together. This decision is strongly influenced by the *drawing power* of the retailer.

Drawing Power and Cumulative Attraction

If the correct mix of retailers cluster together, they will tend to draw more total customer traffic as a whole than could be obtained individually. When this occurs, the retailers are said to benefit from cumulative attraction. *Cumulative attraction* is an increase in the total *drawing power* of a retail property. Cumulative attraction is created when *complementary retail establishments* locate next to each other so all the retailers can benefit from the increased number of customers drawn to the cluster of retail establishments. Accordingly, the whole is greater than the sum of its parts. This market phenomenon encouraged the combination of complementary retail establishments into a clustered retail property.

Cumulative Attraction and Shopping Centers

The most-well-known type of clustered retail properties are shopping centers. The origins of the shopping center industry can be traced back to the 1950s with the development of the Country Club Plaza Shopping Center in Kansas City, Missouri, and the Westwood Village in Los Angeles, California. However, the first completely enclosed shopping center was Southdale Mall in Minneapolis, Minnesota. Today, shopping centers can be categorized as either traditional shopping centers or specialty shopping centers. The difference between these two centers is the type of retailers that are utilized to create the most drawing power to the clustered property.

Traditional Shopping Centers

A *shopping center* is a clustering of retailers within one property. This retail property is designed and developed to be owned, leased, and managed as a single entity. If the shopping center is to be successful, it must address the type of retailers that best serves its trade area, as well as the size and location of the property. The retailers selected for the shopping center must provide goods and services that are demanded by consumers within that market area. Because shopping centers are expected to have increased drawing power, they must also provide for increased on-site parking, pedestrian-friendly walkways, and building flexibility relating to the types and sizes of stores.

Within any given trade area, the total consumer demand is expressed by the dollars that consumers spend on goods and services. Accordingly, the more accurately this demand can be estimated, the more likely the correct retailer will be selected for a property, and the more likely that the retailer will be successful. This is because the retailer is satisfying the demand within the trade area.

From its origins in the 1950s, the traditional shopping center has evolved into five basic types of retail properties: (1) the convenience center, (2) the neighborhood center, (3) the community shopping center, (4) the regional shopping center, (5) and the super-regional shopping center. Table 3.1 summarizes the distinguishing characteristics of traditional types of shopping centers, as categorized by the Urban Land Institute.

The development concept of the retail experience determines the type of shopping center to be built. The development concept must be responsive to the needs of the market it will serve. Once the type of shopping center to be built is determined, the anchor tenants can be selected. The type of shopping center also determines both the size of the site that is required and the size of the improvements to be built.

The anchor tenants as well as other tenants are entering the market area to provide goods and services that are demanded by consumers within that market area. In order to generate the sales necessary to support the retailers, a certain consumer population base is required. The consumer population base can satisfy its demand for the retail goods and services offered by making purchases.

Table 3.1

Characteristics of
Traditonal Shopping Centers

Center	Required Population Base	Anchor Tenant	Square Feet Range–GLA	Square Feet Average-GLA	Site Size Range-Acres
Convenience	3,000 to 40,000	Minimarket	5,000 to 30,000	15,000	⅓ to 3
Neighborhood	3,000 to 40,000	Supermarket and drugstore	30,000 to 100,000	50,000	3 to 10
Community	40,000 to 150,000	Junior department store large variety or discount store, or full-time department store	100,000 to 300,000	150,000	10 to 30
Regional	150,000 or more	One or more full-line department stores	300,000 to 1,500,000 or more	400,000	10 to 60
Super-regional	300,000 or more	Three or more full-line department stores	500,000 to 1,500,000 or more	800,000	15 to 100 or more

Following is a summary overview of each of the five types of traditional shopping centers:

1. *Convenience center.* Provides for the sale of personal services and convenience goods similar to those of a neighborhood center. It contains a minimum of three stores, with a total gross leasable area of up to 30,000 square feet. Instead of being anchored by a supermarket, a convenience center is usually anchored by some other type of personal/convenience service such as a minimarket.

2. *Neighborhood center.* Provides for the sale of convenience goods (foods, drugs, and sundries) and personal services (laundry and dry cleaning, barbering, shoe repair, etc.) for the day-to-day living needs of the immediate neighborhood. It is built around a supermarket as the principal tenant and typically contains a gross leasable area (GLA) of about 50,000 square feet. In practice, it may range in size from 30,000 to over 100,000 square feet.

3. *Community center.* Provides the convenience goods and personal services offered by a neighborhood center. Additionally, this type of center provides a wider range of soft lines (wearing apparel for men, women, and children) and hard lines (hardware and appliances). The community center makes merchandise available in a greater variety of sizes, styles, colors, and prices. Many centers are built around a junior department store, variety store, superdrugstore, or discount department store as the anchor tenant, in addition to a supermarket. Although a community center does not have a full-line department store, it may have a strong specialty store or stores. Its typical size is approximately 150,000 square feet of GLA, but in practice, it may range from 100,000 to 300,000 or more square feet.

a. Centers that fit the general profile of a community center but contain more than 250,000 square feet are classified as *super–community centers*. These centers contain more than 1,000,000 square feet. As a result, the community center is the most difficult to estimate for size and drawing power.

b. A **power center** is a type of super–community center. It contains at least four category-specific, off-price anchors of 20,000 or more square feet. These anchors typically emphasize hard goods such as consumer electronics, sporting goods, office supplies, home furnishings, home improvement goods, bulk foods, drugs, health and beauty aids, toys, and personal computer hardware/software. They tend to be narrowly focused but deeply merchandised "category killers" together with the more broadly merchandised, price-oriented warehouse club and discount department stores. Anchors in power centers typically occupy 85 percent or more of the total GLA.

4. *Regional center.* Provides general merchandise, apparel, furniture, and home furnishings in depth and variety, as well as a range of services and recreational facilities. It is built around one or two full-line department stores of generally not less than 50,000 square feet. Its typical size is approximately 500,000 square feet of gross leasable area, but in practice, it may range from 250,000 to more than 900,000 square feet. The regional center provides services typical of a business district yet not as extensive as those of the super-regional center.

5. *Super-regional center.* Offers extensive variety in general merchandise, apparel, furniture, and home furnishings, as well as a variety of services and recreational facilities. It is built around three or more full-line department stores generally not less than 75,000 square feet each. The typical size of a superregional center is about 1,000,000 square feet of GLA, but in practice, the size ranges from approximately 500,000 to more than 1,500,000 square feet.

A major concern of all of the above shopping centers is the ability for customers and employees to readily access the property, including the ability to park. Vehicular parking capacity is based on standardized parking ratios, or indexes, in relation to the total gross leasable area of the property.

Shopping Centers and Anchor Tenants

All of the five traditional types of shopping centers have a tenant or grouping of tenants that are responsible for most of the drawing power to the clustered property. For example, local minimart grocers, regional grocers, national drugstores, and department stores are considered to exert the most drawing power in convenience, neighborhood, regional, and super-regional shopping centers. These tenants are called anchor tenants. An **anchor tenant** is the retail store within a shopping center that attracts the most consumer traffic to the property. An anchor tenant has enough drawing power to stand alone and is effective in attracting visits from beyond the primary trade area.

A retail property cannot expect to be economically successful unless there are anchor tenants that generate the most customer visits to a shopping center. For whatever reason, if the anchor tenant closes for business and a reasonably complementary replacement cannot be found within a reasonable period of time, the shopping center will most likely begin a decline in market desirability. Patrons will begin to visit alternative retail properties with similar anchors. This decline in patrons will eventually lead to additional closures and vacancies, resulting in a downward market spiral at the property that will be difficult to reverse.

Specialty Shopping Centers

Not all shopping centers have traditional types of anchor tenants. Shopping centers with nontraditional types of anchor tenants are known as specialty shopping centers. A **specialty shopping center** is a shopping center that is characterized by a lack of a traditional anchor tenant. The role of the anchor will be filled by another type of tenant, or by a group of tenants that when clustered together will function as an anchor tenant.

Another distinguishing feature of specialty centers is the type of merchandise they offer—impulse goods and specialty goods. *Impulse goods* are products that shoppers do not actively or consciously seek; they are purchased without a prior decision to shop for them. *Specialty goods* are products that a shopper will examine more carefully and make a greater effort to purchase. Specialty centers include festival centers, fashion centers, off-price and outlet centers, discount centers, and hypermarkets. Following is a summary overview of each type of specialty shopping center, as categorized by the Urban Land Institute:

1. *Festival center.* A shopping center that contains stores that sell impulse goods, either exclusively or as a high percentage of their total merchandise mix. A large portion of its gross leasable area is devoted to restaurants and food vendors that offer ethnic authenticity and uniqueness. Frequently, there is a blend of on-site food service and specialty food retailing. A festival center may also have a strong entertainment theme featuring informal performances by street musicians, acrobats, jugglers, and mimes. Festival centers are generally oriented toward customers most comfortable making purchases in a midpriced range.

2. *Fashion shopping center.* A concentration of apparel shops, boutiques, and custom shops that carry special, high-quality merchandise. A fashion center includes a mixture of both smaller international boutiques and larger national higher-quality fashion stores. Fashion centers are generally oriented toward customers most comfortable making purchases in an upper-priced range.

3. *Off-price and factory outlet shopping center.* Two different types of shopping center concepts combined into one property. An *off-price retailer* functions as a discount store that sells brand-name merchandise at lower prices than can be found elsewhere. A *factory outlet retailer* is owned and operated by the manufacturer and sells goods directly to the public. Off-price and factory outlet shopping centers offer better-quality merchandise than discount stores and are generally oriented toward customers most comfortable making purchases in an upper-priced range.

4. *Discount shopping center.* A community shopping center that is anchored by a discount department store and is smaller than a regional mall. Discount shopping centers differ from other types of shopping centers because they are smaller than a regional mall, have a lower percentage of national or regional tenants, and have a higher percentage of local

tenants. Discount shopping centers are generally oriented toward customers most comfortable making purchases in a discounted price range.

5. *Hypermarket.* A horizontally integrated community shopping center with typical retail establishments, such as a supermarket, drugstore, apparel store, and general merchandise store operated by a single owner under one roof. Such centers have a centralized checkout for all goods and enter market areas offering a quasimonopoly position. Discount shopping centers are generally oriented toward customers most comfortable making bulk purchases in a discounted price range.

Location of Retail Buildings

The location, physical configurations of the space, property amenities, quality of construction, and degree of on-site management are all driven by tenant mix, which must be responsive to the defined market area. Retail buildings must be located within a market where they can capture demand. This demand must be in the form of effective demand. Within a defined market, the consumers' ability to buy retail products from tenants and the availability of those retail products within the market area determine how successful a retail property may be to the market in which it exists and serves. Therefore, retail buildings and their tenants must relate their location, size, and type of tenant to the trade area that it serves.

The decision as to where a retail property will be located is dependent upon the economics of a retail market area. Retail properties must be located within a retail market area that has the necessary levels of effective demand for the retailers that occupy the properties to be successful. For these retail businesses to remain profitable, they must then be able to capture an increasing portion of this effective demand from the market area. In order to capture an increasing portion of effective demand, the retail market area cannot be subject to excessive competitive forces. A market trade area determines a retailer's profit or loss. Accordingly, a retail building's physical location and economic market area are inseparable concepts. A retailer's market area is called a *trade area*.

Trade Area

A retail property's trade area defines its location. A **trade area** is the geographical area that surrounds a retail property. Trade areas are further separated into primary or secondary trade areas. A primary trade area (PTA) may be described in three ways: (1) in terms of travel time, (2) in terms of percentage of total customers, or (3) in terms of percentage of total sales. These three defined areas are estimated individually and then overlaid one upon another. The common area where they overlap is considered the property's PTA. While there is a relationship between these three criteria, they may not result in the same areas:

1. The primary trade area can be the geographic area immediately surrounding the retail property determined by travel time of certain duration. Different retail properties have unique driving times.

2. The primary trade area can be the geographic area immediately sur-rounding the retail property that provides 60 percent to 70 percent of its customer base.

3. The primary trade area can be the geographic area immediately sur-rounding the retail property that generates 60 percent to 70 percent of its total sales.

The area immediately surrounding the PTA is known as a secondary trade area (STA). Secondary trade areas are always viewed by their relative location to the adjoining PTA. A secondary trade area may be described in three ways: (1) in terms of travel time, (2) in terms of percentage of total customers, or (3) in terms of percentage of total sales. These three defined areas are estimated individually and then overlaid one upon another. The common area where they overlap is considered the property's STA. While there is a relationship between these three criteria, they may not result in the same areas:

1. The secondary trade area can be the geographic area surrounding the primary trade area that can be determined by travel time of certain duration. Different retail properties have unique driving times.

2. The secondary trade area can be the geographic area surrounding the primary trade area that provides an additional 20 percent to 30 percent of its total customers.

3. The secondary trade area can be the geographic area surrounding the retail property that generates an additional 20 percent to 30 percent of its total sales.

Figure 3.1 is an illustration of a retail property located within its trade area. That trade area consists of a primary and secondary trade area.

Figure 3.1

Retail Property Primary and
Secondary Trade Areas

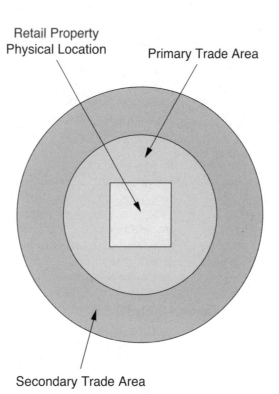

Retail Property
Physical Location

Primary Trade Area

Secondary Trade Area

For a retail property trade area to be viable, its location must be readily accessible, in close proximity to customers, and near complementary but not competitive retail properties.

Readily accessible.   The location of street systems and the intensity of traffic patterns differ by retail property type. A retail property's location is determined by the street patterns and flow of potential customers based on traffic counts past the site. This implies that traffic counts past a retail property should increase in direct proportion to the size of the retail property. However, just the opposite is the case. The smaller the retail establishment, the more significant traffic counts become. For a small strip center or freestanding retail property, traffic counts are a key determinant of gross sales. However, for a large super-regional shopping center, its anchor tenants generate traffic flow to the site from a wide trade area.

Point of origin of potential customers.   The point of origin of potential customers is an important factor in the location of a retail property. The type and amount of the surrounding residential and employment population base is the principal source of potential customers for retail properties. This population base should be located within the primary trade area or secondary trade area of the property. Points of origin are also concerned with the time-distance relationship between the property and customers. This is why driving time is a key consideration.

Complementary not competitive retail properties.   Retail properties operate within a dynamic market environment. A retail property should be located near complementary properties, thereby creating a complementary cluster of retailers. When complementary retail establishments locate next to each other so all the retailers can benefit from the increased number of customers drawn to the cluster of retail establishments, cumulative attraction is said to exist. All of the properties benefit from an increased volume of business as they capture more consumer demand.

A retail property should avoid being located near competitive properties. When competitive retail establishments locate next to each other, all the retailers compete for the same market share, thereby reducing the number of customers drawn to any one retailer. All of the properties suffer from a decreased volume of business as they capture less consumer demand.

Table 3.2 links the locational relationships between street system and traffic patterns, points of origin of potential customers, time-distance relationships, geographic areas, and leakage attributable to competitive properties. The combination of these factors determines both the relative location and geographic area of the retail property's primary trade area. The table is partially based on benchmarks established by the Urban Land Institute and provides general guidelines only. Because each property has specific locational issues, they must be addressed individually.

■ Retail Building Design Standards

A retail property's site and building characteristics will most certainly affect its long-term financial success. The very nature of retailing demands that

Table 3.2

General Guidelines for
Estimating the
Primary Trade Area

Center	PTA Population Base	PTA Radius Distance in Miles	PTA Driving Time in Minutes
Convenience	3,000 to 40,000	1.5	5 to 10
Neighborhood	3,000 to 40,000	1.5	5 to 10
Community	40,000 to 150,000	3 to 5	10 to 20
Regional	150,000 or more	8	20
Super-regional	300,000 or more	12	30

properties be both currently functional and integrate flexibility for future growth. The particular design of a retail property is contingent on the type of retail property to be developed. There are differences between the development criteria for freestanding retail, clustered shopping centers, and specialty centers. Generally, there are three main criteria to be considered in retail design: (1) site characteristics, (2) exterior building characteristics, and (3) interior building characteristics.

Site Characteristics

A retail property is dependent on the physical location within its trade area for customers. Accordingly, an important development element for a retail property is its site characteristics. Following are site characteristics that should be considered for retail property:

- *Size of the site.* A retail site should be large enough to accommodate the footprint of the building and the necessary parking. However, consideration should also be given to setback requirements, buffer zones, outparcels and commercial pads, site circulation, merchandise delivery areas, and land for future expansion.

- *Shape of the site.* The designed shape of retail properties including their sites is usually rectangular or square. However, due to the location of the surrounding streets and roadways, sites tend to include irregularly shaped areas as well. The physical location of the retail buildings within a site must consider its relationship to the adjoining street and roadway network. Consideration should be given to the building's visibility, accessibility, and curbside appeal.

- *Location within the trade area.* To maximize market share and capture consumer dollars, a retail property's site should be at the center of its primary trade area radius to draw equally from all areas within the trade area.

■ *Relationship to street patterns.* Retail access and visibility depends on accessibility from adjoining roadways. A site location at an intersection of two primary roadways offers traffic controls, enhanced visibility, and high traffic counts.

■ *Ability to access.* The site should allow for easy entry to and exit from the property. The site's relationship to the surrounding roadways, the proximity of the site to a traffic-controlled intersection, and well-located curb cuts and turning lanes are important considerations. Site circulation should provide easy access to necessary parking and merchandise delivery areas.

■ *Design and visibility.* Visibility is important to the success of a retail property. Once a site is selected, a retail building should be designed and placed within the site to maximize visibility from the adjoining roadways. A structure should be built on a site that is at least level with the surrounding area for adequate visibility. A challenge for perimeter buildings is to be placed so not to obstruct the visibility of the main buildings. The elevation level of portions of the site itself can improve visibility of interior buildings.

■ *Signage and visibility.* Signage enhances visibility and identification of a property. There are two types of signage: the property's identification signage and the individual tenants' signage. The property's identification signage should be larger monuments that provide name recognition for the property. The signage should be located in areas that offer maximum visibility and exposure for the entire property. The individual tenants' signage is typically placed on the building above the space occupied by the tenant. The signage provides the tenant name recognition within the property and provides the property with tenant identification. Ideally, property management should control all signage. A coordinated signage program offers consistency in signage height, color, and lighting, which provides a visually uniform appearance to prospective customers.

■ *Landscaping and visibility.* Attractive landscaping not only enhances visibility and recognition of a property, but also enhances the "shopping experience." Perimeter landscaping should be colorful and attention getting, yet low enough to not obstruct the property's visibility from the surrounding roadways. Site interior landscaping should be complementary, utilized as a buffer, and add significant visual aesthetics to the shopping experience.

■ *Topography and drainage.* The most efficiently designed structures and property amenities are usually located on a site that is level and at grade, or slightly above grade. These sites have improved visibility and drainage characteristic. Level sites also allow for simple entry to and exit from the property.

■ *Utilities, zoning, planning, permitting, and construction codes.* Retail properties are usually large users of utility services. The availability, proximity, and cost of water, sewer, gas, electricity, telephone service, cable, and fiber optics are of concern to developers and investors. If adequate levels of utilities are not available to the site, development is not possible. The zoning-use code applicable to the site is important because it determines if retail development is permissible. If retail is permissible, zoning will define what type of retail is permissible.

Exterior Building Characteristics

Retail buildings are either successes or failures in the design stage, years before they are opened for business. The design and configuration of retail buildings are as varied as the retail uses of those buildings. Yet according to studies undertaken by the Urban Land Institute, there are only three general shapes and two configurations for shopping centers recognized by the retail industry. The shapes are linear, the "L," and the "U." The configurations are the mall and the cluster. Following is a brief explanation of each:

- *Linear shape.* Resembles a thin rectangle shape and is a line of stores tied together by a canopy over the sidewalk, which runs along the fronts of the stores. It is most functional and economical in the design of small stores. However, linear shapes must be kept to a reasonable length to avoid excessive walking distances and difficult merchandising.

- *"L" shape.* Resembles the letter "L" and is a basic linear layout but with one end turned. This design is used for corner locations.

- *"U" shape.* Resembles the letter "U" and is a basic linear layout with both ends turned in the same direction.

- *Mall configuration.* A pedestrian way between two facing linear buildings. The mall may also take another shape; for example, it may be made up of a series of interlocking linear and L-shaped buildings.

- *Cluster configuration.* A group of pedestrian buildings separated by small pedestrian malls or courts.

Interior Building Characteristics

Trends in retailing are inherently designed to change regularly and rapidly. The interiors of retail properties clearly reflect these trends. The interior design of retail buildings should strive to incorporate flexibility in current and future uses.

Storefronts provide a strong marketing and advertising statement for the retail tenant, and are a prime reason that a customer enters the merchant's store. An attractively designed storefront enhances the customer's opinion of the merchant as well as the retail property in which the merchant is located.

Store size is a function of the total interior area of the retail building and the developer- or investor-desired individual store allocation of square footage. A developer or investor should seek to maximize the income-generating capacity of the retail property by efficiently using the available space. Although there is no standard or typical store width, tenants have a significant influence in space allocations, including the width and depth of store sizes. And the more successful the tenant is, the more control they have on their store size. Some tenants have elevated store size into an art form by requiring prototype store sizes based on their own market research. Store sizes should factor the width, depth, and height of the space. Accordingly, a successful multiple-tenant retail property will be able to offer a variety of store sizes.

Building flexibility as it pertains to the physical configuration of interior space is a key to the long-term viability of any retail property. Accordingly, consideration to flexibility, future expansion, and long-term functionality should be designed into the retail property from its conception. Building flexibility also concerns itself with the costs associated with reconfiguration of space. A building designed with the flexibility to reconfigure interior space will be able to do so efficiently and at a lower cost.

Multiple-level retail properties, also referred to a "vertical malls," present unique interior design, functionality, and logistical challenges that require special consideration for both developers and investors. Tenants should be strategically distributed to create synergies between floors. Visibility of tenants on the floor above or below is very important. The ability of tenants to easily access various locations of the upper floors using walkways, sky bridges, or other means is important because it allows for uninterrupted pedestrian flows. Multiple-level retail properties also have unique tenant and parking requirements. Many vertical malls have become the focus of interest as candidates for adaptive reuse when their original development use has failed. These properties have been readapted to huge "back office" operation centers, call centers, telecom hotels, charter schools, and residential loft redevelopments among other uses.

Food courts are commonplace in virtually any retail property of significant size. They are a major component of specialty, regional, and super-regional centers. Yet a food court is a clustering of food establishments and is based on the same principal as other retail clustering. Food courts may be designed as a convenience to shoppers or a destination "composite anchor tenant." The tenant mix itself defines the development concept of the food court. The food court's hours of operation also impact its development concept, tenant mix, and interrelationship with the property. If the food court will remain open after retailers close, it should be positioned to take advantage of an on-site movie theater or late night patrons who would consider it as an alternative to other dinning choices.

Retail Building Measurement Standards

The proper measurement of a retail building is an important consideration for owners, tenants, investors, appraisers, and lenders. If a retail building is to be properly measured, three factors must be considered:

1. The accurate measurement of the space
2. Identification of all common areas utilized by tenants and patrons, known as the **"common area factor"**
3. Determination of the floor area's configuration, and whether it is functional

The Urban Land Institute has established a set of standards for retail building measurement. Generally accepted in the industry and endorsed by the International Council of Shopping Centers, these standards are used in most areas nationally. Retail buildings are measured in terms of gross building area, gross leasable area, total floor area, common area, and parking indexes.

GBA equals the total of all space within the building including the exterior walls.

Measurement factor 1: the accurate measurement of the space. Gross building area is determined by computing the entire square footage contained within the exterior walls, which includes the building envelope. A retail property's gross building area is measured as the distance between the outer surfaces of the building's exterior walls. This area is also referred to as GBA.

Gross leasable area is the total floor area designed for a retail tenant's occupancy and exclusive use. This includes any basement, mezzanines, or upper floors of the retailer's space. Gross leasable area is measured from the centerline of joint partitions that face outward toward the outside wall. This area is also referred to as GLA.

Total floor space comprises all areas held by the center owner and any areas that are independently managed or owned but that are physically a part of the shopping center. It includes GLA and all other enclosed space in the shopping center as well as outparcels.

Common area is the total area within a retail property that is not designed for rental to tenants but that is available for common use by all tenants, their customers, and adjacent retailers. Common areas include parking areas, courtyards and plazas, sidewalks, landscaped areas, public restrooms, and truck and service facilities.

Parking area refers to the space devoted to car parking, including on-site roadways, aisles, stalls, islands, parking structures, and all other features incidental to parking. Parking areas are part of common area.

Parking index refers to the number of car parking spaces made available per 1,000 square feet of GLA. Parking index is the standard comparison used to indicate the relationship between the number of parking spaces and the GLA.

Measurement factor 2: identification of a "common area factor." Retail tenant leases usually contain a clause requiring the tenant to pay its fair share of defined costs associated with the operation and maintenance of common areas. Common area charges are defined as well as the basis by which costs are incurred. There are three generally accepted methods by which tenants pay common area costs:

1. A *prorated charge* based on the tenant's leased area
2. A *fixed charge* for a stated period of time
3. A *variable charge* based on a percentage of sales

Measurement factor 3: configuration of the floor area or areas. Floor area configurations are important to the property manager in determining how marketable the space is, as well as the types of tenants who might be attracted to it. The practical uses to which various floor layouts can be put are important. Certain floor configurations allow better use of the space by tenants than others. As a practical matter, the more unusual a space configuration is, the less desirable it is to prospective tenants and, therefore, the greater the difficulty a property manager will have in leasing it. As mentioned, the flexibility of the retail building design determines how successfully a space can be configured and reconfigured.

GLA equals the total of all space within the building as measured to the centerline of exterior walls.

Total floor area equals the total of all retail GLA including outparcels.

Common areas equal the total of all areas provided for common use by tenants and customers.

Parking areas are part of common area.

Parking index equals the number of parking spaces per 1,000 square feet of GLA.

Table 3.3

Determining Gross
Leasable Area

Type of Tenant	Retail Category	GLA Leased Sq. Ft.	GLA % Sq. Ft.
Anchor	Regional Grocer	45,000	38%
Anchor	National Drugstore	12,500	11
Local	In-line Shop Tenants	50,000	43
Total Main Building		107,500	91
Anchor—Outparcel	National Bank	5,000	4
Anchor—Outparcel	National Fast Food	5,000	4
Total Freestanding Outparcels		10,000	9
Total GLA Shopping Center		117,500	100

An Example of Building Measurement

Determining gross leasable area.   Consider a neighborhood shopping center. This retail property contains a regional grocer, a national drugstore, in-line shop tenants, and two freestanding outparcel buildings. This retail property has a total measured gross leaseable area of 117,500 square feet as determined in Table 3.3.

To determine the GLA for the retail buildings, all of the space within the buildings is measured to the centerline of the exterior walls. However, GLA excludes the exterior walls.

■   The main building contains the grocer, drugstore, and in-line shop tenants. The measured gross leasable area for these tenants equates to 107,500 square feet, which represents 91 percent of the total GLA for this property.

■   The freestanding outparcel buildings contain a bank and a fast-food restaurant. The measured gross leasable area for these tenants equates to 10,000 square feet, which represents 9 percent of the total GLA for this property.

■   The total measured gross leasable area for all the tenants equates to 117,500 square feet, which represents 100 percent of the total GLA for this property.

Determining gross building area.   The total of all space within the building, *including* the exterior walls, is considered the gross building area. This retail property has a total measured GBA of 131,750 square feet as determined in Table 3.4.

■   The main building contains the grocer, drugstore, and in-line shop tenants. The measured gross building area for these tenants equates to 120,750 square feet, which represents 92 percent of the total GBA for this property.

Table 3.4

Determining Gross
Building Area

Type of Tenant	Retail Category	GBA Sq. Ft.	GLA % Sq. Ft.
Anchor	Regional Grocer	51,750	39%
Anchor	National Drugstore	14,000	11
Local	In-line Shop Tenants	5,500	42
Total Main Building		120,750	92
Anchor—Outparcel	National Bank	5,500	4
Anchor—Outparcel	National Fast Food	5,500	4
Total Freestanding Outparcels		11,000	8
Total Shopping Center Floor Space		131,750	100

■ The freestanding outparcel buildings contain a bank and a fast-food restaurant. The measured gross building area for these tenants equates to 11,000 square feet, which represents 8 percent of the total GBA for this property.

■ The total measured gross building area for all the tenants equates to 131,750 square feet, which represents 100 percent of the total GBA for this property.

Determining loss in leasable area.

■ The total measured gross building area for all the tenants equates to 131,750 square feet, which represents 100 percent of the total GBA for this property.

■ The total measured gross leasable area for all the tenants equates to 117,500 square feet, which represents 100 percent of the total GLA for this property.

■ The difference between the GBA and the GLA represents a loss in leaseable area, and is measured as 14,250 square feet as determined in Table 3.5.

This nonleaseable square footage is necessary for the structural integrity of the building, but is incidental to a retail tenant's occupancy. It is considered a loss of leasable area. However, it is considered important because the total site area that a building will occupy is based on ground-floor GBA. Ground-floor GBA is sometimes referred to as the building's "footprint" on the site.

Determining total floor area. The total floor area for this retail property consists of all retail building gross leaseable area, inclusive of outparcels. The total floor area for this retail property is measured to be 117,500 square feet, as determined in Table 3.6.

Determining common area. In this example, the total common area for the retail property consists of all area within the property that is available for

Table 3.5

Determining Loss in
Leasable Area

Type of Tenant	Retail Category	Loss Sq. Ft.	Loss % Sq. Ft.
Anchor	Regional Grocer	6,750	47%
Anchor	National Drugstore	1,500	11
Local	In-line Shop Tenants	5,000	35
Total Main Building		11,250	93
Anchor—Outparcel	National Bank	500	4
Anchor—Outparcel	National Fast Food	500	4
Total Freestanding Outparcels		1,000	7
Total Shopping Center		14,250	100

Table 3.6

Determining Total
Floor Area

Floor Area Tenant Location	Retail Category	GLA Leased Sq. Ft.	GLA % Sq. Ft.
Total Main Building	Anchors/In-line	107,500	91
Total Freestanding Outparcels	Anchors	10,000	9
Total Floor Area Shopping Center		117,500	100

common use by all tenants, their customers, and adjacent retailers. Common areas include parking areas, courtyards and plazas, sidewalks, landscaped aareas, property setback areas, public restrooms, and truck and service facilities. The common areas provide support to the retailers that are contained within the gross building area. Determining the total common area requires a review of the entire shopping center development. The common area for this retail property is measured to be 454,550 square feet, as determined in Table 3.7.

We have already established the GBA for our neighborhood shopping center to be 131,750 square feet. However, the common area for this neighborhood center is 454,550 square feet, or approximately 3½ times the GBA. The total site area required for this neighborhood center is 586,300 square feet. The total common areas represent 78 percent of this square footage. The building's "footprint" of 131,750 square feet is its GBA and represents less than one-quarter of the total site area.

Table 3.7

Determining Total
Common Area

Site Use	Comments	Sq. Ft.	% Sq. Ft.
Building Footprints	Gross Building Area	131,750	22%
Plaza and Sidewalks	Adjoin Buildings	26,000	4
Parking Lot	Access Buildings	279,300	48
Landscaped Area	Buffer Zone	100,000	17
Site Setbacks, Road Access	Design Requirements	49,250	8
Total Site Area Sq. Ft.		586,300	100%
Total Site Area Acres		13.46	

Common Area Elements	Comments	Sq. Ft.	% Sq. Ft.
Plaza and Sidewalks	Adjoins Buildings	26,000	4%
Parking Lot	Access Buildings	279,300	48
Landscaped Area	Buffer Zone	100,000	17
Site Setbacks, Road Access	Design Requirements	49,250	8
Total Common Area Sq. Ft.		454,250	8

Determining parking spaces and parking area.   Parking areas are part of common area. The parking area includes the number of parking spaces required for the property, which is based on a parking index. If five parking spaces were required for each 1,000 square feet of GLA, then 588 spaces would be required, as calculated in Table 3.8.

The parking area is the space devoted to the 588 car parking spaces plus on-site roadways, aisles, stalls, islands, parking structures, and all other features incidental to parking. If the average square footage for the parking spaces plus the features incidental to parking approximates 475 square feet each, then the total parking area in square feet would approximate 279,300 square feet.

Table 3.8

Determining Total
Parking Spaces and
Parking Area

Site Use	Comments	#
Floor Area Shopping Center	GLA	117,500
divided by:		
Parking Index Per 1,000 Sq. Ft–GLA 5 per 1,000.		6
equals:		
Required Parking Spaces		588
multiplied by:		
Average Sq. Ft. or Space and Related		475
equals:		
Total Parking Area Sq. Ft.		279,300

Example of a Prorated Charge Based on the Tenant's Leased Area

Now that we have calculated the shopping center's GBA, GLA, loss area, and total floor area, we can use this information to allocate property operating expenses back to the each tenant, as appropriate. A prorated charge is based on the percentage relationship of a tenant's leased (GLA) area as a portion of a retail property's total leasable (GLA) area. Alternatively, it may be based on linear exposure in store frontage. Both methods employ a *common area factor.*

For example, let's say a neighborhood shopping center contains 117,500 square feet of gross leasable area. There are 20 local in-line tenants, each occupying 2,500 square feet. Each individual local tenant would have a prorated common area factor of 2.13 percent, calculated using the equation below:

Tenants gross leasable area ÷ total gross leasable area = common area factor.

In our example:

2,500 square feet ÷ 117,500 square feet = 2.13 percent.

The common area factor would be applied to the total expenses applicable to the maintenance of the common areas, which is known as **common area maintenance.** Common area maintenance is often referred to as CAM. Common area maintenance expenses (CAM expenses) are the operating expenses associated with maintaining common areas. Common area charges (CAM charges) are the billing of CAM expenses to tenants for recovery of the common area expenses.

- From a property owner's perspective, CAM recovery is considered additional income collected from tenants.

- From a property tenant's perspective, CAM charges are considered an additional expense billed to the tenants.

- From a profit and loss statement perspective, CAM charges (expenses) are mostly offset by CAM recovery (income) and will have a negative or positive impact, or no impact at all, on net operating income (NOI).

Examples of CAM charges and CAM recoveries are discussed within the following section.

■ Retail Building Leasing, Rental, and Expense Standards

To a retail building owner and property manager, rent and recovery of expenses represent a return on the real estate investment. To a tenant, rent and expense payments represent a cost of business operations. Most retail building leases are based on a form of payment of rent and recovery of expenses that falls into one of the following categories:

1. *Base rent.* This is considered the traditional and least complex method of setting the rent. It calls for the rent to be a fixed dollar amount per annum, payable monthly in advance. It may also be the basis for the calculation of additional or escalation rent. Tenants prefer this type of lease provision because they know exactly what the rent obligation is

Table 3.9

Base Rent Payment

Lease Year	Base Rent	Total Rent
1	$50,000	$50,000
2	50,000	50,000
3	50,000	50,000
4	50,000	50,000
5	50,000	50,000
6	50,000	50,000
7	50,000	50,000
8	50,000	50,000
9	50,000	50,000
10	50,000	50,000
Total	$500,000	$500,000

during the term of the lease. Owners and property managers take the opposite view as it subjects the owner to inflation risk. The primary disadvantage of a base rent–only lease is that it does not have an adjustment mechanism for inflation, and, accordingly, represents an income stream with decreasing purchasing power over time.

For example, let's say the tenant has leased 2,000 square feet of GLA at a base rent of $25 per square foot, equating to $50,000 per year. The lease term is ten years. The total rent during the term of the lease is $500,000 attributable to base rent, as shown in Table 3.9.

2. *Escalation rent.* This is an additional rent to be paid over and above the base rent. Escalation rent is based on an escalation clause in a lease. Additional, or escalation, rent is based on increases in a predetermined index. These indexes are often referred to as *cost-of-living adjustments,* or COLAs. Increases over and above the base rent occur when the cost-of-living index increases. These COLAs usually occur annually.

A popular index for COLAs is the consumer price index (CPI). This lease provision has the benefit of its simplicity. Escalation rent would be the additional rental payment based on increases in the CPI. There are variations to escalation rent calculation formulas. For example, a lease may call for either the annual increase in the CPI or some other stated percentage, say 3 percent, whichever is greater. Another typical variation would be an annual increase based on a certain portion or percentage of the annual increase to the index, say the CPI. For example, the partial increase may be 75 percent of the CPI. The purpose of escalation rent is to ensure that rental income retains its purchasing power.

Table 3.10 presents an income stream from a base rent plus escalation rent scenario. The tenant has leased 2,000 square feet of GLA at a base rent of $25 per square foot, equating to $50,000 per year. The lease term is ten years. The escalation rent is based on a COLA and the index employed is the CPI. In this example, the CPI is 3 percent per annum,

Table 3.10

Base and Escalation
Rate Payments

Lease Year	Base Rent	CPI Growth	COLA Rent	Total Rent
1	$50,000	0.00%	$ —	$50,000
2	50,000	3.00	1,500	51,500
3	50,000	6.09	3,045	53,045
4	50,000	9.27	4,636	54,636
5	50,000	12.55	6,275	56,275
6	50,000	15.93	7,964	57,964
7	50,000	19.41	9,703	59,703
8	50,000	22.99	11,494	61,494
9	50,000	26.6	13,339	63,339
10	50,000	30.48	15,239	65,239
Total	$500,000		$573,194	$573,194

and the CPI adjustment is applied cumulatively to the base rent each year. The total rent during the term of the lease is $573,194, allocated to $500,000 in base rent and $73,194 in escalation rent.

3. *Percentage rent.* This is rental income received in accordance with the terms of a percentage clause in a lease. Rent, or a portion of it, represents a specified percentage of the volume of retail sales or retail profitability achieved by the tenant. Typically, a retail store tenant will pay **percentage rent** based on a certain percentage of its retail sales volume. Accordingly, the obligation of the tenant to pay additional rent to the landlord only occurs when a predetermined percentage of gross sales is achieved. Percentage rent clauses in a lease usually consider a threshold level of sales that the tenant must reach prior to the commencement of percentage rent. This threshold level of sales is referred to as a **breakpoint,** which is the sales threshold at which percentage rent payable commences. Determining the breakpoint can be ascertained in various ways. For example, it may be a *natural breakpoint,* which is determined by dividing a gross sales percentage by the base rent. Another variation would be a stepped percentage lease, whereby the percentage of gross sales applicable to the rental income decreases as gross sales increase.

The mathematics of establishing breakpoints and percentage rents are straightforward. However, the determination of the appropriate level of gross sales at which percentage rent commences is more difficult. This is because percentage rental income requires an accurate forecast of the retailer's trade area, the trade area's current and forecasted retail expenditures, and a retail property and retail tenant's capture rate of those expenditures.

Table 3.11 presents an income stream from a base rent plus percentage rent. This tenant has leased 2,000 square feet of GLA at a base rent of $25 per square foot, equating to $50,000 per year. The lease term is ten years. The percentage rent is based on 10 percent of gross sales with a gross sales threshold of a natural breakpoint. In other words, when gross sales are greater than $500,000 (i.e., $50,000 divided by 10 percent) percentage rent would be due. The total rent during the term

Table 3.11

Base and Percentage
Rent Payments

Lease Year	Base Rent	Percentage Rent	Threshold Gross Sales	Actual Gross Sales	Overage Gross Sales	Percentage Rent	Total Rent
1	$50,000	10%	$500,000	$200,000	$ –	$ –	$50,000
2	50,000	10	500,000	275,000	–	–	50,000
3	50,000	10	500,000	325,000	–	–	50,000
4	50,000	10	500,000	400,000	–	–	50,000
5	50,000	10	500,000	475,000	–	–	50,000
6	50,000	10	500,000	525,000	25,000	2,500	52,500
7	50,000	10	500,000	585,000	85,000	8,500	58,500
8	50,000	10	500,000	625,000	125,000	12,500	62,500
9	50,000	10	500,000	675,000	175,000	17,500	67,500
10	50,000	10	500,000	635,000	135,000	13,500	63,500
Total	$500,000					$54,500	$554,500

of the lease is $554,500, allocated to $500,000 in base rent and $54,500 in percentage rent.

4. *Net lease.* In a **net lease** the tenant pays some or all of the operating expenses, in addition to the rent requirements. Operating expenses consist of fixed expenses, variable expenses, and replacement reserves. Accordingly, the rent paid is "net" of expenses. When referring to a retail tenant's obligations for operating expenses, net leases are often referred to by how "net" the lease is. Specifically, these types of leases may be single net, double net, triple net, or absolute net. The difference between theses types of leases is what expenses the tenant will pay.

   a. A *net lease*, often referred to as a *single net lease,* is a lease in which the tenant is responsible for its pro-rata share of property real estate taxes.

   b. A *net-net lease*, often referred to a *double net lease*, is a lease in which the tenant is responsible for its pro-rata share of property real estate taxes and property insurance.

   c. A *net-net-net lease*, often referred to a *triple net lease*, refers to a lease in which the tenant is responsible for its pro-rata share of property real estate taxes, property insurance, and property common area maintenance.

   d. An *absolute net lease* refers to a lease in which the tenant is responsible for all expenses relating to the premises as if the tenant were the owner. In addition to its pro-rata share of property real estate taxes, property insurance, and property common area maintenance, the tenant is also responsible for its pro-rata share of structural/roof/site repairs, reserves for replacements, capital items, and management. If there was only one tenant occupying a single tenant building, then the one tenant would be responsible for all these costs.

   Table 3.12 summarizes the operating expenses associated with each of the four types of net leases.

Table 3.12

Operating Expense
Characteristics of Net Leases

How "Net"	Tenant Responsibility	Usually Based On
Single Net	Real estate taxes	Pro-rata % GLA
Double Net	Real estate taxes, insurance	Pro-rata % GLA
Triple Net	Real estate taxes, insurance, CAM	Pro-rata % GLA
Absolute Net	All fixed, variable, and replacement and reserve expenses, including real estate taxes, insurance, CAM, structural and roof costs, replacement reserves, and management expenses	Generally preferred for single tenant occupancy; also used on a pro-rata % GLA for multiple tenants

The following examples are based on the 2,500-square-foot tenant introduced above. The tenant occupies 2,500 square feet of gross leasable area (GLA), equating to 2.13 percent of the total GLA. That 2.13 percent also equals the tenant's common area factor. The formula and calculation below determines the pro-rata expense for the tenant.

Expenses × tenant's common area factor =
tenant's pro-rata expense.

In our example:

Expense × 2.13 percent = tenant's pro-rata expense.

The tenant's expenses are determined by the type of net lease the tenant has. Let's say, for example, that the tenant has a triple net lease. Accordingly, the tenant is responsible for its pro-rata share of total floor area real estate taxes, total floor area insurance, and total common area maintenance.

Total floor area real estate tax is the total current year real estate tax expense attributable to the shopping center total GLA (117,500 square feet)—which is the same as the total floor area—which equates to $235,000, or $2 per square foot of GLA.

Total floor area insurance is the total current year real estate insurance expense attributable to the shopping center total GLA (117,500 square feet)—which is the same as the total floor area— which equates to $117,500, or $1 per square foot of GLA.

Total CAM is the common area real estate taxes, common area insurance, and common area maintenance attributable to the shopping center's total common area (454,313 square feet), which equates to $1,930,830 (rounded), or $4.25 per square foot of total common area.

The total property real estate, insurance, and CAM expenses equate to $1,033,250. The tenant's pro-rata share of this expense is $22,008 per annum, or $1,834 per month, and $8.80 per square foot of

Table 3.13

Total Property and Tenant's
Pro-rata Expenses

Property Expense	Expense Amount	Tenants Pro-Rata %	Tenant's Expense	
			In Total	PSF GLA
Total Floor Area Real Estate Taxes	$235,000	2.13%	$ 5,006	$2.00
Total Floor Area Insurance	117,500	2.13	2,503	1.00
Total Common Area Maintenance	680,750	13	14,500	5.80
Total	$1,033,250	2.13%	$22,008	$8.80

tenant GLA. Table 3.13 presents the calculations for determining the tenant's pro-rata share of this expense.

The total property real estate, insurance, and CAM expenses are prorated back to the tenant, based on its relative percentage of GLA. For our tenant, 2.13 percent of the property real estate, insurance, and CAM are prorated, resulting in total tenant charges of $22,008. This amount represents an increase in the tenant's cost of occupancy of $8.80 per square foot of gross leaseable area.

5. A *gross lease* is a lease in which the owner/landlord pays the operating expenses. The owner/landlord receives rent and is obligated to pay all or most of the operating expenses of the property from the rent received. Gross leases may incorporate a **stop clause** that would allow for an *expense stop,* which sets a maximum limit to the amount of the operating expense to be paid by the landlord. Any amount above this maximum limit would then be the responsibility of the tenant.

In this example, a tenant occupies 2,500 square feet of gross leasable area, equating to 2.13 percent of the GLA. That 2.13 percent is also equal to the tenant's common area factor. The lease is gross with a base year stop, and all the expenses in the base year of occupancy are the owner's responsibility. In subsequent years, when expenses *exceed the stopped amount*, the tenant would be obligated for its pro-rata share over and above the stopped expenses. The base year property expenses for the property total $1,033,250, or $8.80 per square foot of GLA. These expenses are summarized within Table 3.13 above.

The following year, the property expenses total $1,057,561, or $9.01 per square foot of GLA. These expenses are summarized within Table 3.14.

The gross lease incorporates a stop clause that allows for an expense stop that sets the maximum owner/landlord expense limit to $8.80 per square foot of GLA. However, the current year amount of $9.01 per square foot of GLA exceeds the expense stop amount. This increase over the expense stop would then be charged back to the

Table 3.14

Total Current Year
Property and Tenant's
Pro-rata Expenses

Property Expense	Expense Amount	Tenant's Pro-rata %	Tenant's Expense	
			In Total	PSF GLA
Total Floor Area Real Estate Taxes	$246,750	2.13%	$ 5,256	$2.10
Total Floor Area Insurance	119,850	2.13	2,553	1.02
Total Common Area Maintenance	690,961	2.13	14,717	5.89
Total	$1,057,561	2.13%	$22,526	$9.01

tenant. The charges to the tenant are based on the differences in expenses summarized within Table 3.15.

The increase over the base year expense stop equates to $24,311. The tenant's pro-rata allocation of these expenses results in a stopped expense charge of $518 per annum, or $43.17 per month, or $0.21 per square foot of the tenant's GLA.

The formula and calculation below determines the stopped expenses:

Current year expenses – base year stopped CAE = chargeable expenses.

In our example:

$1,057,561 – $1,033,250 = $24,311.

Once the chargeable expenses have been determined, the tenant would be allocated its pro-rata share of chargeable expenses. The formula and calculation below determines the tenant's pro-rata chargeable expense:

Increase in stopped expenses × tenant's common area factor = tenant's pro-rata stopped expense.

Table 3.15

Increase Over Expense
Stop—Charged Back
to Tenant

Increase Over Base Year Expenses Property Expense	Expense Amount	Tenants Pro-rata %	Tenant's Expense	
			In Total	PSF GLA
Total Floor Area Real Estate Taxes	$11,750	2.13%	$250	$0.10
Total Floor Area Insurance	2,350	2.13	50	0.02
Total Common Area Maintenance	10,211	2.13	217	0.09
Totals	$24,311	2.13%	$518	$0.21

In our example:

$$\$24,311 \times 2.13\% = \$518.$$

In subsequent years, as stopped expenses increase over the base year, the tenant's pro-rata stopped expense charge would also increase.

■ Summary

A retail building is a building that contains retail space. The purpose of having the retail space is to provide a place where a specific type of business activity can occur—retail sales and related business activities. The design and configuration of retail buildings are as varied as the retail uses of those buildings. The most distinguishing feature of retail buildings is that their configurations are a function of their tenant mix.

Retail merchandising is inherently designed to change regularly and rapidly, which has led to increased pressure for retail buildings to evolve at a faster rate. Retail properties may be individually freestanding or they may be clustered together for the purpose of generating more customer traffic than could be obtained individually. There are six major trends impacting retail buildings and their design: (1) changing consumer tastes and preferences, (2) changing building sizes and locations, (3) e-commerce, (4) changing business strategies, (5) the retail entertainment experience, and (6) competitive market forces and the increase in mixed-use properties due to the depletion of suitable land for development. These trends influence a retail building's classification.

Retail properties are classified by the tenant mix in occupancy of the property. There are 19 generally recognized classifications of retailers. This tenant mix represents the development and target marketing concept of the property, and is the key component that directs all other aspects that will determine the success or failure of the property. The location, delineated market area, physical configuration of the space, property amenities, quality of construction, and degree of on-site management are all driven by this tenant mix. Retail buildings are also categorized by size and building amenities.

Probably the most well-known type of retail property is the shopping center. Shopping centers are based on the principle of cumulative attraction. Cumulative attraction is a situation that results when retail establishments locate next to each other so that each establishment can benefit from the increased volume of potential customers drawn to the cluster of retail establishments. Traditional shopping center types include convenience, neighborhood, community, regional, and super-regional. Traditional shopping centers have a range in size from 3,000 square feet to over 1,000,000 square feet of rentable area.

An anchor tenant is the retail store within a shopping center that attracts the most consumer traffic to the property. Traditional shopping centers have grocery or department stores as anchor tenants. Shopping centers that do not have traditional anchor tenants are called specialty shopping centers. A specialty shopping center is a shopping center that is characterized by a lack of a traditional anchor tenant. The role of the anchor will be filled by another type of tenant or by a group of tenants that when clustered together will function as an anchor tenant. Another distinguishing feature of specialty shopping centers is the type of merchandise they offer—impulse goods and specialty goods.

From a retail trade area perspective, location is crucial. Retail buildings and their tenants must relate their location, size, and type of tenant to the trade area that they serve. They must be located within a trade area that has the required effective demand, be able to capture that effective demand, and not be subject to excessive competitive forces. Accordingly, a retail building's physical location and economic market area are inseparable concepts.

A retailer's market area is called a trade area. A trade area is the geographic area that surrounds a retail property. Trade areas are further separated into primary or secondary trade areas. For a retail property trade area to be viable, its location must be readily accessible, in close proximity to customers, and near complementary but not competitive retail properties. Trade areas may be described in terms of travel time, percentage of total customers, or percentage of total sales.

A retail property's site and building characteristics affect its long-term financial success. The very nature of retailing demands that the design of retail properties be both currently functional and integrate flexibility for future growth. The particular design of a retail property is contingent on the type of retail property to be developed. Broadly speaking, there are three main criteria to be considered in retail design: (1) site characteristics, (2) exterior building characteristics, and (3) interior building characteristics.

The three factors in the proper measurement of a retail building are (1) the accurate measurement of the space, (2) the identification of a "common area factor," and (3) the configuration of the floor area or areas. The Urban Land Institute has established a set of standards for retail building measurement. Generally accepted in the industry, these standards are used in most areas nationally. Retail buildings are measured in terms of gross building area, gross leasable area, total floor space, common area, parking area, and parking index.

To a retail building owner and property manager, rent and recovery of expenses represent a return on the real estate investment. To a tenant, rent and expense payments represent a cost of business operations. Most retail building leases are based on a form of payment of rent and recovery of expenses. These rent categories are base rent, escalation rent, and percentage rent. Depending on the type of lease a retail tenant has, they may also be responsible for operating expenses. The type of leases include a gross lease or a net lease. Depending on the type of expenses to be included in a retail tenant lease, net leases may be further classified as single net, double net, triple net, or absolute net.

■ Review Questions

1. A retail property may be
   a. freestanding.
   b. clustered.
   c. a shopping center.
   d. All of the above (A, B, and C)

2. A shopping center
   a. includes neighborhood, community, regional, or super-regional clustered retail stores.
   b. has an anchor tenant or tenants.
   c. can be a festival, fashion, off-price discount, or hypermarket type.
   d. All of the above (A, B, and C)

3.. Cumulative attraction is a situation that results when
   a. a multiple-screen movie theater benefits from the increased volume of potential customers drawn to the cluster of movies.
   b. retail establishments locate next to each other so that each establishment can benefit from the increased volume of potential customers drawn to the cluster of retail establishments or tenant or tenants.
   c. multiple shopping centers benefit from the increased volume of potential customers drawn to the cluster of properties.
   d. All of the above (A, B, and C)

4. An anchor tenant is
   a. the major store within a shopping center that attracts or generates traffic for the property.
   b. the major store within a shopping center that is involved in marine sales and services.
   c. also known as a marine chandelier.
   d. the major store within a shopping center that is most likely to renew its lease.

5. The location of a retail property may be described relative to
   a. the street and traffic pattern.
   b. points of origin of potential customers.
   c. competing retail establishments.
   d. All of the above (A, B, and C)

6. A retail property's primary trade area is the geographic area immediately adjacent to the subject property
   a. that extends out a travel time of certain duration.
   b. from which the property obtains 60 percent to 70 percent of its customer base.
   c. that generates 60 percent to 70 percent of the property's total sales.
   d. All of the above (A, B, and C)

7. A retail property's secondary trade area is the geographic area immediately adjacent to the primary trade area
   a. that extends out a travel time of certain duration.
   b. from which the property obtains an additional 20 percent to 30 percent of its customer base.
   c. that generates an additional 20 percent to 30 percent of the property's total sales.
   d. All of the above (A, B, and C)

8. The three main criteria to be considered in retail design are
   a. design quality, class, and amenities.
   b. functional design, economic design, and feasibility of design.
   c. site characteristics, exterior building characteristics, and interior building characteristics.
   d. site characteristics, building characteristics, and common area utilization.

9. Retail buildings are measured in terms of
   a. gross building area, gross leasable area, total parking area, and common area index.
   b. gross building area, gross leasable area, total floor area, common area, parking area, and parking index.
   c. gross construction area, usable area, rentable area, common area, parking area, and parking index.
   d. gross building index, gross leasable ratio, total floor area factor, parking area, and parking index.

10. A natural breakpoint may be determined by dividing
    a. the base rent by the gross sales percentage.
    b. the gross sales by the base rent percentage.
    c. the gross sales percentage by the base rent.
    d. the base rent percentage by the gross sales.

11. A new retail property has a total anchor GLA of 66,500 square feet and total local shop tenant GLA of 53,500 square feet. If the required parking index were five parking spaces per 1,000 square feet of GLA, how many parking spaces would be required for this property?

    a. 480

    b. 550

    c. 600

    d. 680

12. A shopping center developer is establishing his first-year operating budget for the new shopping center that is discussed in question 11 above. He is basing his budget on a pro-forma common area expense for the parking spaces and incidental areas at $2.50 per square foot. If the average square footage of the parking spaces plus the features incidental to parking is 425 square feet each, what would the pro-forma common area expenses for the parking area be?

    a. $1,530,000

    b. $1,275,000

    c. $1,020,000

    d. $637,500

13. A local shop tenant has just taken occupancy and commenced its lease term in the new shopping center discussed in question 12. The tenant occupies a GLA of 3,250 square feet. What is this tenant's common area factor?

    a. 6.07%

    b. 4.89%

    c. 2.71%

    d. 1.75%

14. The local shop tenant discussed in question 13 has requested an estimate of its common area charges for the parking area. What is this amount?

    a. $17,276.25 per annum

    b. $1,439.69 per month

    c. $5.32 per square foot of GLA

    d. All of the above (A, B, and C)

15. The local shop tenant discussed in question 14 has a base year rent of $30 per square foot, triple net basis. The base rents escalate at a fixed index of 3 percent per annum. This tenant also has a percentage rent clause in its lease. The breakpoint is determined on the basis of an 11 percent rent payable above the threshold established by an annual natural breakpoint. The tenant is now in the second year of its lease. What is its threshold for sales?

    a. $1,000 per square foot

    b. $280.91 per square foot

    c. $1,030 per square foot

    d. $272.73 per square foot

chapter four

COMMERCIAL REAL ESTATE AS AN INVESTMENT

■ **Key Terminology**

appreciation	equity-debt ratio	property enhancements
capital asset	liquidity	risk
cash flow	opportunity cost	taxable income
equity	property depreciation	tax shelter

■ **Overview**

In this chapter, real estate investment is introduced. Commencing from the basic answer to what real estate investors expect, the decision to invest in real estate is presented as a trade-off between its relative advantages and disadvantages. The good news is that these advantages and disadvantages are measurable. As such, the decision to invest in property can be set within a framework that allows for a systematic and quantitative decision-making process that assists in removing guesswork, emotion, and unsupported conjecture. These measurable advantages and disadvantages are discussed in detail.

As we explore this decision-making process, numerous new terms are introduced. The language of investment real estate continues to take shape. The need for the application of practical business and financial mathematics comes to the forefront of the discussion. Multistep calculations for determining cash flow and taxable income are introduced. The ability to quantify monetarily the advantages and disadvantages of investing are seen as fundamental to the decision-making process.

■ **Learning Objectives**

After completing this chapter, the reader should be able to accomplish the following:

1. List the *six tangible benefits* of investing in real estate
2. Explain why investors are interested in a property's *cash flow*

3. Differentiate between a *cash* and *noncash expense*

4. Explain the difference between a *mortgage* and *mortgage note*

5. Define *amortized loan*

6. Describe the two forms of *increases in property value*

7. Explain the economic principle of *scarcity*

8. List the *six tangible disadvantages* of investing in real estate

9. State the *primary reason* that investors purchase commercial real estate

10. Describe *opportunity cost*

■ What Real Estate Investors Expect

Capital is an amount of money available for investment. As is true of all forms of investment, real estate investors expect the return of all their invested capital, which is called a return *of* capital, as well as payment for the use of the capital during the investment, which is called a return *on* capital. When investors acquire real estate, it is commonly referred to as a **capital asset.**

As it applies to real estate, return of capital is the return of the invested capital, usually through *income* and *reversion*. The *income* component of the return of capital consists of the income stream created by the investment. The *reversion* component of the return of capital consists of the net proceeds from the sale of the investment at the conclusion of the investor's holding period. Reversion is a lump-sum payment that an investor receives at the conclusion of an investment. Return on capital is additional received money for the use of an investor's capital until it is returned.

The combination of the return of capital and the return on capital equate to the investment's *rate of return* on capital. The rate of return on capital is measured in terms of an interest rate. Each year of the investment, it is expected to generate a *measurable return* at a certain rate of interest. However, because the income may fluctuate from one year to the next, so will the rate of interest. The rate of interest that the investment generates during the entire investment period is called a yield rate.

There are unique advantages and disadvantages to real estate investments that every investor must consider. The best time to consider these are prior to investing.

■ Advantages of Commercial Real Estate as an Investment

The advantages of investing in commercial real estate are both intangible and tangible. The intangible, or nonmeasurable, advantages of investing in commercial real estate include pride of ownership, a sense of accomplishment, and ego gratification. The tangible, or measurable, advantages of investing in commercial real estate can be quantified monetarily. These monetary benefits fall into the category of either return of capital or return on capital, and include: (1) cash flow, (2) tax shelter, (3) property depreciation, (4) reduction of property debt financing, (5) increases in property value, and (6) equity buildup.

Benefit 1: Cash Flow

Simply stated, a real estate investment generates periodic revenues that are offset by periodic expenses. The difference between these revenues and expenses is periodic income. This income, which is called net operating income (NOI), is then allocated to the interests in the real estate.

For example, if an investor purchases a $550,000 property for all cash (100 percent), the only party that has an interest in the real estate is that investor. However, who would have an interest in that same $550,000 property if the investor purchased it with, say, $137,5000 (25 percent) of his money and $412,500 (75 percent) of a lender's money? In this case, both parties—the lender and the investor—would have an interest in the real estate. The investor would not be entitled to all of the net operating income, but rather the property's cash flow. **Cash flow** refers to the income that remains each accounting period after all property-related revenues are netted against all property-related expenses, including deductions for mortgage debt service (financing), if appropriate.

Cash flow can be measured on a pretax basis and an after-tax basis. Pretax cash flow (PTCF) is the portion of net operating income that remains after mortgage debt service (financing) is paid but before income tax on property operations is deducted. After-tax cash flow (ATCF) is the portion of pretax cash flow that remains after all income tax liabilities have been deducted. Cash flow is measured in accounting periods that are typically stated monthly, quarterly, or annually.

Measuring cash flow. The following discussion pertaining to cash flow is summarized in Table 4.1, Pretax Cash Flow Calculation, which is also referred to as the cash flow "stack." In this discussion, we will be introducing a number of new terms. It may be helpful to refer to Table 4.1 often to understand how these terms fit into our discussion.

For example, let's say that an investor acquired a ten-unit multifamily rental apartment that has a potential gross income (PGI) attributable to base contract and/or market rental income at full occupancy, plus other income of $100,000 per year. *Potential gross income* is the total income attributable to real property at full occupancy before vacancy and collection losses and operating expenses are deducted. Next, a vacancy and collection loss (V&C) factor of 5 percent of PGI, equating to $5,000, is deducted from this potential gross income. This amount represents the normal V&C loss for the property's *market area*. *Vacancy and collection loss* is an allowance for reductions in potential gross income attributable to vacancies, nonpayment of rents, and releasing of space.

Deducting vacancy and collection loss from potential gross income results in the effective gross income (EGI) for the property. *Effective gross income* is the anticipated income from all operations of the real property after an allowance is made for vacancy and collection losses. Effective gross income includes base contract and/or market rental income plus other income generated from the operation of the real property, such as parking income, income from vending machines, and laundry room income.

Sidebar notes (left margin):

Property revenues less property expenses equals net operating income.

Net operating income less mortgage financing equals pretax cash flow.

Potential gross income less vacancy and collection losses equals effective gross income.

Total *operating expenses* for the year, consisting of *fixed* expenses, *variable* expenses, and *replacement allowances* total $40,000.

■ *Operating expenses (OE)* are the *recurring periodic expenditures* necessary to maintain the property and continue production of revenues.

■ *Fixed expenses (FE)* are those *recurring periodic expenditures* that are usually unaffected by the level of occupancy and that would continue even if the property were totally vacant. Traditional examples of fixed operating expenses include real estate (property) taxes and property insurance.

■ *Variable expenses (VE)* are those *recurring periodic expenditures* that usually vary in relation to the level of occupancy and may decline or discontinue if the property were totally vacant. Traditional examples of variable expenses include management fees, administrative charges, payroll, advertising and promotion, telephone, utilities (including water, sewer, and electric), trash removal, repairs and maintenance, general supplies, pool maintenance, landscape maintenance, and pest control, among others.

■ *Replacement reserves (RR)* are *amortized periodic expenditures* of major property components that have a useful life of more than a year but are wearing away each year. All building components wear out over time. The period of time that a building component is expected to wear out is called its estimated useful life. A replacement reserve accounts for those building components that wear out faster than others. These building components include the building, everything that is contained within and attached to the building, and any site improvements. However, land does not depreciate or wear out and, accordingly, the allocated cost of land is excluded from a replacement reserve. Replacement reserves are also known as replacement allowances, reserves for replacements, and reserves.

Effective gross income less operating expenses equals net operating income.

Total operating expenses are the sum of all fixed and variable operating expenses and replacement allowances. Deducting total operating expenses from effective gross income results in the property's NOI.

Net operating income is the income that remains after all operating expenses are deducted from EGI but before mortgage debt service and depreciation are considered. It can be calculated before or after deducting replacement reserves, depending on what is considered customary for a property type or market area.

Let's say that the property was purchased for $550,000. The property was acquired with a combination of the owner's cash, known as equity, and borrowed funds from a lender, known as debt. A first mortgage financing in the amount of $412,500 was used to acquire the property. That loan amount would equate to 75 percent of the purchase price, and that 75 percent would also represent the loan-to-value ratio.

The *loan-to-value ratio (LTV)* is a basic yet important ratio that expresses the relationship of borrowed funds as a percentage of the value of the property. From a lender's perspective, the LTV is usually the lesser of acquisition price or the appraised value of property. LTVs are an important risk measure for lenders because the property is usually pledged as security for the loan.

The formula below determines the loan-to-value ratio of a property:

$$\text{Loan} \div \text{value} = \text{LTV}.$$

In our example:

$$\$412{,}500 \div \$550{,}000 = 75\%.$$

The loan is fully amortizing to be repaid over 25 years, payable monthly, at an interest rate of 7 percent per annum. The annual debt service for principal and interest totals $35,000. The pretax cash flow from this property after debt service but before taxes is $20,000. Real estate investors are interested in a property's calculated pretax cash flow as it provides a simple yet fundamental measure of the investment's capability of

1. paying the borrowed funds debt service without coming "out of pocket"; and
2. providing a positive return on capital and a return of capital to the investor. The pretax cash flow calculations are summarized in Table 4.1.

Benefit 2: Tax Shelter

A **tax shelter** is an investment feature of real estate that provides relief from income taxes or allows the investor to claim deductions from **taxable income.** Real estate offers the advantage of a noncash expense deduction from taxable income for the property itself in the form of a depreciation allowance. In accounting, a *depreciation allowance* refers to the amount of a noncash expense that is deducted from the property's income to write off the cost of the property. It is an expense "only on paper."

Table 4.1

Pretax Cash Flow Calculation

Potential Gross Income		$100,000
less:		
Vacancy and Collection Losses	5%	(5,000)
equals:		
Effective Gross Income		95,000
less:		
Operating Expenses (Including Reserves)		(40,000)
equals:		
Net Operating Income		55,000
less:		
Mortgage Interest Expense	28,685	
Mortgage Principal Reduction	6,315	
Total Mortgage Payments		(35,000)
equals:		
Pretax Cash Flow		$ 20,000

A tax shelter refers to the income tax savings that a real estate investor can realize by deducting depreciation from the property. Although depreciation is a deductible expense, it is a noncash expense. Because it is a noncash expense, the effect is to shelter an equivalent amount of income from taxes; hence the term *tax shelter.*

To illustrate the operation and benefits of the tax shelter aspects of investment real estate, let's continue with our presentation that we began in Table 4.1. Let's say the federal and state (as applicable) income tax obligations of our investor place him in the 35 percent tax bracket. Furthermore, assume that based on our analysis (which follows) of property depreciation, 85 percent of the purchase price of $550,000 can be allocated to depreciable property. That means that $467,500 (i.e., $550,000 × 85 percent) is subject to a depreciation allowance.

Using the depreciation methods and their recovery periods discussed in the next section, a first-year depreciation of $22,165 can be claimed for the improvements. Land does not depreciate and is excluded from calculations.

The calculations for taxable income are presented in Table 4.2.

Comparing Table 4.1 and Table 4.2 for similarities and differences (see Table 4.3) will illustrate the financial power of tax shelters as they relate to investment real estate.

Both tables are similar up to and including the calculations resulting in effective gross income. Now let's focus on the differences. In Table 4.1, for the purposes of calculating pretax cash flow, net operating income includes reserves for replacement. From net operating income we then deduct the incurred expenses of mortgage interest and principal payments to arrive at a cash flow amount of $20,000. Pretax cash flow really represents the actual cash that "flows" from the real estate investment prior to tax considerations.

Table 4.2

Taxable Income Calculation

Potential Gross Income		$100,000
less:		
Vacancy and Collection Losses	5%	(5,000)
equals:		
Effective Gross Income		95,000
less:		
Operating Expenses (Excluding Reserves)		(35,000)
equals:		
Adjusted Net Operating Income		60,000
less:		
Mortgage Interest Expense		(28,685)
less:		
Depreciation		(22,165)
equals:		
Taxable Income		$ 9,150

Table 4.3

Comparison of Pretax Cash Flow and
Taxable Income Calculations

Potential Gross Income			$100,000
less:			
Vacancy and Collection Losses @		5%	(5,000)
equals:			
Effective Gross Income			95,000
less:			
Operating Expenses (Including Reserves)			(40,000)
equals:			
Net Operating Income			55,000
less:			
Mortgage Interest Expense	28,685		
Mortgage Principal Reduction	6,315		
Total Mortgage Payments			(35,000)
equals:			
Pre-Tax Cash Flow			$ 20,000

Potential Gross Income			$100,000
less:			
Vacancy and Collection Losses @		5%	(5,000)
equals:			
Effective Gross Income			95,000
less:			
Operating Expenses (Excluding Reserves)			(35,000)
equals:			
Adjusted Net Operating Income			60,000
less:			
Mortgage Interest Expense			(28,685)
less:			
Depreciation			(22,165)
equals:			
Taxable Income			$ 9,150

On the other hand, in Table 4.2, for the purposes of calculating taxable income, "adjusted" NOI excludes reserves for replacement. From adjusted NOI we then deduct the incurred expense of the mortgage interest payment and the noncash expense of depreciation to arrive at a taxable income amount of $9,150. What happened? In Table 4.2, the $22,165 noncash deduction for depreciation "shelters" $22,165 of property income that would be subject to taxation. Specifically, the noncash deduction shelters $6,315 of property income that was utilized to pay the mortgage principal reduction and an additional $15,850 of property income that would have otherwise "flowed" to the bottom line. Furthermore, because depreciation is a noncash expense, the value of the $22,165 deduction for depreciation for our investor in the 35 percent tax bracket is $7,758. Stated differently, an advantage or benefit of investing in this commercial real estate is a tax savings to our investor of $7,758.

Tax shelters are actually more valuable to those in higher tax brackets. In our discussion, the value of the $22,165 deduction for depreciation to our investor in the 35 percent tax bracket is a tax savings of $7,758 (i.e., 35 percent of $22,165). If, however, he was in the 40 percent tax bracket, the $22,165 deduction for depreciation is worth $8,866 in tax savings (i.e., 40 percent of $22,165) And if he was in the 50 percent tax bracket, the $22,165 deduction for depreciation is worth $11,083 in tax savings (i.e., 50 percent of $22,165).

Benefit 3: Property Depreciation

Depreciation of a building has no direct effect on cash flow because depreciation is an accounting concept and does not represent actual "out-of-pocket" cash expenditures. However, as previously discussed (in Table 4.2), **property depreciation** is a recognized deduction against taxable income. It has a positive impact on cash available to the investor and also has value due to its tax shelter qualities. These tax shelters are more appealing to those in higher tax brackets.

Depreciation is an accounting concept that allows an investor to recover the cost of the real estate investment property. It provides an accounting deduction to the investor that allows for the setting aside of a sum each year that together with the remaining salvage value of the improvements at the end of the useful life of the real estate will allow the investor to purchase a replacement property. Therefore, in concept, it is grounded in sound economic and investment principles. However, the accounting deduction is a bookkeeping entry rather than an actual cash deposit of funds, and as so there is no real assurance that the money will actually be available to buy the replacement property at the end of the current property's economic life.

The straight-line method writes off equal amounts in all years.

There are various methods for calculating depreciation for income tax purposes. The simplest is to take the price paid for the improvements (land does not depreciate and is excluded from calculations) and divide by the number of years of allowed depreciation; this is called straight-line depreciation. *Straight-line depreciation* is a depreciation method in which the depreciable part of the real estate asset, estimated at cost or some other basis, is written off in equal annual amounts over the estimated useful life of the assets. Effective for properties placed in service after 1986, real estate must be depreciated using the straight-line method of depreciation over a recovery period of 27.5 years for residential real estate and 39 years for nonresidential real estate.

Accelerated depreciation is a depreciation method of cost write-off in which the allowances made for depreciation of the wasting real estate asset are greater in the earlier years and decline in the subsequent years based upon a formula. Technically, the depreciation decelerates over time. The term *accelerated depreciation* refers to the accelerated or faster recovery of capital during the early years of an investment. Accelerated depreciation does not allow an owner to depreciate more than the price paid for the improvements. However, because it does allow the owner to take the depreciation charge sooner rather than later, it is more valuable to him.

The accelerated method writes off greater amounts in the earlier years.

Under the Economic Recovery Act of 1981, the accelerated system adopted was known as the accelerated cost recovery system (ACRS), which had little relationship to the actual using up of the existing real estate. The Tax Reform Act of 1986 modified the ACRS to the current system of accelerated depreciation known as the modified accelerated cost recovery system (MCRS). An MCRS allows for the depreciation of tangible property via a straight-line method or a combination of the straight-line and accelerated methods. To maximize the depreciation and create a tax shelter, most investors use the MCRS method.

MCRS classes.   MCRS breaks down a real estate investment into eight categories of tangible property, also known as classes. There are two broad real property classes based on property type—residential real estate rental property and nonresidential real estate rental property. There also are six broad personal property classes based on the depreciable life of the property ranging from 3 years to 20 years.

Following is a summary overview of the U.S. Internal Revenue Service's tax guidelines for these property classes. Further investigation should be conducted regarding the actual guidelines themselves.

- *Residential real estate.* Generally, residential real estate includes single family residences, condominiums, cooperative units, town homes, duplexes, triplexes, four-plexes, multifamily apartment houses, and similar types of property used as a personal residence by the occupant. Residential real estate employs a 27½-year life for straight-line depreciation.

- *Nonresidential real estate.* Generally, nonresidential real estate is real estate other than residential real estate. Nonresidential real estate includes office properties, retail properties, lodging properties, industrial properties, and certain mixed-use properties containing residential components where the income generated from the residential component is less than 80 percent of the total income generated from the property. For properties purchased subsequent to May 12, 1993, nonresidential real estate employs a 39-year life for straight-line depreciation. For properties purchased between January 1, 1987, and May 12, 1993, nonresidential real estate employs a 31½-year life for straight-line depreciation.

- *Personal property.* There are six classes of MCRSs for personal property. The classes are based on the years of the useful life of the property. The six classes are:

    1.   MCRS class for property with a 3-year life
    2.   MCRS class for property with a 5-year life

Table 4.4

Depreciation Schedule

	Allocation	% Allocation	Depreciable Life in Years	Year 1 % Factor $Dollars	Year 2 % Factor $ Dollars	Year 3 % Factor $ Dollars
Purchase Price	$550,000	117.65%	N/A			
less:						
Land Value	82,500	17.65	N/A			
equals:						
Depreciable Improvements	467,500	100.00	N/A			
less:						
Apartment Unit Property	20,000	4.28	5.00	20.0%	20.0%	20.0%
				$4,000	$4,000	$4,000
Common Washers and Dryers	2,500	0.53	5.00	20.0%	20.0%	20.0%
				$500	$500	$500
Hallway Artwork, Furniture	1,500	0.32	5.00	20.0%	20.0%	20.0%
				$4,000	$4,000	$4,000
Site Improvements	60,000	12.83	15.00	6.67%	6.67%	6.67%
				$300	$300	$300
Building Improvements	383,500	82.03	27.50	3.485%	3.636%	3.636%
				$13,365	$13,944	$13,944
Yearly Depreciation				$22,165	$22,744	$22,744

3. MCRS class for property with a 7-year life

4. MCRS class for property with a 10-year life

5. MCRS class for property with a 15-year life

6. MCRS class for property with a 20-year life

A practical example. Let's use our ten-unit, multifamily rental apartment acquired for $550,000 as the basis for the property depreciation schedule shown in Table 4.4.

Based on a real estate appraisal, the allocated land value, excluding site improvements, is estimated at $82,500. Each unit has property consisting of refrigerators, stoves, microwaves, kitchen cabinetry, etc., with a per unit value of $2,000. Miscellaneous income is generated with two commercial washers and two commercial dryers with an allocated total cost of $2,500. The apartment has $1,500 worth of common area furniture and artwork located throughout the interior corridors of the building. Site improvements, consisting of perimeter fencing, landscaping, sprinkler system, parking area paving, walkways, on-site lighting, and drainage, have an allocated cost of $60,000. The remainder is allocated to the long-lived components of the building, equating to $383,500. Table 4.4 summarizes these allocations and depreciation percentages for the first three years of the investment's holding period.

The calculations indicate that the property can generate $22,165 in tax shelter and depreciation during the first year, and $22,744 during the second and third years. Other than the building improvements of $383,500, the IRS

Table 4.5

Straight-Line Depreciation
Table for Residential
Real Estate

Straight-Line Depreciation Method for "27.5-Year" Residential Real Property												
Month Placed in Service	1	2	3	4	5	6	7	8	9	10	11	12
Recovery Period in Years												
1	3.485%	3.182%	2.879%	2.576%	2.273%	1.970%	1.667%	1.364%	1.061%	.758%	.455%	.152%
2–9	3.636	3.636	3.636	3.636	3.636	3.636	3.636	3.636	3.636	3.636	3.636	3.636
10, 12–26	3.637	3.637	3.637	3.637	3.637	3.637	3.637	3.637	3.637	3.637	3.637	3.637
28	3.636	3.636	3.637	3.636	3.636	3.636	3.637	3.637	3.637	3.637	3.637	3.637
29	0.00	0.00	0.00	0.00	0.00	0.00	.152	.455	.758	1.61	1.061	1.667
Total	100%	100%	100%	100%	100%	100%	100%	100%	100%	100%	100%	100%
The appropriate percentage is indicated by using the column for the month in the first year the property was placed in service												

Source: Internal Revenue Service

considers the remaining property elements nonstructural property, even though in certain instances they may be permanently affixed to the property.

What about the building improvements? Those improvements would be depreciated using IRS tables for straight-line depreciation of residential real estate similar to the presentation in Table 4.5.

As this presentation demonstrates, tax laws, including reference to the tax code, is a complex and sophisticated area of real estate investing.

Benefit 4: Reduction of Property Mortgage Debt

The majority of commercial investment property acquisitions involve a combination of equity, which is the investor's cash, and debt, which is the lender's financing. Relative to the purchase price, the combination of the equity component and debt component results in an equity-debt ratio. An **equity-debt ratio** is the ratio of the equity invested in a property to the amount of debt borrowed for that property.

Table 4.6 presents the first three years of the equity-debt ratios and declining debt component of the multifamily rental apartment property introduced in Table 4.1.

The equity-debt ratio is always described in relation to the total purchase price of the property, which may or may not be subject to adjustment for appreciation. For example, the multifamily rental apartment property referred to in Table 4.2 was acquired for a cost of $550,000, which represents the total purchase price. The equity invested at the beginning of the investment period,

Table 4.6

Mortgage Loan
Amortization and Changing
Equity-debt Ratios

End of Year	Purchase Price	Equity Component	Equity %	Debt Component	Debt %
Begin Year 1	$550,000	$137,500	25%	$412,500	75%
End Year 1	$550,000	$143,810	26	$406,190	74
End Year 2	$550,000	$150,577	27	$399,423	73
End Year 3	$550,000	$157,833	29	$392,167	71

In this example, purchase price and total value are the same.

for the beginning of year 1, was $137,500, which equates to 25 percent of the total purchase price. The debt, or loan obtained, was $412,500, which equates to 75 percent of the total purchase price. The combination of these two components represents the total purchase price. The equity-debt ratio is therefore 25 percent to 75 percent.

At the end of the first year, total principal reduction of the outstanding debt equated to $6,310, which reduced the principal outstanding to $406,190. This amount represents 74 percent of the acquisition price. Because the acquisition price has not changed, the equity component benefits by an increase to 26 percent. The equity-debt ratio has changed to 26 percent to 74 percent. This reduction of the outstanding debt occurs during the second and third years as well, resulting in an equity-debt ratio of 29 percent to 71 percent at the end of the third year.

The debt component is based on a mortgage note and a mortgage. The mortgage note and a separate mortgage are evidence of the lender's financing of a property. A mortgage note is a written promise to pay back the money borrowed from the lender. It contains the specific terms and conditions, such as the length of the loan, the interest rate to be charged, and when the money is to be repaid. It is secured by a mortgage. A mortgage is a conveyance of an interest in real property that is given as security for the payment of the loan.

A reduction in the amount outstanding of the mortgage note occurs periodically, and the investor uses the property's income stream to pay both the mortgage interest expense and the mortgage principal reduction. This process is called amortizing the loan. An amortized loan is a loan requiring periodic payments that include both interest and partial repayment of principal. As the loan amortizes, the loan balance declines. Because the total purchase price remains unchanged and the debt component is declining, the equity component is increasing in relation to the purchase price.

Benefit 5: Increase in Property Value

One of the primary monetary benefits of investing in real estate is the expectation of an increase in the value of the property over and above the purchase price. An increase in value provides a greater rate of return of the invested capital because upon reversion there will be more capital returned to the investor over and above the purchase price. Additionally, an increase in a property's value is usually linked to a property's increasing income stream.

As the property's income stream increases, the amount received as compensation for the use of the investor's capital also increases and, accordingly, the rate of return on an investor's capital increases.

Increases in property value may originate from either property appreciation or property enhancements. **Appreciation** is an increase in value due to the market forces of supply, demand, and inflationary trends. Because these market forces and trends are beyond the control of the investor, an increase in value due to appreciation is considered a passive form of increase in value. Appreciation occurs when there is excess demand for a property or a property type over and above the supply of the property or property type. When this market condition occurs it is called scarcity. Scarcity is the present or anticipated undersupply of a property or property type relative to the demand for it. Scarcity usually leads to an increase in value. Appreciation may occur to both vacant undeveloped land and improved property.

> Appreciation is a passive increase in value due to market forces.

Although it has the same effect on property value, property enhancements differ from property appreciation. **Property enhancements** are improvements and upgrades to the property and its operations that are implemented by the property owner. A property enhancement program's core purpose is to increase the desirability and efficiency of the property, which ultimately equate to an increasing property income stream and an increasing property value. Because the owner is directly involved in the decision-making process, property enhancements are considered an active form of increase in value.

Property enhancements may be in the form of physical changes to the property itself, including additions, renovations, or retrofitting. Another form of property enhancement is the integration of "smart building" technology into an older property. Alternatively, the owner may improve the property's management and maintenance programs. Perhaps the owner may decide to combine different types of enhancements.

> Property enhancement is an active increase in value due to ownership.

In the case of undeveloped land, the owner may enhance the property by obtaining a more valuable zoning for the property. Perhaps the owner may bring in utilities to the perimeter of the land, have a development plan approved for the land, or have the land annexed into a city or town. Accordingly, property enhancements may also occur to both vacant undeveloped land and improved property.

Benefit 6: Equity Buildup

Equity is the value of an ownership interest in property over and above all other claims against the property. These claims may be in the form of liens or mortgages. Equity may also be defined as the total value of a property less all other claims against the property. Equity is as directly linked to market value as it is to purchase price. The total value of a property is equal to the sum of the owner's equity in a property plus the liens and claims against the property. The formulas for calculating the owner's equity position, total value, and lien position for a property are shown below:

Owner's Equity = Total Value – All Liens and Claims
Total Value = Owner's Equity + All Liens and Claims
All Liens and Claims = Total Value – Owner's Equity

Table 4.7

Calculations for Equity
Buildup with No Value
Change

Equity Begin Year 1		Equity End Year 3		Equity Buildup	
Purchase Price	$550,000	Total Value	$550,000	Equity Year 3	$157,833
Debt Balance	(412,500)	Debt Balance	(392,167)	Equity Year 1	(137,500)
Equity Year 1	$137,500	Equity Year 3	$157,833	Equity Buildup	$ 20,333

Equity buildup is the change in equity that occurs over time. It is the increase in the equity investor's share of total property value. This increase results from gradual debt reduction through periodic repayment of principal on a mortgage loan, an increase in total property value, or both.

To understand how equity buildup really works, let's continue with our example of the multifamily rental apartment property we introduced at the beginning of this chapter. As Table 4.1 summarized, our investor acquired the property for a purchase price of $550,000, using $137,500 of equity and borrowing the remainder in the form of a new first mortgage in the amount of $412,500. At the beginning of the investment, his equity is $137,500. After three years, the loan was paid down to $392,167, the property had not appreciated, and the purchase price and total value both equaled $550,000. At this point, the investor's equity would be $157,833. Because the initial equity investment was $137,500, the equity buildup is $20,333. Table 4.7 summarizes these calculations.

The previous calculation for equity buildup is based on a total value that is the same as the purchase price. To see the true power of equity buildup, the following example adds an increase in total value to the equity buildup formula.

Let's say that the property increased in value by approximately 5 percent per year. At the end of the third year the property would have a total value of approximately $637,000. If after three years the loan was paid down to $392,167 and the property had a total value of $637,000, the investor's equity would be $244,833. Because the initial equity investment was $137,500, the equity buildup is $107,333. Table 4.8 summarizes these calculations.

While equity buildup alone is a powerful tool for increasing the investor's wealth position in the property, combining it with an increase in value multiplies the effect.

Table 4.8

Calculations for Equity
Buildup with Increase
in Value

Equity Begin Year 1		Equity End Year 3		Equity Buildup	
Purchase Price	$550,000	Total Value	$637,000	Equity Year 3	$244,833
Debt Balance	(412,500)	Debt Balance	(392,167)	Equity Year 1	(137,500)
Equity Year 1	$137,500	Equity Year 3	$244,833	Equity Buildup	$107,333

■ Combining the Advantages of Commercial Real Estate as an Investment

Investors are motivated by one, some, or all of the advantages of commercial real estate as an investment. Table 4.9 summarizes our discussion of these advantages and puts the discussion into perspective. The table presents the calculations for pretax cash flow, taxable income, and after-tax cash flow.

1. Within the *pretax cash flow section* of the table, operating expenses have been presented in greater detail to highlight the different types of fixed, variable, and replacement allowance expenses.

2. Within the *taxable income section* of the table, the investor's taxable income has been determined and, with the tax rate known, the tax liability determined.

3. Within the *after-tax cash flow section* of the table, cash flow that is available to the investor after taxes has been considered are determined. (After-tax cash flow is equal to pretax cash flow plus replacement reserves less the tax liability.) Notice that thanks to the tax shelter qualities of the depreciation charge, after-tax income is approximately equal to or greater than pretax cash flow.

The first three years of the investment have been "modeled" to present the typical mind-set of investors. Notice how income is trending upward while expenses are trending downward.

Table 4.9 presents our investor's ten-unit, multifamily rental apartment in an expanded presentation, summarizing pretax cash flow, taxable income, and after-tax cash flow calculations into one efficient income and expense statement. The property is also presented in a three-year pro-forma to forecast "best estimates" of the property's probable performance. These types of presentations are typically prepared for five- to ten-year periods, and include a property reversion. They also employ technically advanced discounted cash flow analysis utilizing electronic spreadsheet software or financial and investment analysis lease-by-lease software.

Table 4.9

Three-Year Income and Expense Analysis

10 Unit Apartment Building - Income and Expense Analysis

			Units	10
			Living Area Square Feet	10,500

Period	Current Year 2004				Forecast 2005				Forecast 2006			
Category	Amount	Amount Per Unit	Amount Per SF	% Total PGI	Amount	Amount Per Unit	Amount Per SF	% Total PGI	Amount	Amount Per Unit	Amount Per SF	% Total PGI
PRE-TAX CASH FLOW												
Scheduled Base Rent	$ 99,400	$ 9,940	$ 9.47	99.40%	$ 102,382	$ 10,238	$ 9.75	99.39%	$ 107,245	$ 10,725	$ 10.21	99.36%
Market Rent for Vacant Units	$ -	$ -	$ -	0.00%	$ -	$ -	$ -	0.00%	$ -	$ -	$ -	0.00%
Subtotal: Adjusted Base Rent	$ 99,400	$ 9,940	$ 9.47	99.40%	$ 102,382	$ 10,238	$ 9.75	102.38%	$ 107,245	$ 10,725	$ 10.21	99.36%
Other Income												
Laundry	$ 600	$ 60	$ 0.06	0.60%	$ 630	$ 63	$ 0.06	0.61%	$ 690	$ 69	$ 0.07	0.64%
Subtotal: Other Income	$ 600	$ 60	$ 0.06	0.60%	$ 630	$ 63	$ 0.06	0.61%	$ 690	$ 69	$ 0.07	0.64%
Potential Gross Income @ 100% Occupancy	$ 100,000	$ 10,000	$ 9.52	100.00%	$ 103,012	$ 10,301	$ 9.81	100.00%	$ 107,935	$ 10,793	$ 10.28	100.00%
Vacancy & Collection Loss @ 5%	$ 5,000	$ 500	$ 0.48	5.00%	$ 5,151	$ 515	$ 0.49	5.00%	$ 5,397	$ 540	$ 0.51	5.00%
Effective Gross Income	$ 95,000	$ 9,500	$ 9.05	95.00%	$ 97,861	$ 9,786	$ 9.32	95.00%	$ 102,538	$ 10,254	$ 9.77	95.00%
Operating Expenses — Fixed (% Total EGI)	Amount	Per Unit	Per SF	Total EGI	Amount	Per Unit	Per SF	Total EGI	Amount	Per Unit	Per SF	Total EGI
Real Estate Taxes	$ 11,000	$ 1,100	$ 1.05	11.58%	$ 11,000	$ 1,100	$ 1.05	11.24%	$ 11,165	$ 1,117	$ 1.06	10.89%
Insurance	$ 1,750	$ 175	$ 0.17	1.84%	$ 1,750	$ 175	$ 0.17	1.79%	$ 1,500	$ 150	$ 0.14	1.46%
Subtotal Fixed	$ 12,750	$ 1,275	$ 1.21	13.42%	$ 12,750	$ 1,275	$ 1.21	13.03%	$ 12,665	$ 1,267	$ 1.21	12.35%
Variable												
Management Fee @ 4%	$ 3,800	$ 380	$ 0.36	4.00%	$ 3,914	$ 391	$ 0.37	4.00%	$ 4,102	$ 410	$ 0.39	4.00%
Advertising & Promotion	$ 825	$ 83	$ 0.08	0.87%	$ 800	$ 80	$ 0.08	0.82%	$ 700	$ 70	$ 0.07	0.68%
Telephone	$ 900	$ 90	$ 0.09	0.95%	$ 900	$ 90	$ 0.09	0.92%	$ 800	$ 80	$ 0.08	0.78%
Utilities (Water, Sewer, Electric)	$ 1,600	$ 160	$ 0.15	1.68%	$ 1,600	$ 160	$ 0.15	1.63%	$ 1,575	$ 158	$ 0.15	1.54%
Trash Removal / Refuse	$ 1,000	$ 100	$ 0.10	1.05%	$ 1,000	$ 100	$ 0.10	1.02%	$ 1,030	$ 103	$ 0.10	1.00%
Repairs, Maintenance & Supplies	$ 11,000	$ 1,100	$ 1.05	11.58%	$ 11,000	$ 1,100	$ 1.05	11.24%	$ 10,000	$ 1,000	$ 0.95	9.75%
Unit Interior Redecorating	$ 1,475	$ 148	$ 0.14	1.55%	$ 1,425	$ 143	$ 0.14	1.46%	$ 1,275	$ 128	$ 0.12	1.24%
Landscape, Lawn & Grounds	$ 1,200	$ 120	$ 0.11	1.26%	$ 1,200	$ 120	$ 0.11	1.23%	$ 1,250	$ 125	$ 0.12	1.22%
Pest Control	$ 450	$ 45	$ 0.04	0.47%	$ 450	$ 45	$ 0.04	0.46%	$ 400	$ 40	$ 0.04	0.39%
Subtotal Variable	$ 22,250	$ 2,225	$ 2.12	23.42%	$ 22,289	$ 2,229	$ 2.12	22.78%	$ 21,132	$ 2,113	$ 2.01	20.61%
Replacement Allowances	$ 5,000	$ 500	$ 0.48	5.26%	$ 5,000	$ 500	$ 0.48	5.11%	$ 5,000	$ 500	$ 0.48	4.88%
Subtotal Replacement Allowances	$ 5,000	$ 500	$ 0.48	5.26%	$ 5,000	$ 500	$ 0.48	5.11%	$ 5,000	$ 500	$ 0.48	4.88%
Total Operating Expenses	$ 40,000	$ 4,000	$ 3.81	42.11%	$ 40,039	$ 4,004	$ 3.81	40.91%	$ 38,797	$ 3,880	$ 3.69	37.84%
Net Operating Income	$ 55,000	$ 5,500	$ 5.24	57.89%	$ 57,822	$ 5,782	$ 5.51	59.09%	$ 63,742	$ 6,374	$ 6.07	62.16%
Mortgage Loan												
Interest Expense	$ 28,694	$ 2,869	$ 2.73	30.20%	$ 28,238	$ 2,824	$ 2.69	28.86%	$ 27,749	$ 2,775	$ 2.64	27.06%
Principal Reduction	$ 6,306	$ 631	$ 0.60	6.64%	$ 6,762	$ 676	$ 0.64	6.91%	$ 7,251	$ 725	$ 0.69	7.07%
Total Debt Service	$ 35,000	$ 3,500	$ 3.33	36.84%	$ 35,000	$ 3,500	$ 3.33	35.76%	$ 35,000	$ 3,500	$ 3.33	34.13%
Pre-Tax Cash Flow	$ 20,000	$ 2,000	$ 1.90	21.05%	$ 22,822	$ 2,282	$ 2.17	23.32%	$ 28,742	$ 2,874	$ 2.74	28.03%
TAXABLE INCOME												
Net Operating Income	$ 55,000	$ 5,500	$ 5.24	57.89%	$ 57,822	$ 5,782	$ 5.51	59.09%	$ 63,742	$ 6,374	$ 6.07	62.16%
add: Reserves	$ 5,000	$ 500	$ 0.48	5.26%	$ 5,000	$ 500	$ 0.48	5.11%	$ 5,000	$ 500	$ 0.48	4.88%
less: Interest Expense	$ 28,694	$ 2,869	$ 2.73	30.20%	$ 28,238	$ 2,824	$ 2.69	28.86%	$ 27,749	$ 2,775	$ 2.64	27.06%
less: Depreciation	$ 22,165	$ 2,216	$ 2.11	23.33%	$ 22,744	$ 2,274	$ 2.17	23.24%	$ 22,744	$ 2,274	$ 2.17	22.18%
Taxable Income	$ 9,141	$ 914	$ 0.87	9.62%	$ 11,840	$ 1,184	$ 1.13	12.10%	$ 18,249	$ 1,825	$ 1.74	17.80%
multiply: Tax Rate @ 35%	$ 3,199	$ 320	$ 0.30	3.37%	$ 4,144	$ 414	$ 0.39	4.23%	$ 6,387	$ 639	$ 0.61	6.23%
Tax Liability	$ 3,199	$ 320	$ 0.30	3.37%	$ 4,144	$ 414	$ 0.39	4.23%	$ 6,387	$ 639	$ 0.61	6.23%
AFTER TAX CASH FLOW												
Pre-Tax Cash Flow	$ 20,000	$ 2,000	$ 1.90	21.05%	$ 22,822	$ 2,282	$ 2.17	23.32%	$ 28,742	$ 2,874	$ 2.74	28.03%
add: Reserves	$ 5,000	$ 500	$ 0.48	5.26%	$ 5,000	$ 500	$ 0.48	5.11%	$ 5,000	$ 500	$ 0.48	4.88%
less: Tax Liability	$ 3,199	$ 320	$ 0.30	3.37%	$ 4,144	$ 414	$ 0.39	4.23%	$ 6,387	$ 639	$ 0.61	6.23%
After Tax Cash Flow	$ 21,801	$ 2,180	$ 2.08	22.95%	$ 23,678	$ 2,368	$ 2.26	24.20%	$ 27,355	$ 2,735	$ 2.61	26.68%

■ Disadvantages of Commercial Real Estate as an Investment

The disadvantages of investing in commercial real estate are also both intangible and tangible. The intangible, or nonmeasurable, disadvantages of investing in commercial real estate include the possible sense of personal failure and embarrassment if the investment fails for any reason. The tangible or measurable disadvantages of investing in commercial real estate can be quantified monetarily and include that it is: (1) capital intensive, (2) long term in nature, (3) nonliquid, (4) management intensive, (5) subject to economic-, market-, and property-related risks, and (6) has an opportunity cost of capital.

Disadvantage 1: Capital Intensive

Commercial real estate requires a significant capital expenditure for purchase. Capital is accumulated wealth. It may also be described as a sum of money available for an investment. The concept of capital is related to but not the same as the concept of a capital expenditure. A capital expenditure represents an investment to acquire or to improve real estate. The sum of money for investment may consist entirely of the investor's money, which is called equity. Alternatively, it may consist of a combination of equity and money borrowed from a lender, which is called debt.

The price range of commercial real estate is as varied as the type and quality of property available. While the term *expensive* is relative, it is reasonable to say that commercial property is capital intensive to acquire, manage, and maintain. Consider our investor who acquired the multifamily apartment building for a purchase price of $550,000. In this investment, the equity of $137,500 represents 25 percent of the total purchase price and the debt borrowed and invested was $412,500, which represents 75 percent of the total purchase price. We may debate if this purchase price is a bargain, justifiable, or overpriced, but clearly the acquisition represents a significant capital expenditure.

There is also a "price of entry" into the real estate arena. Before a decision to purchase the property was reached, the investor had to expend additional resources in the form of time and money. Prior to the investor purchasing the apartment property, he had to find the opportunity, prepare and submit a letter of intent, and when agreement was reached, prepare a contract for purchase and sale. The investor then conducted a buyer's inspection, also known as due diligence. Some of the information the investor reviewed during his due diligence period prior to committing to buy the property were leases, historical and current operating results, budgets, service contracts, existing title information, surveys, parking agreements, environmental tests, and studies such as structural, HVAC, roof, and mechanical reports and so forth. In addition to the investor, other professionals such as attorneys, engineers, and technicians were required to review portions of this information. If, based on the due diligence, the investor decided not to purchase the property, he would still have incurred expenses associated with these activities.

Because the investor was going to use debt as part of his capital base, he also had to consider and resolve issues of mortgage financing to acquire the property. Prior to committing to provide financing for the property, the selected lender was required to conduct its own due diligence, also know as a lender's underwriting. The lender's underwriting required most of the information the investor reviewed in his due diligence. Additional information, including an appraisal was required, and those and other costs were charged to the investor. In addition to the lender, other professionals such as attorneys, engineers, and technicians were required to review portions of this information. The investor was charged for these services through lender application, administrative, and/or underwriting fees. If, based on the underwriting, the lender decided not to finance the property, the investor would still have incurred these expenses associated with these activities. Once the lender decided to provide financing for the property, other expenses incurred by the investor included loan origination fees and charges for discount points.

Disadvantage 2: Long Term in Nature

In order to maximize the total return to the investor, acquired property must generally be held for a number of years. It usually takes from three to five years to obtain meaningful increases in cash flow and property value from the combination of property enhancement and property appreciation. Investors may hold property for seven to ten years or longer to meet their investment and capital recapture objectives. Other investors buy but don't sell. *Capital recapture* is the return of equity in an investment as distinguished from the return on equity. Invested capital is usually recaptured through annual income and resale of the property at the conclusion of the investment. The tax laws also encourage long-term investments.

Disadvantage 3: Nonliquidity

The total value of a real estate investment is usually not immediately convertible to cash without a loss in value. This characteristic of real estate makes it a nonliquid or illiquid asset. **Liquidity** refers to the ability of an asset value to be converted into an equivalent cash amount. The long-term nature of commercial real estate investments is consistent with its illiquid conversion characteristics. Commercial properties tend to be complex in nature. Usually, as a property increases in size so does its complexity and value. These characteristics further impede the cash convertibility of real estate.

To illustrate the illiquid nature of real estate, let's assume that the following properties each had a 90-day sales and marketing period, and that the buyers and sellers are finally in agreement as to the purchase terms and price. There are no financing contingencies, and the price is all cash to the seller. All that is required now is the completion of the buyer's due diligence and inspection prior to closing. The timing between the commencement of the sales and marketing period and the closing highlights the illiquid nature of real estate.

- In smaller commercial properties, a 60-day due diligence period followed by a 30-day closing period is not uncommon. Factoring in a 90-day sales and marketing period, the total time to convent this real estate asset to cash without a loss in value is 180 days, or six months.
- In larger commercial properties, a 90-day due diligence period followed by a 30-day closing period is not uncommon. Factoring in a 90-day sales and marketing period, the total time to convent this real estate asset to cash without a loss in value is 210 days, or seven months.
- For a special purpose property being acquired for a new use, a 180-day due diligence period followed by a 30-day closing is not uncommon.

Factoring in a 90-day sales and marketing period, the total time to convent this real estate asset to cash is 300 days, or 10 months.

■ For a major parcel of land that has a sales price contingent on a rezoning and site plan approval, a 270- to 360-day due diligence period followed by a 30-day closing is not uncommon. Factoring in a 90-day sales and marketing period, the total time to convent this real estate asset to cash without a loss in value is 390 to 480 days, or 13 to 16 months.

These examples highlight the considerable time required to convert a real estate asset to its cash value. A property owner who has an immediate requirement for cash may be forced to sell his property at a discounted price and give up asset value in the process.

Disadvantage 4: Management Intensive

Successful real estate investments are dependent on the capable management of every aspect of the real estate. Generally speaking, real estate management consists of expertise in property maintenance and operations, human resources, marketing and leasing, financial operations, asset management, and legal and risk management. Although fundamental business management is necessary for all investment property, the time, effort, and number of individuals required to carry out these tasks increases in relation to the size, scope, and number of tenants in an investment property.

Once the real estate is acquired, it must be managed. With smaller properties or a small portfolio of properties, the investor may act as manager. As the complexities of management grow, investors may develop their own staffs. However, other investors decide not to divert their valuable time and creative energies to management. These investors employ professional managers or management companies to take on this responsibility. In addition to the expense associated with valuable time and creative energies, there is also a monetary expense.

Investors purchase real estate for the anticipated financial returns.

The primary reason investors retain competent property management is to supervise every aspect of the property's operation so as to produce the greatest achievable financial return for the longest period of time. This fact underlies the primary reason for the investment in the first place: investors purchase commercial real estate for what it provides them, namely the anticipated financial returns desired, and not necessarily the property's physical and location attributes. Accordingly, real estate is a capital asset. A capital asset has two distinguishing characteristics: it is used to produce income and it has physical permanence.

Disadvantage 5: Economic-, Market-, and Property-Related Risks

Risk is the probability that foreseen events will not occur. Risk may be incurred as a result of general economic and market conditions upon the performance of a property, the interaction of a group of real estate investments in a portfolio, or the operation of the real estate enterprise as an independent venture. In real estate, risk is linked to uncertainty. *Uncertainty* is the probability that unforeseen events will occur.

Regardless of the type of risk, all investors attempt to mitigate or reduce the effect of risk. The forces that shape economic trends are constantly in motion within neighborhoods, districts, localities, regions, and among nations. Similarly, the influences on the characteristics of supply and demand that create market conditions are dynamic and always in motion. These forces that create economic and market risk conditions are beyond the control of the investor in commercial real estate and are only indirectly manageable. To a significant degree, property-related risk is directly manageable by the investor. That is why prudent property management is fundamental to the success of a real estate investment.

Disadvantage 6: The Opportunity Cost of Capital

An **opportunity cost** is the theoretical cost associated with selecting one investment opportunity as compared to another. It may also be described as the theoretical cost associated with investment options foregone once another investment option or options have been selected.

Ideally, commercial real estate investors will have alternative properties to analyze and consider before selecting one to bid on and purchase. However, while many properties will look similar, their anticipated rates of return and the risk associated with those returns will most certainly differ. Accordingly, investors must first determine their desired level of risk associated with their desired level of return. Risk and return normally move in the same direction, at the same time. For a real estate investor, the greater the anticipated risk associated with a monetary return, the greater the monetary return necessary to induce an investor to accept that greater risk. The combination of risk and return that the investor selects becomes part of his investment objectives.

Opportunity cost may manifest itself in a number of ways. Consider the following example that is based on actual events. An investor has selected an area in which to invest and decides he would like to purchase a freestanding building leased to a national drugstore chain. The lease must be a minimum of 20 years, with the drugstore tenant responsible for all expenses including property taxes, insurance, structural repair, and maintenance. Therefore, the rent actually paid to the investor-landlord is net of all expenses and the predictability of the periodic net rent payments is similar to a dividend or an annuity.

The investor desires the drugstore tenant occupying the property to pay a lease rate of a minimum of $25 per square foot net of all expenses. The investor desires a high degree of certainty that the payment of rent will occur as promised within the lease. The higher the degree of certainty, the lower the degree of risk. The investor will accept returns as evidenced in the market.

The investor finds two such alternative properties to analyze and consider before selecting one to bid on and purchase. Both properties are occupied by national drugstore chains. They are located on opposite and equally desirable corners of the main intersection in the area and are similar in every way. Both buildings are 7,500 square feet each and are located on 30,000-square-foot corner lots. Both investment properties are being sold with 20 years remaining on their leases with the tenant paying identical lease rates of $25 per square foot net of all expenses. Because the properties are the same size, total rent payments are the same, with the current annual rents being $187,500 each. These two alternative properties—drugstore 1 and drugstore 2—are presented in Figure 4.1.

Figure 4.1

Alternative Investment
Locations

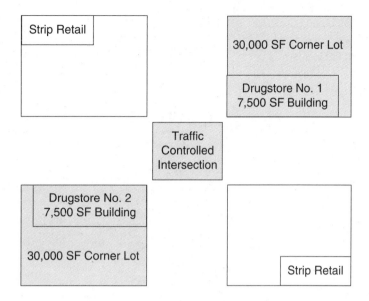

The investor learns that drugstore 1 is wholly owned by a major U.S. corporation. This corporation has had a profitable business year and its creditworthiness remains rated AAA+ (excellent) by a national rating agency. Because the corporation guarantees the lease, the rent default risks associated with this drugstore lease are considered minimal. Based on the review of a number of comparable sales of this drugstore chain within the region, other investors are willing to accept a return of 8 percent on the current rent payments of this national chain drugstore.

Upon further investigation, the investor finds that drugstore 2 is also wholly owned by a major U.S. corporation. This corporation has had financial problems and its creditworthiness has been rated BBB- (fair to poor) by a national credit rating agency. Because this corporation also guarantees the lease, the rent default risks associated with this drugstore lease are considered greater than the default risk associated with drugstore 1. Based on the review of a number of comparable sales of this drugstore chain within the region, other investors are willing to accept a return of 9.75 percent on the current rent payments of this national chain drugstore.

With this information, the investor prepares the figures in Table 4.10. The table summarizes for the investor the investment alternatives available to him. He will also consider this purchase on an all-cash basis and a leveraged basis.

The investor's analysis can be compared to the annual interest desired for a savings account. If the investor has $2,343,750 to deposit at his local bank, and he desires to place it into an account paying 8 percent simple interest per annum on the principal, the investor could determine that he would receive a total of $187,500 in interest income at the end of one year, by the calculation below:

Principal deposited × simple interest rate per annum =
Interest income per annum.

Table 4.10

Alternative
Investment Pricing

Description	Drugstore No. 1	Drugstore No. 2
Sq. Ft. Building	7,500	7,500
Rent Per Sq. Ft.	$25.00	$25.00
Annual Rent	$187,500.00	$187,500.00
Credit Rating	AAA+	BBB–
Return Rates	8.00%	9.75%
Total Bid Price	$2,343,750.00	$1,923,075.00
Bid Price Sq. Ft.	$312.50	$256.41

In our example:

$$\$2,343,750 \times 0.08 = \$187,500.$$

However, because the investor knew the amount of income he would receive on his principal investment and the rate of interest on his investment (i.e., the rate of return on the investment), he simply solved for the principal investment amount of the deposit by the following calculation:

Interest income per annum ÷ simple interest rate per annum = principal deposited.

In our example:

$$\$187,500 \div 0.08 = \$2,343,750.$$

Opportunity cost based on an all-cash offer.   This investor prefers less risk and more safety. Based on these preferences, the investor prefers the AAA+ credit-rated tenant and must accept the lower return of 8 percent on his investment. This means he can bid, or offer to pay, $2,343,750 for the annual rent stream of $187,000, and still receive an 8 percent return on his investment. Moreover, because investing in drugstore 1 will require $2,343,750 while investing in drugstore 2 will require only $1,923,075, the investor must spend $420,673 more for the same income stream, given his risk-return preferences. This additional $420,675 represents the opportunity cost of unleveraged capital because these additional funds are no longer available for alternative investments. (See Table 4.11.)

Opportunity cost based on a leveraged offer.   The investor presents both drugstores to a lender for financing consideration. The lender will provide financing on either of the two drugstores. The loan has a term of 25-year amortization, with a balloon payment at the end of the 20th year, at a fixed 5 percent interest rate. Because drugstore 1 has a lease guaranteed by a corporation with AAA+ (excellent) credit, the lender will provide an 80 percent loan-to-value ratio loan. However, because drugstore 2 has a lease guaranteed by a corporation with BBB- (fair to poor) credit, the lender will only provide a 60 percent loan-to-value ratio loan.

Based on this loan quote, the investor prepares Table 4.12.

Table 4.11

Opportunity Cost—
Unleveraged Basis

Description	Equity
Drugstore No. 1—Unleveraged	$2,343,750
less:	
Drugstore No. 2—Unleveraged	$1,923,075
equals:	
Opportunity Cost—Unleveraged	$ 420,675

Table 4.12

Determining the
Equity Required for a
Leveraged Purchase

Description	Drugstore No. 1		Drugstore No. 2	
	$	%	$	%
Price	$2,343,750	100%	$1,923,0750	100%
less:				
Debt	1,875,000	80	1,153,845	60
equals:				
Equity	$ 468,750	20%	$ 769,230	40%

The investor discovers that the lender also prefers less risk and more safety. Based on theses preferences, the investor will have to use $769,230 of equity to buy "less expensive" drugstore 2, but only $468,750 of equity to buy "more expensive" drugstore 1. Ironically, the "cheaper" purchase will actually cost the investor $300,480 more from an equity position. (See Table 4.13.)

This additional $300,480 represents the opportunity cost of leveraged capital because these additional funds are no longer available for alternative investments.

Table 4.13

Opportunity Cost—
Leveraged Basis

Description	Equity
Drugstore No. 2—Leveraged	$769,230
less:	
Drugstore No. 1—Leveraged	468,750
equals:	
Opportunity Cost—Leveraged	$300,480

■ Summary

The purchase of commercial real estate is an investment in an income-producing capital asset. Real estate investors expect a return of all their invested capital, as well as a return on their invested capital. Because real estate is a capital asset, investors are concerned with the probability of recovery of all their capital investment, as well as the probability of receiving payment for the use of the invested capital. In all real estate investments, there are measurable and nonmeasurable advantages and disadvantages that must be considered. The tangible, or measurable, advantages of investing in commercial real estate can be quantified monetarily. These monetary benefits fall into the category of either return of capital or return on capital and include: (1) cash flow, (2) tax shelter, (3) property depreciation, (4) reduction of property debt financing, (5) increases in property value, and (6) equity buildup.

Due primarily to the disadvantages associated with an investment in real estate, sophisticated investors gather as much relevant information as possible for their decision-making process. The tangible, or measurable, disadvantages of investing in commercial real estate can be quantified monetarily and include that it is: (1) capital intensive, (2) long term in nature, (3) nonliquid, (4) management intensive, (5) subject to economic-, market-, and property-related risks, and (6) has an opportunity cost of capital.

The decision to invest in commercial real estate is made more reliably when the decision is set within a framework that allows for a systematic and quantitative decision-making process that assists in removing guesswork. Although an investor should obtain as much relevant measurable and non-measurable information as possible, he should rely primarily on the measurable information because the investor is concerned with the risks associated with both the return of capital and the return on capital. Pride of ownership and a sense of accomplishment are certainly advantages of investing in real estate. However, investors purchase commercial real estate primarily for what it provides them—the anticipated financial returns desired—and not necessarily what the property's physical and location attributes are.

Investors should not only be familiar with the advantages and disadvantages of investing, but should know how to quantify them for their decision-making process. The decision to invest in commercial real estate is really a business decision with financial implications. Accordingly, investors should be sufficiently fluent in practical business, management, and organizational structures, as well as mathematics and finance. These advantages and disadvantages are always considered in terms of the risk associated with a particular investment, the alternative investment choices available to the investor, and the opportunity cost of selection of one investment in lieu of another.

■ Review Questions

1. The six tangible advantages of investing in real estate are
   a. (1) cash flow, (2) tax shelter, (3) property depreciation, (4) reduction of property debt financing, (5) increases in property value, and (6) equity buildup.
   b. (1) capital intensive, (2) long term in nature, (3) nonliquid, (4) management intensive, (5) subject to economic-, market-, and property-related risks, and (6) has an opportunity cost of capital.
   c. (1) cash flow, (2) nonliquid, (3) property depreciation, (4) capital intensive, (5) increases in property value, and (6) ego buildup.
   d. None of the above

2. Reasons that investors are interested in a property's cash flow include that it provides a simple yet fundamental measure of an investment's capability of
   a. paying the borrowed debt without coming out of pocket.
   b. providing a positive return on capital.
   c. providing a positive return of capital.
   d. All the above (A, B, and C)

3. Depreciation is a noncash expense that may be described as
   a. an accounting concept that allows an investor to deduct the cost of the investment property.
   b. an accounting concept that allows an investor to deduct "out-of-pocket" cash expenditures to recover the cost of the investment property.
   c. an accounting deduction that in concept allows an investor to recover the cost of the investment property.
   d. None of the above

4. The difference between a mortgage and a mortgage note is
   a. a mortgage is a note.
   b. a mortgage note is a written promise to convey an interest in real property.
   c. a mortgage is a conveyance of payback money.
   d. a note is a written promise to pay and a mortgage is a conveyance of an interest in real property.

5. An amortized loan is a loan requiring periodic payments that include both
   a. income and partial expenses.
   b. income and partial interest.
   c. interest and partial principal.
   d. income and partial appreciation.

6. Increases in property value
   a. may originate from either property appreciation or property enhancements.
   b. may originate from market forces and trends that are beyond the control of the investor.
   c. may originate from programs implemented by the property owner.
   d. All the above (A, B, and C)

7. The economic principle of scarcity is
   a. the undersupply of demand for a property relative to the supply of it.
   b. the undersupply of a property relative to the demand for it.
   c. the oversupply of a property relative to the demand for it.
   d. the oversupply of demand for a property relative to the supply of it.

8. The six tangible disadvantages of investing in real estate are
   a. (1) cash flow, (2) tax shelter, (3) property depreciation, (4) reduction of property debt financing, (5) increases in property value, and (6) equity buildup.
   b. that it is (1) capital intensive, (2) long term in nature, (3) nonliquid, (4) management intensive, (5) subject to economic-, market-, and property-related risks, and (6) has the opportunity cost of capital.
   c. (1) cash flow, (2) nonliquidity, (3) property depreciation, (4) capital intensive, (5) increases in property value, and (6) ego buildup.
   d. None of the above

9. The primary reason that investors purchase commercial real estate is

   a. to supervise every aspect of the property's operation so as to produce the greatest achievable financial return for the longest period of time.

   b. the anticipated financial returns.

   c. the property's physical and location attributes.

   d. liquidation.

10. The opportunity cost of capital is

   a. the theoretical cost associated with selecting one investment opportunity as compared to another.

   b. the theoretical cost associated with investment options foregone once another investment option has been selected.

   c. interrelated with an investor's risk and return profile.

   d. All the above (A, B, and C)

11. An investor acquired an office building that contains 15,000 square feet of rentable area. The building has an occupancy rate of 100 percent and the average rent in the building is $25 per square foot. In addition to the lease rental income, there is other annual income generated from the operation of the real estate, such as $1,200 from reserved parking income and $800 from vending machines. Other annual income is considered before vacancy and collection losses. For analysis purposes, a 5 percent vacancy and collection loss factor is used. Using this information, determine the property's total potential gross income, vacancy and collection loss, and effective gross income.

   a. The property's total annual lease rental income is $375,000, the total annual other income is $2,000, and the total annual potential gross income is $377,000. The annual vacancy and collection loss is $18,850 and the annual effective gross income is $358,150.

   b. The property's total annual lease rental income is $375,000, the total annual other income is $2,000, and the total annual potential gross income is $377,000. The annual vacancy and collection loss is $18,750 and the annual effective gross income is $358,250.

   c. The property's total annual lease rental income is $375,000, the total annual other income is $2,000, and the total annual potential gross income is $375,000. The annual vacancy and collection loss is $18,850 and the annual effective gross income is $356,250.

   d. The property's total annual lease rental income is $375,000, the total annual other income is $2,000, and the total annual potential gross income is $373,000. The annual vacancy and collection loss is $18,650 and the annual effective gross income is $354,350.

12. For the property in question 11, the investor has budgeted $6 per square foot of rentable area for total fixed and variable expenses. Replacement reserves have been budgeted at $0.25 per square foot of rentable area. For analysis purposes, a 5 percent vacancy and collection loss factor is used. Using this information, determine the property's total annual fixed and variable expenses, replacement reserves expense, and net operating income.

    a. The property's total annual fixed and variable expenses are $89,062.50, total annual replacement reserves expense is $3,562.50, and net operating income is $265,525.

    b. The property's total annual fixed and variable expenses are $93,750, total annual replacement reserves expense is $3,562.50, and net operating income is $260,837.50.

    c. The property's total annual fixed and variable expenses are $89,062.50, total annual replacement reserves expense is $3,750, and net operating income is $265,337.50.

    d. The property's total annual fixed and variable expenses are $90,000, total annual replacement reserves expense is $3,750, and net operating income is $264,400.

13. Continuing with the office building presented in question 12, the investor purchased this property on the basis of a 10 percent rate of return. What was the purchase price of this office building?

    a. $3,770,000

    b. $3,750,000

    c. $3,581,500

    d. $2,644,000

14. Continuing with the office building presented in question 13, the investor purchased this property with a combination of the investor's equity and lender's debt. The lender's debt equated to 75 percent of the purchase price. What would the debt amount be based on this LTV?

    a. $2,827,500

    b. $2,812,500

    c. $2,686,125

    d. $1,983,000

15. Continuing with the office building presented in question 14, the lender will provide debt financing based on the following terms: 25-year fully amortizing loan at a fixed rate of 7 percent, payable monthly, with annual debt service totaling $168,185 for principal and interest. What would the pretax cash flow from this investment be?

    a. $116,215

    b. $106,215

    c. $96,215

    d. $86,215

chapter five

MARKET ANALYSIS FOR COMMERCIAL REAL ESTATE

■ Key Terminology

buyer's market	highest and best use	seller's market
competitive supply	market analysis	submarket
demand	market leakage	supply
effective demand	market share	

■ Overview

In this chapter, market analysis is introduced as a core tool for both investors and decision makers in real estate. Market analysis provides fundamental answers to investors' questions and concerns about their established investment objectives and goals. The various steps in the preparation of a market analysis are presented in detail. The interdependence between economic principals and market forces that impact market analysis are emphasized.

Market analysis is presented as both a self-contained tool for investors and part of the foundation of other, more complex forms of analysis. It is important to complete one form of analysis as the foundation for the next, more complex form of analysis. These analyses form a continuum of analysis that provides a great deal of insight into the historical, current, and projected market conditions for real estate.

■ Learning Objectives

After completing this chapter, the reader should be able to accomplish the following:

1. Define *market analysis*
2. Describe the *various steps* in preparing a market analysis
3. Explain why the market for real estate is *inefficient*
4. Explain the *characteristics of demand*
5. Differentiate between *demand* and *effective demand*
6. Explain the *characteristics of supply*

7. Differentiate between *supply* and **competitive supply**
8. Differentiate between a *buyer's* and *seller's market*
9. Explain the concept of *market share*
10. Differentiate between a *market analysis,* a *marketability study,* a *feasibility study,* a *highest and best use study,* and an *investment analysis*

■ What Is Market Analysis?

Market analysis is a term that has been misused and misinterpreted. Generally speaking, market analysis tends to become more complex as one proceeds along the hierarchy of market studies. The study of market analysis embraces the study of economics. For these reasons, many investors prefer not to study the subject at all. Yet when these same investors speak in terms of a buyer's market or a seller's market, they are not only speaking in terms of market analysis, but in terms of an even more complex subject: real estate market cycles. As such, investors, whether they know it or not, are already talking and thinking in terms of market analysis. So, it is not a question of should investors know about market analysis, but how to go about it in a way that does not drive us into information overload and frustration.

Market Analysis Defined

Market analysis is the study of real estate market conditions for a specific property type. Simply stated, market analysis is the study of real estate market conditions. If the focus is on a specific type of property within a specific real estate market, then the analysis also becomes more focused. So market analysis can have either a broad or narrow focus.

Real Estate Markets

Generally, a *market* is a gathering of people for the buying and selling of things. The individuals gathered for this purpose comprise the market. For example, consider the origins of the New York Stock Exchange. In 1792, 24 of New York City's leading merchants would regularly gather under a buttonwood tree on the streets of New York City for the purpose of buying and selling securities. These 24 merchants had formed a securities *market.*

When buyers and sellers gather and are interacting for the purchase and sale of real estate, they have formed a market for real estate. For example, consider LoopNet, which exists in cyberspace on the Internet (*www.loopnet. com*). Simply stated, LoopNet connects buyers and sellers for the purpose of facilitating real estate transactions. LoopNet is a leading commercial real estate information services provider that offers products and services to satisfy the needs of both the national and local commercial real estate industry. LoopNet operates the largest commercial real estate listing service online. In early 2006, LoopNet boasted $270 billion of real estate for sale, over 2.7 billion square feet of real estate for lease, 3 million acres of land for sale, and over 1.1 million members who are *gathering and interacting in cyberspace.* These 1.1 million members have formed a real estate *market.* These members, who normally do not meet personally to conduct business, use mobile telephones, laptops with wireless connections, e-mail, and scanners and e-faxes to conduct business.

A *real estate market* is a gathering of individuals who are in contact with one another to buy and sell real property rights for money and other assets. A real estate market may also be described in terms of individuals, groups, or firms that are in contact with one another to conduct real estate transactions. Market participants often use the terms *real estate market, the market for real estate*, and *the market* interchangeably.

Selection Process

Land and improvements are immobile; they are in a fixed geographical *location* that cannot be changed. As such, the universal *geographic* market for real estate must be delineated into its component real estate markets. Commercial land and improvements are also *property specific*. As such, the universal market for commercial property must be delineated into its *component property types*. The following six real estate markets are distinguishable commercial property types:

1. Office market
2. Retail market
3. Multifamily apartment properties market
4. Lodging market
5. Industrial market
6. Vacant commercial land market

The universal market for real estate is separated into four broad market categories:

1. Location
2. Property types
3. Property class
4. Market participants

A **submarket** is a division of the universal real estate market that reflects the preferences of buyers and sellers.

Market location.   A real estate market can be subdivided into international, national, regional, or local markets. For example, an investor from the state of New York may be interested in an investment of a retail property within the southeastern United States. He believes that current and projected population growth and migration into the "Sunbelt" will provide for long-term growing demand for retail products and services. However, a location within the Sunbelt is much too vague. The investor would have to be more location specific. If the investor decided to focus on, say, the coastal area of Palm Beach County within the state of Florida, which is part of the Sunbelt, then he would have located a particular submarket. This subdivision of a real estate market into its component parts is known as a *submarket analysis*.

Property type within a market.   Additionally, a real estate market may be further subdivided from the broad classification of commercial property into a type of property, such as office, retail, or lodging. For example, the investor from New York has to select in what specific type of retail property he is interested. Based on his individual investment preferences, he considers properties occupied by a national drugstore tenant, strip centers occupied by local area merchants, and regional grocery-anchored shopping centers. Upon review, he further refines his preferences and decides on regional grocery-anchored shopping centers. This subdivision of the retail real estate into its component property types classification is known as a *submarket analysis*.

Property class within the market.   Commercial property varies significantly in class, quality, location, and income within any given market. Based on his individual investment preferences and financial constraints, if any, the investor must decide if he will pursue institutional-quality or noninstitutional-quality real estate assets. *Institutional real estate* is usually the best in class, quality, location, and income within any given market. An example of an *institutional investor* is a national pension fund, insurance company, or private real estate entity, as well as the advisors who provide acquisition services to those investors. They invest and manage the most "pristine" of real estate, which is usually the most marketable and demanded within any given market.

Because institutional real estate is considered best in class, quality, location, and income, it is also considered to possess less risk than noninstitutional real estate. *Noninstitutional real estate* is all real estate assets other than institutional real estate assets. Accordingly, there is more risk associated with noninstitutional real estate. This subdivision of the retail real estate into its component property quality classification is another type of *submarket analysis*.

Market participants.   Market participants include the buyers, investors, sellers, users, and service providers within the commercial real estate business for the property type. The commercial real estate business consists of the varied professions that have developed a specialization within the commercial real estate industry and within a commercial property type as well. This subdivision of the universe of real estate market participants into their professions and specialty classification is also known as a *submarket analysis*.

The Market for Real Estate Is Inefficient

It has been estimated that approximately two-thirds of the total tangible wealth in the United States is held in the form of real property. Because the vast majority of wealth is held in real estate assets, it would seem reasonable to assume that real estate markets are efficient. Actually, just the opposite is the case.

The characteristics of the goods and services traded within a market, along with the motivation and actions of the buyers and sellers, determine the relative efficiency of a market. The global market for real estate is comprised of characteristics that render it inefficient. Accordingly, the individual property markets that comprise the global real estate market are also inefficient. The inherent characteristics of real estate preclude its differing markets from operating efficiently. Following are the eight primary reasons why the real estate market is considered inefficient:

1. In an efficient market, the goods and services that are bought and sold can be readily exchanged into their cash equivalent amount rapidly and without a loss in value. However, within a real estate market, the conversion of an investment to its cash equivalent value requires time.

To avoid a loss in value, real estate must be marketed for a reasonable amount of time. This characteristic of real estate makes its investment long term in nature, and nonliquid or illiquid, and is considered a disadvantage of real estate.

2. In an efficient market, there are centralized exchanges that allow for orderly entry to and exit from the market. For example, in the stocks and bonds market, the New York Stock Exchange provides an efficient centralization of markets and its participants. Within the real estate industry, there is no centralized exchange, mechanism, or market. Some properties may be marketed through Internet-based Web sites while others may be marketed through Internet-based broadcasted e-mail. Still others are marketed to a select group of highly qualified market participants on a personal basis. Entering one area of a real estate market does not guarantee access to all available property, and entering the appropriate market area takes time.

3. In an efficient market, such as the New York Stock Exchange, information is transmitted immediately and is readily available to all market participants simultaneously. Within the real estate market, information is not always readily available. When information does become available, it is not immediately transmitted throughout the market because there is no centralized market mechanism to disseminate the information. Market participants usually operate with differing amounts of information, and that information may not be current or correct. These "information gaps" sometimes result in underpricing real estate on the selling side, overpaying on the buying side, or missing opportunities completely by misinterpreting the market.

4. In an efficient market, the demand for goods and services are moving toward a balance with the supply of those same goods and services. Efficient markets are always moving toward the direction of balance. Within real estate markets, changes in demand occur more rapidly than changes in supply. A single event, such as a favorable change in real estate tax laws or a favorable decline in interest rates, can result in an almost instantaneous increase in demand. Yet it can take years to complete and deliver additional supply of real estate to the market to meet that demand. As a result, real estate markets are usually moving toward or away from balance but are seldom in balance. These supply and demand trends interact and impact the direction and velocity of prices. Conditions leading to an oversupply of real estate can decrease its relative demand and lead to a decrease in price. Conversely, conditions leading to excess demand for real estate can cause rapid upward pressure on pricing.

5. In an efficient market, there is usually no need for regulation because the market is self-regulating through efficient market operations. Within the real estate markets, there is significant regulatory impact from all levels of government. Federal, state, county, and local government bodies and agencies exert tremendous regulation on the real estate market. Within the context of real estate, free market economics are always "subject to" regulatory review.

6. In an efficient market, prices are generally uniform at similar quality levels and are a primary consideration in a purchase decision. Within real estate markets, prices may vary significantly for similar properties and price is not always the primary consideration in a purchase decision. Real estate is expensive and usually requires financing. Because real

estate is usually not acquired for all cash, changes within the financial markets can have a significant and immediate impact on the cost of borrowed funds, loan-to-value ratios, debt-coverage ratios, financial feasibility, and, ultimately, prices paid. This characteristic of real estate makes it capital intensive and is considered a disadvantage of real estate.

7. In an efficient market, centralized marketplaces and efficient market mechanisms encourage a large number of market participants to be interacting, and competitive market forces preclude any one individual or group from exerting a significant influence on the price of goods and services. Within real estate markets, not all of the potential buyers and sellers are interacting at any given time. There may be few or none operating within any particular real estate market at a given time. These seemingly unrelated shifts in the supply and demand for real estate interact and cause shifts in pricing.

8. In an efficient market, prices of goods and services are generally uniform at similar price levels and are easily substituted for one another. Within real estate markets, no two properties are identical due to geographical differences. Acquiring a property that has reasonably similar physical characteristics does not guarantee it has reasonably similar investment characteristics or a reasonably similar acquisition price.

The inefficient nature of real estate markets is summarized in Table 5.1.

Example of Market Analysis

Let's say an investor is interested in purchasing a retail property. The investor has selected a submarket: the coastal area of Palm Beach County within the state of Florida. Within this area, the investor has selected his preferred property type: regional grocery-anchored shopping centers. He also prefers

Table 5.1

Efficient Market versus
Inefficient Real Estate Market

Efficient Market	Real Estate Market
Readily exchanged into cash equivalent	Conversion to cash equivalent takes time
Centralized and orderly markets	Decentralized and disorganized markets
Information readily available	Information disseminated slowly
Market usually moving toward balance	Market usually moving toward imbalance
Efficient, generally self-regulating market	Inefficient market requiring significant regulation
Uniform prices for similar quality	Variation in prices for similar quality
Significant control and influence not possible	Significant control and influence possible
Uniform goods, easily substituted	Unique goods, not easily substituted

institutional-quality real estate. The investor finds such a property. This shopping center contains a total of 107,500 square feet of gross leasable area.

The investor commences with an aspect of market analysis. The purpose of this particular market analysis is to determine the primary and secondary trade areas of the property and then to determine the total comparable square footage of retail space within those trade areas. The investor plots the geographic market location of the shopping center within its market area. The shopping center is located within a defined retail market that contains 1,127,500 square feet of *comparable* existing retail space, including the investor's property. A retail market analysis would study the entire 1,127,500 square feet of retail space within this market, which includes the 107,500-square-foot grocery-anchored shopping center. The investor's retail submarket analysis is presented in Figure 5.1.

The investor's targeted shopping center has the tenant, square footage, and income characteristics noted in Table 5.2.

From this partial market analysis, the investor determines the following facts:

1. The grocery center has a primary trade area of three miles and a secondary trade area of ten miles.

2. There exists a total of 161,250 square feet of retail space within the primary trade area, of which the investor's grocery center accounts for

Figure 5.1

Current Supply Analysis
of Retail Submarket

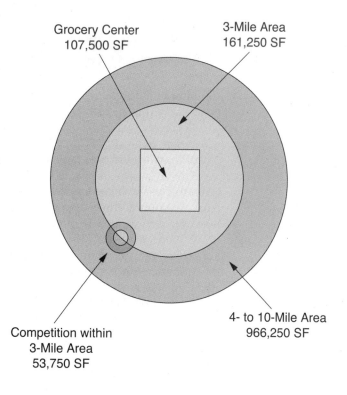

Total 10-Mile Submarket Contains 1,127,500 SF

Grocery Center
107,500 SF

3-Mile Area
161,250 SF

Competition within
3-Mile Area
53,750 SF

4- to 10-Mile Area
966,250 SF

Table 5.2

Grocery-anchored
Shopping Center Tenant Mix

Investor's Targeted Neighborhood Shopping Center				
Tenant Type	**Leased Sq. Ft.**	**% Leased Sq. Ft.**	**NNN Rent Per Sq. Ft.**	**Annual NNN Rent**
Regional Grocery Chain	45,000	42%	$10.00	$ 450,000
National Drugstore Chain	12,500	12	17.50	218,750
Local Shop Tenants	50,000	47	25.00	1,250,000
Total/Average	107,500	100%	$17.85	$1,918,750

107,500 square feet, or 67 percent, of the comparable retail space. This means the grocery center is the dominant property within its market, which is good from an investment perspective.

3. The only competitive property within the primary trade area is a smaller, older 53,750-square-foot strip retail property that has a mini-food mart, not a grocery store. Because this property is located at the fringe of the primary trade area, it is considered only indirectly competitive. This means that the vast majority of the primary trade area should visit the grocery center, which is good from an investment perspective.

4. The primary market area contains 14 percent of the total submarket space of 1,127,500 square feet. This means that the grocery center has little competition within its most important primary market, which is good from an investment perspective.

5. The investor's property represents the newest and largest retail property in the primary trade area.

6. Most of the comparable retail space is located outside of the three-mile area. Within a four- to ten-mile radius, the secondary trade area contains 86 percent of the total submarket space of 1,127,500 square feet. This means that most of the competition is located further away from the primary trade market, which is good from an investment perspective.

From this preliminary market analysis, the investor concludes that the retail market supports the long-term viability of the grocery center as an investment. He decides this property merits further consideration.

When investors buy real estate, they buy a part of the real estate market.

For any given real estate market, a market analysis is concerned about all of the property—not a specific property—within a real estate market. For a specific property type, if real estate market conditions are concluded to be moving in the direction of equilibrium and improvement, all of the property type within that market should also move toward equilibrium and improvement. A property or the property management, not the market, would therefore cause variations in a particular property's performance. Accordingly, when investors buy real estate, they buy a part of the real estate market.

Who Uses Market Analysis?

Market analysis is a fundamental tool utilized by market participants, which include real estate owners, investors, and developers. Because it is universal in its application, the real estate appraisal, investment, advisory, counseling, management, and brokerage professions also use it extensively. Market analysis is one of many interrelated types of analysis that are utilized by market participants.

Market analysis involves the research, analysis, and projection of the determining factors of demand and supply as they relate to a select property type within a select market. Although market analysis is demand based it would be meaningless without an analysis of supply. It is the study of a defined market area, and focuses on how the interaction of the supply of a given property type and the demand for that same property type impact its value. Market analysis is a powerful investment tool because it determines if the contemplated investment decision is justified by market evidence and what alternatives might otherwise be considered.

Relevance to Commercial Real Estate Investment

Owners, investors, and developers in commercial real estate establish investment objectives and goals, which then become the reason for their investment activities. Once these investment objectives have been determined, decisions such as to buy, hold, sell, develop, reposition, lease, sublease, or leaseback commercial real estate are based on market analysis. This market analysis may be as informal as the investor acting on "gut intuition" where no formal report containing the analyses is ever prepared. In the alternative, the investor may obtain a formalized market analysis with a report prepared by experts in this area of real estate investment. In this case, the investor is relying on a third-party consultant to interpret and determine market characteristics. In either circumstance, the investor is basing his decision on an implied and understood set of facts, assumptions, and conclusions concerning the general market conditions of supply and demand.

Along with most other areas of real estate, market analysis has evolved with highly specialized and sophisticated tools and techniques. Figure 5.2 illustrates the process or steps in market analysis.

■ Approach to Market Analysis

Generally speaking, the eight *separate* potential findings of a market analysis are the following:

1. Economic information
2. Characteristics of demand
3. Characteristics of supply
4. Effects of the interaction of supply and demand
5. Property market share
6. Management strategies
7. Alternative uses and exit strategies
8. Forecast of the performance of the investment property

Figure 5.2

Market Analysis Flow Chart

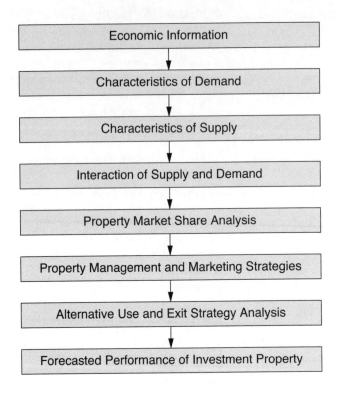

Market analysis plays a central role in all eight potential findings noted above. However, those eight steps do not all have to be performed for a market analysis. *The decision of where the analysis begins and ends is determined by the purpose and use of the market analysis.* For example, an investor may say, "The purpose of this market analysis is simply to determine the competitive supply of retail space within a primary and secondary trade area." In this case, only activities related to item 3 would have to be undertaken.

Economic Information

An economic overview should correspond to the market area in which the property type will be found and will compete. Because all property is geographically specific, an economic overview usually begins with the location and area of the property type under consideration. Because local, district, regional, national, and international economies are both interlinked and interdependent, market analysis seeks to uncover the existing and potential cause and effect economic relationships that ultimately will impact supply, demand, and price for the property. Figure 5.3 presents the interrelationship of economies as they relate to the property type under consideration.

The United States is part of the global economy, and international events may impact the national economy. Accordingly, an overview of global events that may impact the national/local economy should also be addressed. Even if an investor monitors world events, he is always exposed to hidden risk and uncertainty. The following recent international and national events shed

Figure 5.3

Interrelationship of
Economies and
Property Type

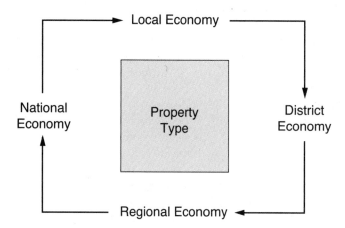

light on just how vulnerable national, regional, and local economies are to
seemingly unrelated events:

- In mid-November 2001 the National Bureau of Economic Research confirmed that the economy had sunk into a recession that had commenced
in March 2001. The bureau also reported that the September 11, 2001,
terrorist attacks accelerated and deepened the contraction.

- The bureau stated that it is possible that the decline would have been
too mild to qualify as a recession prior to the attacks, but the attacks
combined with the slowdown were important factors in turning the
economy into a recession.

- The combination of a recession and the traumatizing effects of the terrorist attacks lead to a rapid decline in national travel for business and lei-
sure. National airline passenger revenue plunged forcing many airlines
to lay off employees, restructure their business, or declare bankruptcy.

- The decline in travel resulted in a decline in national travelers need
for lodging at hotels. Nationally, hotel guest revenue plunged forcing
many hotels to lay off employees, restructure their business, or declare
bankruptcy.

- The occupancy and income for hotel properties declined nationally,
causing the risk associated with hotel acquisition to increase. The
national real estate market for hotels became inactive and it became a
buyer's market. Many prospective buyers exited the market while other
prospective buyers demanded significantly discounted prices.

- Questions about loan underwriting and high property values put the
commercial hotel lending market in a holding pattern and sent lenders
running to the sidelines to "wait and see." The lending risk associated
with new hotel development increased causing lenders to step out of
that sector of the market. Loanable funds for existing hotels became
scarce and for proposed properties it became virtually nonexistent.

- Because occupancy and income declined for hotels, hotel management scrambled to stabilize income by chopping expenses. Variable
expenses included portions of the staff, which were subsequently laid
off. In resort and destination areas, such as Miami Beach, Florida, this
unemployed and unemployable staff then vacated their apartments

causing vacancies in the multifamily rental apartment market to rapidly increase.

■ This decline in the local rental market population caused a decrease in the amount of money spent on retail services. The retail industry began to suffer flat or declining earnings.

And so on . . .

In each circumstance, it was the *change in demand* that caused all the other changes.

Characteristics of Demand

When consumers are hungry and have a need to eat, they have options as to how to satisfy their desire to eat. They may go to a grocery store located in a popular neighborhood shopping center. Perhaps they desire to go to a gourmet restaurant located on the top floor of a downtown office tower offering spectacular views of the city. Or perhaps they are in a rush and they prefer to go to a freestanding fast-food restaurant's drive-thru window. In these circumstances they are exercising their options as consumers, and are fulfilling their need to satisfy a desire. Collectively, they are expressing their demand for food and beverages by the dollars spent on these retail sales.

If an investor is interested in purchasing a grocery-anchored neighborhood shopping center, he will want to know what the demand for groceries is in the property's market area. He knows that the greater the demand for groceries within the property's market area, the greater the shopping center's capture rate of grocery demand. Also, the greater the demand for groceries at the shopping center, the more desirable the property becomes to the grocer tenant because it will have higher retail sales and become more profitable. The grocer tenant will have an increased desire and demand to be located at the property and, accordingly, the owner-landlord can charge more rent.

The investor is acquiring information about demand for grocery services that originates from the potential consumers located within the property's trade area. He needs to know this because the tenants at the property are paying rent based on their expected success as retailers at this location. If he desires to purchase the property, he wants to know the advantages and disadvantages of investing in this property. If the neighborhood shopping center contains the mix of tenants, square footages, and triple net rent (i.e., NNN rent), shown in Table 5.3, the investor wants to know the probability that these tenants will continue to occupy space and pay rents.

Each tenant offers retail goods or services. It is the demand for these goods and services that will determine their business success. **Demand** is the desire for goods and services.

| Consumer demand is the desire for goods and services. |

However, it is not only the desire but also the ability to purchase goods and services that determine a retailer's success. **Effective demand**, also referred to as *effective purchasing power*, is the ability to purchase goods and services. Effective demand is the desire to buy combined with the ability to pay.

| Consumer effective demand is the desire for goods and services combined with the ability to pay for them. |

Table 5.3

Neighborhood Shopping
Center Tenant Mix

Investor's Targeted Neighborhood Shopping Center				
Tenant Type	**Leased Sq. Ft.**	**% Leased Sq. Ft.**	**NNN Rent Per Sq. Ft.**	**Annual NNN Rent**
Regional Grocery Chain	45,000	42%	$10.00	$ 450,000
National Drugstore Chain	12,500	12	17.50	218,750
Local Shop Tenants	50,000	47	25.00	1,250,000
Total/Average	107,500	100%	$17.85	$1,918,750

Within the context of real estate, demand is the amount of a type of real estate desired for purchase or rent at various prices in a given market for a given period of time.

An analysis of demand focuses on the users of the property type under consideration. These include the tenants who may occupy the property, such as retail or office property tenants; the customers who may visit the property and the property's tenants, such as retail shoppers or office tenant clients; and the investors who may acquire the property itself. In each case, the analysis links these users of the property to the respective goods and services they are demanding.

So what does demand look like? Stated differently, what are the characteristics of demand? How does a market analysis extract these characteristics from the marketplace?

■ For *retail properties*, characteristics of demand include the per-capita and household incomes combined with the population base within a trade area. The age distribution of households would provide insight into what goods and services are demanded. The rate of increase or decrease in the population and households would provide insight into the rate of growth in demand for goods and services. The location, ability to access the property, and the time-distance relationship of the property from the customer affect demand. The more positive these characteristics are, the better the performance of the property.

■ For *office properties*, characteristics of demand include the state of the economy, including the rate of increase or decrease in employers and employees within a given office market. The office building class—A, B, or C. The location, ability to access the property, and the time-distance relationship of the property from the employers and employees affect demand. The more positive these characteristics are, the better the performance of the property.

■ For *residential properties*, characteristics of demand include residential population migration into the area and the per-capita and household incomes. The affordability of the residential property affects demand.

Table 5.4

Characteristics of Demand

Retail Properties	Office Properties	Residential Properties
Characteristics of trade area: size and number of households, rate of increase or decrease in household formation, composition and age distribution of households, percentages of owners and renters, per-capita and household incomes	Characteristics of trade area: size and number of employers, rate of increase or decrease in employers and employees	Characteristics of trade area: size and number of households, rate of increase or decrease in household formation, composition and age distribution of households, percentages of owners and renters, per-capita and household incomes
Employment and economic base: types, distribution, and unemployment rates	Employment and economic base: types, distribution, and unemployment rates	Employment and economic base: types, distribution, and unemployment rates
Rental rate trends and concessions	Rental rate trends and concessions	Rental rate trends and concessions
Percentage of household income spent on retail purchases, in total and by retail category		Affordability
Average square footage of retail space required by retailer: factors employees, location of property, and category of retailer	Average square footage of office space required by business: factors office workers, location of property, and category of business and work	
Rate of sales retention in area, rate of leakage factor in area		
Rate of sales captured from outside trade area		
Sales volume per square foot: current existing versus proforma required for retailers		
Retail vacancy rate in market, in total and by property class	Office vacancy rate in market, in total and by property class	Residential housing turnover rate in market; multifamily residential vacancy rate in market, in total and by property class

The location, ability to access the residential area, and the time-distance relationship of the residential area from retail, employment, and related services affect demand. The more positive these characteristics are, the better the performance of the property.

These are only a few of the characteristics of demand. Table 5.4 summarizes additional characteristics of demand for these three primary property types.

Characteristics of Supply

In the discussion above regarding demand, reference was made to consumers who had a desire to eat, and the options available to them to satisfy their desire to eat. Options available included grocery stores, gourmet restaurants, and fast-food restaurants. There are, of course, other choices. The number and diversity of these choices address the concept of supply.

Supply. If an investor is interested in purchasing a grocery-anchored neighborhood shopping center, he will want to know what the number of such properties are in his market area, because he will then be able to evaluate these alternative properties in relation to his contemplated purchase. He will want to know about the supply of that property type. As it pertains to real estate, **supply** refers to the amount of a type of real estate available for sale or lease at various prices in a given market at a given time. Accordingly, supply is type, location, and time sensitive. As mentioned, LoopNet operates the largest Internet-based commercial real estate listing service. Offering properties for sale and lease on a national-market level, it is an excellent source of national real estate supply. However, LoopNet also allows for a local submarket analysis for most property types within the United States. It lists the amount of a type of real estate available for sale or lease at various prices in a given market at a given time. It lists supply.

Competitive supply. The investor would also want to analyze the competitive supply of grocery-anchored shopping centers. A **competitive supply** analysis is a market analysis that identifies the supply of properties competitive with a subject property within a defined area. As it applies to a retail property, once a trade area is determined, a competitive supply analysis is utilized to determine the amount of competitive space within that trade area. The analysis may also rank the competitive properties against a subject based on factors such as size, rental rates, operating expenses, net operating income, occupancy rates, location attributes, and amenities.

Estimating the supply of real estate also considers a time period. The current estimated competitive supply of real estate includes all existing property within a defined area. The future estimated supply of the property should be adjusted, usually increased, for the rumored, announced, planned, approved, permitted, financed, under construction, newly completed, converted, and retrofitted real estate. Another consideration is that not all future projects will be completed because some will not be *financially feasible* due to factors such as cost, oversupply, and lack of demand. Of those completed, not all will be *marketable* due to factors such as poor location, inappropriate tenant mix, and lack of demand.

An analysis of the competitive supply of a property type provides a quantifiable measure of the degree of competition that a property faces. The existing supply represents the current competition with which the subject property must contend.

However, the future competitive environment must also be considered because it provides an indication of the future competition with which the subject property must contend. Real estate purchases are capital intensive, long term in nature, illiquid, and directly influenced by economic-, market-, and property-related risks. Understanding changes to the future

> The supply of real estate is type, location, and time sensitive.

> Not all proposed future supply will be completed because some projects will not be financially feasible and some will not be marketable.

> Existing supply represents a property's current competition.

> Future supply represents a property's future competition.

Table 5.5

Forecast of Competitive
Shopping Center Supply

Year of Delivery to the Marketplace			2003	2004	2005	2006	2007
Type of Supply	Total Sq. Ft.	% Sq. Ft.	Allocated By Year of Delivery to the Marketplace				
Existing Supply							
Subject Property	107,500	7.06%	107,500				
Other Existing	1,020,000	66.95%	1,020,000				
Total Existing Supply	1,127,500	74.01%	1,127,500				
Future Supply							
Rumored, Announced, Planned	102,000	6.70%				–	102,000
Permitted	99,000	6.50%			99,000		
Financed; Under-Construction	120,000	7.88%		120,000			
Newly Completed		0.00%					
Converted and Retrofitted	75,000	4.92%	75,000				
Total Future Supply	396,000	25.99%	75,000	120,000	99,000	–	102,000
Total Existing and Future Supply	1,523,500	100.00%	1,202,500	1,322,500	1,421,500	1,421,500	1,523,500
Growth in Supply							
Supply Beginning of Year			1,127,500	1,202,500	1,322,500	1,421,500	1,421,500
Additions During Year			75,000	120,000	99,000	–	102,000
Supply End of Year			1,202,500	1,322,500	1.421.500	1,421,500	1,523,500
% Increase from Prior Year			6.65%	9.98%	7.49%	0.00%	7.18%
Average Annual % Change			4.21%	4.21%	4.21%	4.21%	4.21%

competitive supply is key to evaluating the advantages and disadvantages
of real estate. Table 5.5 provides an analysis of the competitive supply for the
neighborhood shopping center introduced earlier in Table 5.2. That property,
referred to as the subject property, is included as part of the existing supply of neighborhood shopping centers within the defined trade area. The
prospective future supply is also examined. This supply analysis provides
useful information for the investor's decision-making process.

Following is an explanation of the information that is presented in Table 5.5.

Year of delivery to the marketplace ("pipeline"). Delivery to the marketplace is a term
used to describe the completion and availability of new supply. The investor
is considering a purchase of the subject property in 2003. The calendar years
under review are from January 2003 through December 2007, equating to
five years. Forecasting tends to become less accurate as the forecast period
increases. The future supply allocation by year of expected completion to the
marketplace is sometimes referred to as the supply "pipeline."

Type of supply. There are two types of supply: existing and future. The total
of the existing and future supply is then allocated by year of delivery to the
marketplace. Supply is evaluated in terms of total square feet and percent of
square feet. This supply includes all neighborhood shopping centers within
the primary trade area, considered to be within a three-mile radius of the
subject property; the secondary trade area is considered to be within a ten-
mile radius of the subject property.

Existing supply. The existing supply of competitive neighborhood shopping centers is estimated as of January 2003 and includes the subject property because it is part of the market. The other existing supply includes all neighborhood shopping centers within the primary trade area and the secondary trade area of the subject property. As of January 2003, the existing supply equated to 1,127,500 square feet. However, the existing supply represented only ±74.01 percent of the total existing supply plus future supply of competitive space. The subject property represented ±7.06 percent of the total forecasted five-year supply.

Future supply. The future supply of competitive neighborhood shopping centers includes five categories of property: (1) rumored, announced, and planned; (2) permitted; (3) financed and under construction; (4) newly completed; and (5) converted and retrofitted. A future supply equated to 396,000 square feet. The future supply represents an additional ±25.99 percent of the total existing supply plus future supply of competitive space. The subject property represented ±7.06 percent of the total forecasted five-year supply. It is the future supply that is allocated by year of delivery to the marketplace. In 2003, supply is expected to increase by 75,000 square feet. In 2004, supply is expected to increase by an additional 120,000 square feet, and so on. This allocation by year of delivery to the marketplace represents the "pipeline" of future supply, as shown in Figure 5.4.

Total future supply. As of January 2003, the total future supply equates to 396,000 square feet. The future supply represents a ±25.99 percent increase in the supply of competitive space.

Growth in supply. The growth in supply quantifies the current annual supply and increases to the annual supply expected during the market analysis period. This information allows for the projection of percent increases from the prior year. It also allows for the projection of average in annual percent growth rate. Although increases in supply fluctuate from year to year, the average annual increase in supply is determined to be 4.21 percent per annum.

Figure 5.4

Pipeline of Future Supply

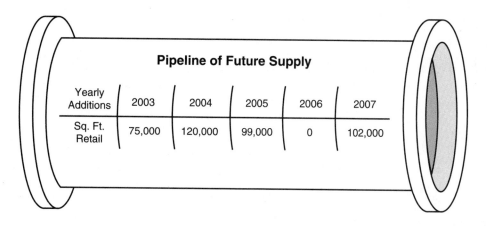

Pipeline of Future Supply

Yearly Additions	2003	2004	2005	2006	2007
Sq. Ft. Retail	75,000	120,000	99,000	0	102,000

Figure 5.5

Current and Future
Supply Analysis of
Retail Supermarket

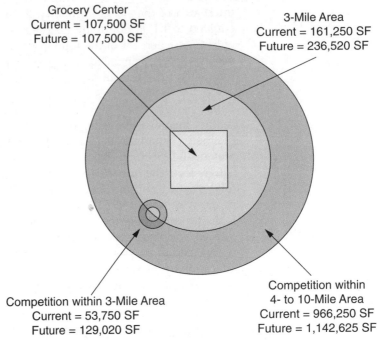

Total 10-Mile Submarket
Current = 1,127,500 SF
Future = 1,523,500 SF

Grocery Center
Current = 107,500 SF
Future = 107,500 SF

3-Mile Area
Current = 161,250 SF
Future = 236,520 SF

Competition within 3-Mile Area
Current = 53,750 SF
Future = 129,020 SF

Competition within
4- to 10-Mile Area
Current = 966,250 SF
Future = 1,142,625 SF

Figure 5.5 provides a summary of information relating to supply. It is an update of Figure 5.1 because it considers not only current supply but also future additions to supply. If the investor were going to acquire the subject grocery center he would have to consider the impact that a growing supply of competitive space would have on the financial feasibility and marketability of his purchase.

To illustrate the characteristics of supply, Table 5.6 summarizes core determinants of supply for the three primary property types. The table focuses on the similarities of market analysis across property types, as well as the differences. As the table reveals, characteristics of supply tend to be similar across property types.

■ The Interaction of Supply and Demand

The supply of real estate moves in its own unique cycle. As discussed, there are unique characteristics and factors of supply. During a given period of time, the supply of property within the real estate market will vary. This variation in supply will inevitably lead to conditions of undersupply, stable supply, expansion of supply, oversupply, and declining supply. On its own, supply is never in balance because it does not have anything with which to be in balance. So supply is always measured in terms of its relationship, or interaction, with demand.

Table 5.6

Characteristics of Supply

Retail Properties	Office Properties	Residential Properties
Existing supply of property type	Existing supply of property type	Existing supply of property type
Future additions to supply of property type	Future additions to supply of property type	Future additions to supply of property type
Future reductions to supply of property type	Future reductions to supply of property type	Future reductions to supply of property type
Future gross and net additions to supply of property type by year and by percent	Future gross and net additions to supply of property type by year and by percent	Future gross and net additions to supply of property type by year and by percent
Existing and future occupancy and vacancy rates and causes for fluctuations	Existing and future occupancy and vacancy rates and causes for fluctuations	Existing and future occupancy and vacancy rates and causes for fluctuations
Singletenant properties versus multiple-tenant properties	Single-tenant properties versus multiple-tenant properties	Single-tenant properties versus multiple-tenant properties
Owner-occupied properties versus tenant-occupied properties	Owner-occupied properties versus tenant-occupied properties	Owner-occupied properties versus tenant-occupied properties
Barriers to market entry: availability of land, concurrency and development issues, and market saturation	Barriers to market entry: availability of land, concurrency and development issues, and market saturation	Barriers to market entry: availability of land, concurrency and development issues, and market saturation
Threshold and feasibility issues: cost of land, labor, materials, and developer's incentive	Threshold and feasibility issues: cost of land, labor, materials, and developer's incentive	Threshold and feasibility issues: cost of land, labor, materials, and developer's incentive
Financing terms and availability	Financing terms and availability	Financing terms and availability
Existing and future demand generators that would warrant an increase in supply	Existing and future demand generators that would warrant an increase in supply	Existing and future demand generators that would warrant an increase in supply
Price, investment criteria, and sales velocity of competitive properties for sale	Price, investment criteria, and sales velocity of competitive properties for sale	Price, investment criteria, and sales velocity of competitive properties for sale

The supply of and demand for real estate moves in cycles.

Similarly, the demand for real estate moves in its own unique cycle. As discussed, there are unique characteristics and factors of demand. During a given period of time, the demand of property within the real estate market will vary. This variation in demand will inevitably lead to conditions of stable demand, increasing demand, excess demand, and declining demand. On its own, demand for real estate is never in or out of balance because it does not have anything with which to be in balance. So demand is always measured in terms of its relationship, or interaction, with supply.

The interaction of real estate supply and demand creates real estate pricing.

Changing market forces such as the employment and economic base, land-use patterns, and affordability impact demand for real estate. At the same time, changing market forces such as availability of land, demand generators that would warrant supply, and alternative choices impact supply of real estate. Market forces are at constant work, separately impacting supply and demand. However, real estate supply and real estate demand, also interact within the real estate marketplace. When these two complementary counterparts interact, they create pricing for real estate.

The price of real estate is the result of the interchange of supply and demand with one another. Within the context of real estate, the principle of supply and demand states that the price of real property varies directly, but not necessarily proportionately, with demand, and inversely, but not necessarily proportionally, with supply.

If Demand Increases Outpacing Supply, Prices Will Eventually Increase

Let's say, for example, that an investor has an effective demand to purchase neighborhood shopping centers located in the Palm Beach County retail market within the state of Florida in the United States. Other investors enter the market and create a competitive environment by demanding to purchase this property type within the same market. The competing investors' effective demand will cause upward pressure on the price for that property type. The more these competing investors demand this property type, the more the upward influence on pricing will occur. In this circumstance, prices are rising because *demand is increasing, relative to supply*. This cause-and-effect relationship occurs because the price of real property varies directly, but not necessarily proportionately, with demand.

The price of real property varies directly with demand.

If Supply Increases Outpacing Demand, Prices Will Eventually Decrease

Now let's say that as prices continue to increase, this catches the attention of owners of neighborhood shopping centers within the same market area. Many of these owners may decide to become sellers of their property and enter the market in anticipation of selling into a market of rising prices that will increase their overall profit on a sale. As more sellers enter the market, the supply of that property type increases and outpaces demand, which has the effect of placing downward pressure on the price for that property type. In this circumstance, prices are decreasing because *supply is increasing, relative to demand*. This cause-and-effect relationship occurs because the price of real property varies inversely, or opposite, but not necessarily proportionately, with supply.

The price of real property varies inversely with supply.

Supply and Demand Are Constantly Interacting

If the demand for neighborhood shopping centers continued to outpace the supply of this property, eventually sales prices would increase to the level where new construction would become *economically feasible*. Developers would enter the market and begin the usually lengthy development process in anticipation of participating in the market. Due to the length of time associated with development, market conditions may change. Demand might also shift in the opposite direction for reasons unrelated to supply. For example, rising interest rates will eventually slow demand for real estate because the cost of financing will become increasingly more expensive and render some purchases *economically infeasible*.

Buyer's and Seller's Markets

The supply of and demand for real estate moves in separate cycles. It is the interaction of these separate cycles that results in pricing of real estate. Because shifts in demand occur much faster than shifts in supply, the markets are seldom in balance or equilibrium. These market imbalances result in what is often referred to as either a buyer's market or a seller's market.

In a **buyer's market,** buyers benefit from excess supply relative to demand and purchase their properties at a discount. In a buyer's market, prices are falling because demand is falling relative to supply.

In a **seller's market,** sellers of property benefit from excess demand relative to supply and sell their properties at a premium. In a seller's market, prices are rising because supply is becoming scarce relative to demand.

A characteristic of a buyer's or seller's market is that usually in the short term, supply is fixed, and changes in the direction and rate of change in pricing is usually completely due to shifts in demand. This characteristic underlies the economic principle upon which market analysis is based. Specifically, that market analysis is demand based.

■ Property Market Share Analysis

What It Is and How It Works

As it pertains to real estate, **market share** represents the portion of effective demand that is captured by a particular property. Market share represents *captured demand.* For example, let's say we were talking about a retail property. A retail property's captured market share would represent the portion of consumers' expenditures spent on goods and services at that particular property. What draws these consumers to the property are its tenants, especially its anchor tenants. The greater the drawing power of the tenants, the greater the market share captured by the retail property. So market share represents the portion of a given market's potential expenditures that are captured by a property in that market. *The consumer expenditures represent effective demand, and consumer expenditures that occur at a particular property represent captured demand.*

The terms market share, capture rate, and penetration rate are used interchangeably.

Market analysis is demand based. The terms *market share, capture rate,* and *penetration rate* are used interchangeably.

Determining Market Share for Existing Properties

There is no universally accepted method to estimate market share. Because of this, estimating market share is as much an art as a science. For existing properties, market share is equal to the portion of the total market potential captured by the total existing competitive supply, including a subject property.

Generally, in order to determine market share for existing retail properties, the following six steps are taken:

1. Determine where the market area is, including primary and secondary market areas. This is a geographic location and area.

2. Determine the market area's actual level of consumer expenditures for goods and services.

3. Determine the market area's potential level of consumer expenditures for goods and services.

4. Compare the results of step 2 with step 3. The actual level of consumer expenditures divided by the potential level of consumer expenditures is the capture rate, expressed as a percentage.

5. If the actual level of consumer expenditures is less than 100 percent of the potential level of sales,

    a. consumers are either traveling outside of the delineated market area or acquiring the services some other way, which is known as **market leakage;** and

    b. there may be an opportunity for a new development that would capture the untapped consumer potential.

6. If the actual level of consumer expenditures is greater than 100 percent of the potential level of sales,

    a. consumers are traveling into the delineated market area from outside areas; and

    b. there may be an opportunity for a new development that would capture the excess consumer potential.

In the case of capture rates being less than 100 percent, the cause may be either positive or negative. For example, if a new superhighway system replaces a local roadway and provides new entry and exit points that change traffic patterns, this may lead to a shifting away of household and business formation in a retail market area. Although the retail potential still exists and is measurable within the market area, it is shifting away from the core market area. In this circumstance, the existing retail supply is receiving a decreasing percentage of total demand, which may continue to decline for the foreseeable future. Due to this decreasing demand, new retail development would probably be *economically infeasible and not the highest and best use of the land*.

In the case of capture rates being more than 100 percent, the cause may also be positive or negative. A retail market's trade area may have a capture rate greater than 100 percent of the market due to the tremendous drawing power of a super-regional mall. The mall may pull in shoppers from outside the trade area, outside the region, and even outside the country. As the mall continues to increase its drawing power, the capture rate increases. The top super-regional malls in the United States have a capture rate of more than 100 percent of the designated market area. Other retailers usually scramble for sites located in close proximity to such sales-generating magnets, expecting to capture part of this demand. In this circumstance, there is a definite opportunity for potential new development.

Market Area Supply

If an investor is interested in purchasing a grocery-anchored neighborhood shopping center, he will want to know where that property's primary and secondary trade areas are. He will want to know about the *competitive supply* of similar properties within that trade area because those properties are competing for the same sales revenues as his property. He will conduct a competitive supply analysis to determine both the existing and future supply of competitive properties within that market area. For the investor to address the market area's supply of competitive properties, he must accomplish two goals. First, he must determine the total *existing* competitive supply. Second, he must determine the total *future* competitive supply.

Market Area Demand

The investor will also want to know about the *amount of demand for goods and services* within that trade area because a portion of this demand will be *captured* by the competitive supply of shopping centers within the trade area. He will conduct a demand analysis to determine both the existing and future demand for goods and services within the market area. For the investor to address the market area's demand for goods and services he must accomplish two goals. First, he must determine the total existing and forecasted demand of goods and services. Second, he must determine what part of the demand for goods and services his property will *capture.*

Leakage

If the capture rates within a market area are less than the total market potential within that same market area, leakage is said to exist. Leakage may result from the market population traveling outside the market area or from "importing" the good or service.

- *As leakage pertains to a retail market*, portions of the consumer population (i.e., households) could simply travel outside the market area to another market. Importing may take the form of buying goods and services on the Internet or through direct mail catalogs.

- *As leakage pertains to an office market*, portions of the consumer population (i.e., employees and employers) could travel outside the market area to another office market. Importing may take the form of telecommuting, whereby the employer and the employee do not necessarily even leave their homes to attend to work.

- *As leakage pertains to a residential market*, portions of the consumer population (i.e., residential purchasers) could relocate from one delineated market area to another.

An Example of Determining Market Share for Existing Properties— No Change in Supply

Let's continue with our example of an investor who is interested in the 107,500-square-foot shopping center introduced earlier. Figure 5.6 shows the three-mile trade area available.

Current status of the three-mile trade area.

1. The three-mile trade area has a capture level of consumer expenditures for shopping center goods and services of $36,281,250 in total. This three-mile area has a total of 161,250 square feet of retail shopping

Figure 5.6

Current Three-Mile
Captured and Potential
Demand in Expenditures

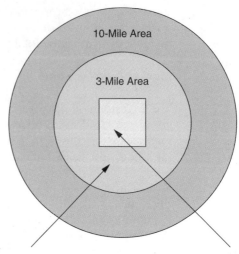

3-Mile Current Expenditures
Captured = $36,281,250 (60%)
Potential = $60,468,750 (100%)

Competition 3-Mile Area
Current = 161,250 SF

10-Mile Area

3-Mile Area

3-Mile Area Captured Sales
Pro-rata Basis
Captured = $225 Sales PSF (60%)
Potential = $375 Sales PSF (100%)

Grocery Center = 107,500 SF
Pro-rata Basis
Captured = $225 Sales PSF (60%)
Potential = $375 Sales PSF (100%)

center space, which equates to a pro-rata capture rate of $225 per square
foot of competitive space.

2. The three-mile trade area has a potential level of consumer expenditures for shopping center goods and services of $60,468,750 in total.
   This three-mile area has a total of 161,250 square feet of retail shopping
   center space, which equates to a pro-rata potential capture rate of $375
   per square foot of competitive space.

3. Comparing the results of 1 and 2, the actual level of consumer expenditures represents 60 percent of the potential level of expenditures so the
   capture rate is 60 percent and the leakage rate is 40 percent.

Future projections of the three-mile trade area. Figure 5.7 shows the projected
information for the three-mile trade area that is available.

1. Over a five-year period, the supply of competitive retail space is projected to increase from 161,250 square feet to of 236,520 square feet.

2. The three-mile trade area has a five-year future projected capture level
   of consumer expenditures for shopping center goods and services
   of $72,562,500 in total. With a projected increase of supply to 236,520
   square feet of retail shopping center space, a pro-rata capture rate of
   $307 per square foot of competitive space is expected.

3. The three-mile trade area has a five-year future projected potential
   level of consumer expenditures for shopping center goods and services
   of $96,750,000 in total. With a projected increase of supply to 236,520
   square feet of retail shopping center space, a pro-rata potential rate of
   $409 per square foot of competitive space is expected.

Figure 5.7

Future Projected Three-Mile Capture and Potential Demand in Expenditures

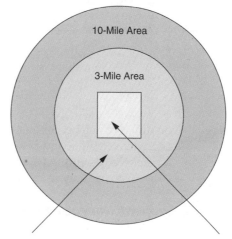

3-Mile Future Expenditures
Captured = $72,562,500 (75%)
Potential = $96,750,000 (100%)

Competition 3-Mile Area
Future = 236,520 SF

10-Mile Area

3-Mile Area

3-Mile Area Future Captured Sales
Pro-rata Basis
Captured = $307 Sales PSF (75%)
Potential = $409 Sales PSF (100%)

Grocery Center = 107,500 SF
Future Pro-rata Basis
Captured = $307 Sales PSF (75%)
Potential = $409 Sales PSF (100%)

4. Comparing the results of 1 and 2, the actual level of consumer expenditures represents 75 percent of the potential level of expenditures, so the capture rate is 75 percent and the leakage rate is 25 percent.

5. A total of $72,562,500 in expenditures is projected to be captured. If the existing supply of shopping center space remained unchanged at 161,250 square feet, the pro-rata capture rate of retail space would have been $450 per square foot. However, because supply is projected to expand to 236,520 square feet, the capture rate will decline to only $307 per square foot.

As is demonstrated by these examples, it is only when demand (expressed in consumer expenditures) interacts with supply (expressed in square feet of retail area) that we can conclude a capture (expressed in expenditures per square foot).

Types of Market Share Analysis

At first glance, estimating market share appears straightforward enough. We can quantify the historical existing rate of retail sales, office rent levels, residential sales prices, or rate of sales of the residential stock either within a given market area or for a specific property type. Projecting future rates becomes more difficult, as does proposed uses and unknown site locations. Table 5.7 summarizes the four types of market share analysis.

As we have seen, market share analysis can be utilized to determine supply and demand in a primary market. A similar analysis could be conducted within the secondary market. Market share analysis can be focused

Table 5.7

Four Types of Market Share Analysis

Existing Property	Proposed Use with Known Site	Proposed Use with Unknown Site	Proposed Site with Unknown Use

Simplest analysis → → *Analysis becomes more complicated and less accurate* →

on different market characteristics to determine how these characteristics will change over time, and how one impacts the other. *Market analysis* is a tool, a means to an end. As we move from what is known to what is unknown, market share analysis becomes more complicated and less accurate.

Property Management and Marketing Strategies

The primary reason investors acquire real estate is for it to produce income. The goal of competent property management should be to supervise every aspect of the property's operation to produce the greatest achievable financial return for the longest period of time. This fact underlies the primary reason for the investment in the first place. Investors purchase commercial real estate primarily for what it provides them—namely, the anticipated financial returns desired—and not necessarily the property's physical and locational attributes.

To ensure that a real estate investment is successful, every aspect of the real estate must be managed. Fundamental business and management skills are necessary for all investment property. The most effective property management and marketing strategies for real estate are comprehensive, well planned, and workable. Successful property management involves strategic thinking. The time, effort, and number of individuals required to carry out these tasks increases in relation to the size, scope, and number of tenants in an investment property.

As an affiliate of The National Association of REALTORS®, The Institute of Real Estate Management (IREM) offers the only comprehensive program exclusively developed for property and asset managers working with large portfolios of all property types. IREM confers the coveted Certified Property Manager (CPM) designation, which is considered to be the industry's premier real estate management credential. Based on IREM's criteria, real estate management consists of the following five functions:

1. *Property maintenance and operations, including legal and risk management.* A property maintenance program manages various types of risk. Efficient property maintenance operations will improve a property's performance. Risk management deals with protection of a property and its occupants. Property insurance, life safety programs, and emergency/disaster plans address risk management are designed to protect a property and its occupants.

2. *Human resources.* This addresses the optimal allocation of human capital to enhance the success of a real estate investment. The larger a prop-

erty, the more likely the challenges of hiring, managing, and evaluating on-site staff. Managers strive to operate a seamless human resources function.

3. *Marketing and leasing.* This function is property type specific. For retail property, developing the right tenant mix for a retail location is vital to its success. For multifamily rental apartments, positioning a property in its market to attract and retain new tenants is vital to its success. For office property, an understanding of the economy and the local marketplace combined with expert marketing and leasing skills are vital to its success. Other major aspects of marketing and leasing include market analysis, effective marketing practices, and successful lease negotiations.

4. *Financial management.* This addresses proper accounting as well as real estate finance and real estate valuation. Effective financial management includes risk assessment, valuation, leverage, and capitalization techniques to maximize profit in real estate investment property. Financial performance and measurement tools, such as discounted cash-flow analysis (DCFA), net present value (NPV), and internal rate of return (IRR), are considered core tools utilized in evaluating, comparing, and achieving the highest potential income for real estate assets.

5. *Asset management.* When the individual management tasks of property maintenance, human resources management, marketing and leasing, and financial management are managed by one entity, that entity is considered an asset manager. (See Figure 5.8.)

Property management and marketing strategies are an inherent part of investment real estate and are especially relevant within the context of market analysis. Market analysis addresses factors of demand and capture as they relate to a select property or property type. It follows that a strategy to maximize a property's demand and capture should evolve from the market analysis process.

Consider the information in Table 5.8 for grocery shopping center containing 107,500 square feet.

Figure 5.8

Core Components of
Asset Management

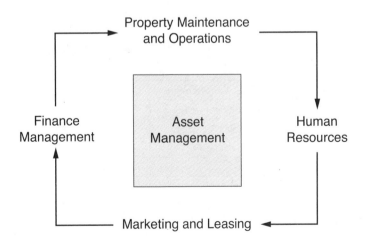

Table 5.8

Neighborhood Shopping
Center Tenant Mix

Investor's Targeted Neighborhood Shopping Center				
Tenant Type	**Leased Sq. Ft.**	**% Leased Sq. Ft.**	**NNN Rent Per Sq. Ft.**	**Annual NNN Rent**
Regional Grocery Chain	45,000	42%	$10.00	$ 450,000
National Drugstore Chain	12,500	12	$17.50	$ 218,750
Local Shop Tenants	50,000	47	$25.00	$1,250,000
Total/Average	107,500	100%	$17.85	$1,918,750

An investor is considering the purchase of this property. He notes that the local shop tenants pay an average of $25 per square foot on a triple net (net of expenses) basis. One of the investor's criteria is the ability to raise local shop tenant rents an average of $1 per square foot per year. Rent is considered an occupancy cost to the tenant and is paid from the tenant's only source of revenue: retail sales. Area surveys have shown that the rent paid per square foot is generally 10.50 percent of captured retail sales per square foot.

With this information and the results from a market analysis, the investor is able to prepare the information in Table 5.9.

Table 5.9

Neighborhood Shopping
Center Tenant Mix

Year	Current	Forecast	Forecast	Forecast	Forecast	Forecast
Period		1	2	3	4	5
Minimum Rent and Captured Sales Requirement						
Proforma Growth Local Shop Tenant Rent—NNN	$ 25	$ 26	$ 27	$ 28	$ 29	$ 30
Proforma NNN as % of Captured Sales Per Sq. Ft.	10.5%	10.5%	10.5%	10.5%	10.5%	10.5%
Proforma Captured Sales Required Per Sq. Ft.	$238	$248	$257	$267	$276	$286
Forecast Rent and Captured Sales						
Proforma Growth Local Shop Tenant Rent—NNN	$ 25	$ 26	$ 27	$ 28	$ 29	$ 30
Proforma NNN as % of Captured Sales Per Sq. Ft.	11.1%	10.9%	10.6%	10.3%	10.0%	9.8%
Proforma Captured Sales Required Per Sq. Ft.	$225	$239	$255	$271	$289	$397

The investor desires to increase rents by $1 per square foot per year. During the investor's five-year forecasted holding period, NNN rents would increase from $25 to $30 per square foot. Ideally, the investor would like rents to represent a maximum of 10.50 percent of captured retail sales per square foot. If that were the case, captured sales would have to increase from $238 to $286 per square foot during the investor's five-year forecasted holding period.

Based on a market analysis, forecasted captured sales are expected to increase from $225 to $307 per square foot during the investor's five-year forecasted holding period. This has a favorable effect on occupancy costs. Rents, which represent 11.10 percent of captured retail sales per square foot, are forecast to decline to 9.80 percent during the investor's five-year holding period. This indicates that forecasted captured retail sales will support the investor's desired increase in rent during the investor's five-year forecasted holding period.

Alternative Use and Exit Strategy Analysis

An analysis of alternative uses and probable exit strategies speaks to the issues of risk, uncertainty, and wealth maximization in investment real estate. Market analysis provides key information for this decision-making process because it determines if a contemplated investment decision is justified by market evidence, and what alternatives might otherwise be considered.

Many investors do not even consider alternative use or exit strategy concepts. Alternative use analysis relates to "what if" scenarios that allow the investor to determine what alternative uses are *economically feasible* and which alternative use produces the greatest economic benefits, referred to as the *highest and best use of the property*. Because alternative uses may involve renovation, retrofitting, or readaptive use, the economic costs and benefits must also be determined. Once the highest and best use and alternative economically feasible uses are known, probable exit strategies are formulated. The alternative use that provides the greatest economic benefit to the investor should be the use considered as the appropriate alternative exit strategy.

For example, consider the following alternative use and exit strategy analysis. A developer commences construction of a ten-unit rental apartment building. His goal is to sell the building shortly after completion, as soon as the property is fully occupied and leased. He expects that he can complete construction and lease all ten units in approximately one year.

The developer's total development costs are $400,000. Based on a market analysis of comparable rental properties, the developer is able to support his assumptions of rental rates, operating expenses, and income and capitalization rates. The developer then prepares a pro-forma profit and loss statement for the property, and anticipates effective gross income of $95,000, total operating expenses of $40,000, and a resultant net operating income of $55,000. He anticipates that the rental property can be sold on the basis of a 10 percent capitalization rate, resulting in a capitalized sales price of $550,000. Because his total development costs are $400,000, he expects to make a profit of $150,000. This information is summarized in Table 5.10.

Table 5.10

Development and
Sale as a Rental

Scenario	Sell as a Rental
Efective Gross Income	$95,000
less:	
Operating Expenses	$40,000
equals:	
Net Operating Income	$55,000
divided by:	
Cap Rate @	10%
equals:	
Sales Proceeds	$550,000
less:	
Total development Costs	$400,000
equals:	
Profit to Developer	$150,000

Shortly after construction commences, the developer learns that there is a growing market demand for condominiums within the affordable housing price range. After consulting with his general contractor and legal counsel, the developer budgets an additional $75,000 for conversion from a rental property to a condominium property. Based on a market analysis of comparable condominium properties, the developer is able to support his assumptions of unit sales prices, sales and marketing costs, and conversion costs from a rental property to a condominium property. The developer then prepares a pro-forma sellout analysis for the condominium property, and anticipates gross sales proceeds of $900,000, or $90,000, per unit, total sales and marketing costs of $100,000, and resultant sales proceeds of $800,000. Because his total development and conversion costs are $475,000, he expects to make a profit of $325,000. This information is summarized in Table 5.11.

Table 5.11

Development and
Sale as a Condo

Scenario	Sell as a Condo
Gross Sales Proceeds	$900,000
less:	
Sales and Marketing Costs	$100,000
equals:	
Net Sales Proceeds	$800,000
less:	
Total Development Costs	$475,000
equals:	
Profit to Developer	$325,000

Table 5.12

Alternative Use Analysis
Development and Sale—
Rental versus Condo

Scenario	A	B
Alternative Use	Sell as a Rental	Sell as a Condominium
REVENUES		
EGI/Gross Sales Proceeds	$95,000	$900,000
less:		
Operating Expenses/Marketing Costs	$40,000	$100,000
equals:		
NOI/Net Sales Proceeds	$55,000	$800,000
divided by:		
Cap Rate @	10%	N/A
equals:		
Sales Proceeds	$550,000	$800,000
less:		
COSTS		
Total Development Costs	$400,000	475,000
equals:		
PROFIT		
Profit to Developer	$150,00	$325,000

The developer conducts an alternative use analysis and "what if" scenarios, summarized in Table 5.12.

This alternative use analysis allows the investor to determine that both alternative uses are *economically feasible*. However, the rental use produces $150,000 profit to the developer and the condominium use produces $325,000 profit to the developer. Accordingly, it is the condominium use that produces the greatest economic benefits and, therefore, represents the *highest and best use* of the property. Because it is the condominium use that provides the greatest economic benefit it is also the appropriate exit strategy for the developer. Alternative use analysis and probable exit strategies address concepts closely related to *feasibility studies* and *highest and best use analysis*.

Forecasted Performance of Investment Property

The purpose of market analysis is to provide a framework for the decision-making process that allows an investor to make informed investment decisions. As part of the decision-making process to purchase the property, a forecasted performance of the investment property must be considered. Forecasting involves a combination of skills that involve the practical application of market and property data. Forecasting concepts incorporate the results of feasibility studies and highest and best use analysis. However, forecasting is also closely associated with investment analysis.

Figure 5.9

Hieracrchy of Studies

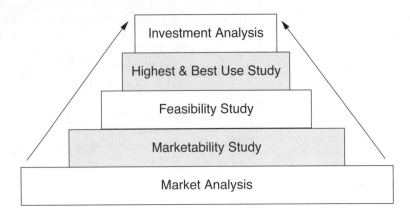

■ Continuum of Market Analysis with Other Forms of Analysis

Market analysis is a primary form of analysis that provides the basis for additional and more sophisticated types of analysis. Accordingly, market analysis is part of a continuum of analysis. It is important to complete one form of analysis as the foundation for the next, more complex form of analysis. These analyses form a continuum of analysis that provides a great deal of insight into the historical, current, and projected market conditions for real estate. Figure 5.9 provides an illustration of the interdependence of these studies.

There are many reasons to conduct these analyses but they all have one central theme: *they provide insight into the anticipated future benefits that investors may expect to derive from their real estate investments.* Accordingly, they are forecasting tools.

Marketability Study

When we progress within the framework of analysis to an investment property's capture rate or to marketing and property management strategies, the framework of analysis also moves forward into the realm of a marketability study.

A *marketability study* investigates how a particular property will be absorbed, leased, or sold under current or anticipated market conditions. It includes *a market study or analysis* of the general class of property being studied. It examines the marketability of a given property or class of property, usually focusing on the market segment(s) in which the property is likely to *generate demand*. Marketability studies are used in determining the *economic feasibility* of alternative uses and the *highest and best use* of property.

A marketability study determines how a specific property is currently positioned and how it may be repositioned in the marketplace. The *supply, demand,* and *price structure* that exists today, as well as in the future, are the subject of the marketability study. Once the determinants of *demand* have been identified and contrasted with *supply,* a marketability study continues the analysis further by identifying the number of units (i.e., apartment units, square feet of office space, cubic feet of industrial space, etc.) that most likely will be absorbed within a market during a specified time period.

A marketability study does not involve the consideration of feasibility, the development costs, or profitability. A marketability study is sandwiched between a market study and a feasibility study. The continuum of analysis progresses from one form of analysis to another along the hierarchy of studies. For example, if demand exists, a proposed development may be marketable but not feasible. If the development costs of the proposed development are greater than the revenues generated by it, it is not feasible.

Feasibility Study

When we progress within the framework of analysis to an investment property's alternative use and probable exit strategies, the framework of analysis also moves forward into the realm of a feasibility study and/or a highest and best use study.

A *feasibility study* is a study of the cost-versus-benefit relationship of a real estate endeavor. It includes a *marketability analysis*. It analyzes whether a property will meet the objectives of a developer, lender, or investor. It is utilized to determine if a development is economically feasible and, if so, estimate the rate of return obtainable by that development. Feasibility studies are usually a prerequisite to any actual development or development funding.

The property may be existing or proposed. A feasibility study also tests the capability of alternative investment scenarios to meet the investor's objectives. The profitability of a specific real estate project is analyzed in terms of the *specific criteria* of a specific market or investor. A feasibility analysis can identify the anticipated results of alternative investment decisions and compares these results with the investor's objectives. It also identifies what may be changed in order to achieve the desired objectives, and what costs and benefits will be obtained by implementing those changes.

A feasibility study would include consideration of the following ten components:

1. A preliminary development concept
2. A known site location
3. A market demand analysis
4. A market supply analysis
5. A refinement of the development concept into a finalized plan
6. A compilation of the development costs to complete the project and stabilize the project, and the operating expenses to operate and maintain the project
7. A compilation and analysis of the capital structure of the development, specifically the equity and debt components of the development costs
8. An estimation of sales price or rental rate of space and the rate of sales or absorption of that space
9. A time-allocated projection of the revenues and income, development costs, and operating expenses into a period-by-period forecast

10. An analysis of the rate of return on capital, the rate of return of capital, and the yield rate on the components of capital

Highest and Best Use Study

Feasibility studies and highest and best use studies are also interrelated. It is difficult to separate the framework of highest and best use analysis from feasibility analysis. A **highest and best use** study seeks the reasonably probable and legal use of either vacant land or an improved property that is physically possible, appropriately supported, and financially feasible, and that results in the highest value.

The four criteria the highest and best use must meet are:

1. Legal permissibility—the use must be allowable
2. Physical possibility—the use must be physically possible
3. Financial feasibility—the use must be economically feasible
4. Maximum profitability—among the financially feasible uses, the use must be the maximally profitable use

Investment Analysis

When we progress within the framework of analysis to the forecasted performance of an investment property, the framework of analysis also moves forward into the realm of investment analysis. *Investment analysis* is a process by which the attractiveness of an investment is determined by analyzing the costs and benefits utilizing time, the value of money, and the use of various ratios. Investment analysis incorporates the results of feasibility analysis and highest and best use analysis.

Figure 5.10 illustrates the continuum of market analysis with other forms of analysis.

Figure 5.10

Continuum of Market Analysis with Other Forms of Analysis

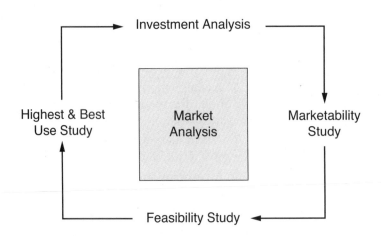

■ Summary

Market analysis is the study of real estate market conditions. It is a tool that provides a framework of analysis for an investor's decision making. Market analysis provides fundamental answers to investors questions and concerns about their established investment objectives and goals. Once these investment objectives have been determined, decisions such as to buy, hold, sell, develop, reposition, lease, sublease, or leaseback commercial real estate are based on market analysis.

A real estate market is a gathering of individuals who are in contact with one another to buy and sell real property rights for money and other assets. That gathering place can be in a physical location such as a real estate brokerage office. It can also be in a virtual location such as an Internet-based Web site. A submarket is a division of the universal real estate market that reflects the preferences of buyers and sellers. The universal market for real estate is separated into submarket categories based on location, property types, property class, and market participants.

The global market for real estate is comprised of characteristics that render it inefficient. Accordingly, the individual property markets that comprise the global real estate market are also inefficient. The inherent characteristics of real estate preclude its differing markets from operating efficiently. Some of the inherent characteristics of real estate that preclude it from operating efficiently include illiquidity, the lack of centralized exchanges, unequal dissemination of information, significant government regulation, and a capital-intensive nature. Market analysis is also an important tool for market participants because the real estate market itself is inefficient.

Because all property is geographic specific, market analysis usually begins with an economic overview of the market area in which the property type will compete. Next, the characteristics of demand are addressed. Demand is the amount of a type of real estate desired for purchase or rent at various prices in a given market for a given period of time. Demand analysis focuses on the users of real estate. Market analysis is demand based but would be meaningless without an analysis of supply. Supply refers to the amount of a type of real estate available for sale or lease at various price levels in a given market at a given time. On its own, supply is never in balance because it does not have anything with which to be in balance. So supply is always measured in terms of its relationship, or interaction, with demand.

Once supply and demand are known, the interaction of the two is analyzed based on the principle of supply and demand. This principle states that the price of a commodity, good, or service varies directly, but not necessarily proportionately, with demand, and inversely, but not necessarily proportionately, with supply. So, the interaction of supply and demand creates real estate pricing. The interaction of supply and demand causes cyclical market fluctuations including a buyer's or a seller's market.

The interaction of supply and demand also causes a gravitational pull toward or away from individual properties. This captured demand, known as market share, represents the portion of effective demand that is captured by a particular property. Market share represents captured demand. Market share can be estimated for both existing and proposed properties. There is no universally accepted method to estimate market share. Because of this, estimating market share is as much an art as a science.

Property management and marketing strategies naturally evolve out of market analysis. The primary reason investors acquire real estate is for it to produce income. The goal of property management and marketing strategies should be to produce the greatest achievable financial return for the longest possible time. A comprehensive property management and marketing program would consist of the following six components: (1) maintenance and operations, (2) risk management, (3) human resources, (4) marketing and leasing, (5) financial management, and (6) asset management. Considerations closely related to property management and marketing include alternative use analysis and probable exit strategies.

An analysis of alternative uses and probable exit strategies speaks to the issues of risk, uncertainty, and wealth maximization in investment real estate. Alternative use analysis relates to "what if" scenarios that allow the investor to determine what alternative uses are economically feasible and which alternative use produces the greatest economic benefits, referred to as the highest and best use of the property. Because alternative uses may involve renovation, retrofitting, or readaptive use, the economic costs and benefits must also be determined. Once alternative uses are known, probable exit strategies are formulated.

The purpose of market analysis is to provide a framework for the decision-making process that allows an investor to make informed investment decisions. As part of the decision-making process to purchase the property, a forecasted performance of the investment property must be considered. Forecasting utilizes a combination of skills that involve the practical application of market and property data. Forecasting concepts incorporate the results of feasibility studies and highest and best use analysis. However, forecasting is also closely associated with investment analysis.

Market analysis is a primary form of analysis that provides the basis for additional and more sophisticated types of analysis. Accordingly, market analysis is part of a continuum of analysis. It is important to complete one form of analysis as the foundation for the next, more complex form of analysis. These analyses form a continuum of analysis that provides a great deal of insight into the historical, current, and projected market conditions for real estate.

Market analysis is a core tool in the hierarchy of analytical tools available for successful real estate investment. There is a clear interrelationship of market analysis with other forms of analysis. The four interlinked forms of analysis are: (1) marketability study, (2) feasibility study, (3) highest and best use study, and (4) investment analysis. Because these studies are all interlinked, a correctly executed market analysis is the crucial building block.

■ Review Questions

1. Market analysis is
   a. the study of real estate market conditions for a specific type of property within a delineated market area.
   b. the study of a specific type of property within a delineated market area, including the market conditions relating thereto.
   c. the study of a delineated market area as it pertains to market conditions that impact a specific property type.
   d. All of the above (A, B, and C)

2. The market for real estate is inefficient because
   a. real estate can be readily exchanged into its cash equivalent.
   b. its markets are centralized and orderly.
   c. there is significant control and influence possible.
   d. property is easily substituted for one another.

3. A characteristic of demand is that it
   a. is a desire for goods and services.
   b. is the ability to pay for goods and services.
   c. varies directly with price.
   d. All of the above (A, B, and C)

4. Effective demand is
   a. the desire and ability to purchase goods and services.
   b. the demand for the ability to purchase goods and services.
   c. the desire for the ability to purchase goods and services.
   d. the demand for the desire to purchase goods and services.

5. A characteristic of supply is that it
   a. refers to the amount of a type of real estate.
   b. is location and time sensitive.
   c. varies inversely with price.
   d. All of the above (A, B, and C)

6. Competitive supply analysis identifies a
   a. supply of properties.
   b. supply of competitive properties.
   c. supply of properties competitive with a subject property.
   d. supply of properties competitive with a subject property within a defined area.

7. In a buyer's market,
    a. buyers benefit from excess demand.
    b. sellers benefit from excess demand.
    c. buyers benefit from excess supply.
    d. sellers benefit from excess supply.

8. In a seller's market,
    a. buyers benefit from excess demand.
    b. sellers benefit from excess demand.
    c. buyers benefit from excess supply.
    d. sellers benefit from excess supply.

9. Market share
    a. is demand based.
    b. is also known as capture rate and penetration rate.
    c. represents captured demand.
    d. All of the above (A, B, and C)

10. A highest and best use analysis supports the use that results in the
    a. highest density.
    b. highest tax base.
    c. highest value.
    d. highest cost.

11. A developer commences construction of a 20-unit rental apartment
    building. His goal is to sell the building shortly after completion, as
    soon as the property is fully occupied and leased. He expects that he
    can complete construction and lease all 20 units in less than one year.
    The developer's total development costs are $800,000. Based on a
    market analysis of comparable rental properties, the developer is able
    to support his assumptions of rental rates, operating expenses, and net
    operating income and capitalization rates. Utilizing this information,
    the developer prepares a pro-forma profit and loss statement for the
    property and anticipates effective gross income of $190,000 and total
    operating expenses of $80,000. He anticipates that the rental property
    can be sold on the basis of a 7 percent capitalization rate.
    Using this information, if the developer can complete the building
    on time and within budget, what are the net operating income, capital-
    ized sale price, and profit to the developer?
    a. NOI is $110,000, sale price is $1,571,430, and profit is $771,430.
    b. NOI is $190,000, sale price is $2,714,285, and profit is $1,914,285.
    c. NOI is $110,000, sale price is $1,571,430, and profit is $1,914,285.
    d. NOI is $110,000, sale price is $2,714,285, and profit is $771,430.

12. Shortly after construction commences, the developer learns that there is a market demand for condominiums within the affordable housing price range. After consulting with his general contractor and legal counsel, the developer budgets an additional $10,000 per unit for conversion from a rental property to a condominium property. Based on a market analysis of comparable condominium properties, the developer is able to support his assumptions of sales prices at $80,000 per unit, and sales and marketing costs at $10,000 per unit.

    Using this information, if the developer can covert the building to a condominium, what are the gross sales proceeds and profit to the developer?

    a. Gross sales proceeds are $1,600,000 and profit is $1,400,000.

    b. Gross sales proceeds are $1,400,000 and profit is $1,000,000.

    c. Gross sales proceeds are $1,600,000 and profit is $400,000.

    d. Gross sales proceeds are $1,400,000 and profit is $200,000.

13. Based on the answers obtained from questions 11 and 12, which of the two alternative uses would provide the most profit to the developer?

    a. Development as a rental

    b. Conversion to a condominium

    c. Neither

    d. There is not enough information to make a decision.

14. The developer learns new information about the proposed alternative uses. Specifically, the capitalization rate that should have been utilized in the rental analysis is 11 percent, not 7 percent. The developer recalculates his alternative use scenarios. Should the developer change the use of the property? Why?

    a. No. The use should remain the same because the capitalization rate is not a factor in the decision-making process.

    b. Yes. The use should change to condominium because when the income is capitalized at the 11 percent rate, the profit from the condominium conversion scenario exceeds the profit from the rental apartment scenario.

    c. No. Increasing the capitalization rate to 11 percent implies that the developer will obtain a higher rate of return than with a capitalization rate of 7 percent.

    d. There is not enough information to make a decision.

15. Based on the answer to question 14, which statement is true?

    a. Given an income stream, as the capitalization rate decreases, the capitalized value increases.

    b. Given a capitalization rate, as the income stream increases, the capitalized value increases.

    c. Capitalization rates and capitalized values move inversely in relation to each other.

    d. All of the above (A, B, and C)

ANSWER KEY

■ **Chapter 1**

Multiple-choice Questions

1. D   2. B   3. D   4. D   5. A   6. C   7. A   8. C   9. D   10. A

Application Questions

11. D

Yes. The lender debt plus owner equity is enough for the capital required for the deal. The negotiated price for the 25-unit rental apartment building is $75,000 per unit, which would equate to a total purchase price of $1,875,000, as follows:

$$\$75,000 \text{ per unit} \times 25 \text{ units} = \$1,875,000.$$

A lender will underwrite a senior loan on the basis of a 75 percent LTV. Accordingly, the lender will lend a maximum of $1,406,250, as follows:

$$\$1,875,000 \text{ purchase price} \times 75\% \text{ LTV} = \$1,406,250 \text{ senior loan.}$$

The investor will be required to provide the remaining 25 percent in the form of equity. This equity amount is determined to be $468,750, as follows:

$$\$1,875,000 \text{ purchase price} - \$1,406,250 \text{ loan} = \$468,750 \text{ equity required.}$$

The investor has $500,000 equity available. This is more than the $468,750 equity required. The lender debt plus the owner equity is enough for the capital required for the deal, as follows:

	Capital Available	= Lender Debt	+ Owner Equity
Acquisition Price	$1,875,000	= $1,406,250	+ $468,750
Percent of Price	100%	= 75%	+ 25%

12. A

The investment of $1,875,000 generates an unleveraged or all-cash return of 10 percent, which equates to $187,500, as follows:

Acquisition Price	$1,875,000
Pro-forma Return %	10%
Pro-forma Return $	$187,500

13. C

The lender's return is 8.87 percent and the investor's return is 13.40 percent. Because the unleveraged return is 10 percent, using debt results in positive leverage for the investor. The lender will provide a loan commitment based on an interest rate of 7.50 percent and a loan amortization period of 25 years. The annual debt service required to service this loan is $124,705. This amount represents an 8.87 percent return on the lender's loan amount of $1,406,250 as follows:

$$\$124,705 \div \$1,406,250 = 8.87\% \text{ return.}$$

The investment generates a pro-forma return of $187,500. The annual debt service required to service this loan is $124,705. Subtracting the annual debt service from the pro-forma return results in a return to the owner's equity of $62,795, which represents a 13.40 percent return, as follows:

Investment return of	$187,500
Less annual debt service of	$124,705
Equals return to owners equity of	$62,795
Divided by owners equity of	$468,750
Equals return on owners equity of	13.40%

Positive leverage occurs because the 10 percent rate of return that the investment generates is greater than the 7.5 percent interest rate charged by the lender for borrowed funds that are utilized to acquire that investment. In this case, the rate of return that the investment generates on an all-cash basis is 10 percent, which is greater than both the 7.50 percent interest rate charged by the lender and the 8.87 percent return to the lender for the borrowed funds utilized to acquire the investment, as follows:

	Capital Available	= Lender Debt	+ Owner Equity
Acquisition Price	$1,875,000	= $1,406,250	+ $468,750
Percent of Price	100%	= 75%	+ 25%
Pro-forma Return $	$187,500	= $124,705	+ $62,795
Pro-forma Return %	10%	8.87%	13.40%
% of Return	100%	= 75%	+ 25%
Pro-forma Weighted Return	10%	= 6.65%	+ 3.35%

The investor expects to make a $15,920 profit on the borrowed funds (i.e., $140,625 less $142,707 equals $15,920 profit). This profit of $15,920 is added to the investor's unleveraged return of $46,875, which has the effect of increasing the return on the investor's cash portion of the investment from $46,875 to $62,795. It also has the effect of increasing the rate of return on the investor's cash portion of the investment from 10 percent to 13.40 percent.

14. A

The DCR for this property is 1.51. The loan exceeds the lender's minimum DCR requirement of 1.25. The formula for DCR is net operating income divided by annual debt service. The NOI for the property is $187,500. The ADS for the loan is $124,705. The DCR for this combination of NOI and ADS is 1.51, as follows:

$$\$187,500 \div \$124,705 = 1.51.$$

The DCR of 1.51 exceeds the lender's minimum requirement of 1.25.

15. B

The seller made a $312,500 profit in this deal. The purchase price for this property is $1,875,000. This price represents 120 percent of the seller'sdeveloper's cost. To determine the cost of this property, divide the price by the 120 percent cost, as follows:

$$\$1,875,000 \div 1.20 = \$1,562,500.$$

The total cost is $1,562,500. Subtracting the cost from the price results in the total profit of $312,500.

■ Chapter 2

Multiple-choice Questions

1. D   2. D   3. C   4. D   5. C   6.D   7. D   8D   9. C   10. B

Application Questions

11. A

The GBA equals 20,000 square feet, the total core space equals 3,000 square feet, and the usable area equals 17,000 square feet.

Determine the GBA: Gross construction area is also referred to as gross building area or GBA. The gross construction area for this floor area is 20,000 square feet. Therefore, the GBA is also 20,000 square feet.

Determine the core space: Core space represents 15 percent of the GBA. Therefore, the core space equates to 3,000 square feet, calculated as follows:

20,000 sq. ft. GBA × 15% core space = 3,000 sq. ft. of core space.

Determine the Useable Area: Useable area is gross building area less core space. Therefore, the useable area equates to 17,000 square feet, calculated as follows:

20,000 sq. ft. GBA – 3,000 sq. ft. of core space = useable area.

12. D

The adjusted core space equals 2,400 square feet and the total rentable area equals 19,400 square feet.

As previously determined, the gross building area has core space of 15 percent, or 3,000 square feet. This resulted in a usable area of 17,000 square feet, calculated as follows:

	Sq. Ft.	% Sq. Ft.
Gr. Construction Area	20,000	100%
less:		
Total Core Space	3,000	15%
equals:		
Usable Area	17,000	85%

A total of 20 percent of the total core space, amounting to 600 square feet, consists of areas for elevators and stairs. Although elevators and stairs are considered part of total core space, they are not considered part of the rentable area of a floor area. Accordingly, the adjusted core space for this floor plate is 2,400 square feet, calculated as follows:

	Sq. Ft.	% Sq. Ft.
Total Core Space	20,000	100%
less:		
Excluded Core Space	600	20%
equals:		
Adjusted Core Space	2,400	80%

Now that the floor area's adjusted core area has been calculated, the rentable area is determined to be 19,400 square feet, calculated as follows:

	Sq. Ft.	% Sq. Ft.
Usable Area	17,000	88%
less:		
Excluded Core Space	2,400	12%
equals:		
Adjusted Core Space	19,400	100%

13. B

If fully leased, the potential annual first-year rent for this floor area would be $388,000.

The rent is quoted at $20 per square foot, full service. The rentable area for this floor plan is 19,400 square feet. Therefore, the potential annual first-year rent for this floor plan would be $388,000, calculated as follows:

19,400 sq. ft. × $20 per sq. ft. = $388,000 potential annual rent.

14. B

$0.40 per square foot, or $7,760, operating expenses can be charged back to the tenants on this floor.

Rents are quoted at $20 per square foot, full service, base year stop. Base year operating expenses represent 25 percent of the $20 per square foot rent, equating to $5 per square foot. During the second year, the $5-per-square-foot operating expenses escalate 8 percent, equating to $0.40 per square foot. Because the operating expenses are "stopped" at $5 per square foot, the $0.40 per square foot can be charged back to tenants. Because the rentable area is 19,400 square feet, the total expense charged to tenants equates to $7,760.

15. D

The COLA rent would be $0.60 per square foot, $11,640 per year, and $970 per month.

The $20-per-square-foot rent is subject to a cost-of-living adjustment, based on the Consumer Price Index. The CPI rises by 3 percent in the second year. The COLA rent is equal to $0.60 per square foot, calculated as follows:

$$\$20 \times 3\% = \$0.60 \text{ per square foot COLA rent;}$$
$$\$0.60 \text{ per square foot} \times 19,400 \text{ square feet rentable area} =$$
$$\$11,640 \text{ per annum;}$$
$$\$11,640 \text{ per annum} \div 12 \text{ months} = \$970 \text{ per month.}$$

■ Chapter 3

Multiple-choice Questions

1. D   2. D   3. B   4. A   5. D   6. D   7. D   8. C   9. B   10. A

Application Questions

11. C

600 parking spaces are required for this new shopping center.

The total anchor GLA in the property is 66,500 square feet. The total local shop tenant GLA is 53,500 square feet. Adding the total anchor and shop tenant GLA represents the total GLA in the property and equates to 120,000 square feet.

The parking index is 5 parking spaces per 1,000 square feet of GLA. By dividing the 120,000 of GLA by 1,000 square feet, it is determined that there are 120 GLA units of 1,000 square feet each. Multiplying the parking index of 5 by the 120 GLA units equates to 600 parking spaces.

12. D

The pro-forma common area expense for the parking lot is $637,500.

The shopping center has 600 parking spaces. The average square footage of the parking spaces plus the features incidental to parking is 425 square feet each. By multiplying the 600 parking spaces by 425 square feet, it is determined that there are 255,000 square feet of parking lot common area. Multiplying the 255,000 square feet of parking lot common area parking by the pro-forma common area expense of $2.50 per square foot equates to $637,500.

13. C

This tenant has a common area factor of 2.71 percent.

The local shop tenant occupies 3,250 square feet of GLA. The shopping center has a total of 120,000 of GLA. Dividing the shop tenant GLA by the shopping center GLA results in a factor of 2.71 percent. This represents the portion of space occupied by the shop tenant as it relates to the total shopping center.

14. D

This tenant has an estimated common area charge of $17,276.25 per year, which would equate to an equivalent monthly amount of $1,439.69 and $5.32 per square foot of GLA.

The tenant has a common area factor of 2.71 percent. The parking lot pro-forma common area expense equates to $637,500. The tenant's 2.71 percent pro-rata share of the $637,500 expense equates to $17,276.25 per annum and $1,439.69 per month. The local shop tenant occupies 3,250 square feet of GLA. The tenant's pro-rata share of the expense equates to $17,276.25 per annum. Dividing the tenant expenses by the tenant's GLA results in an expense of $5.32 per square foot of tenant GLA.

15. B

Because the tenant is in the second year of its lease, its threshold for sales is now $280.73 per square foot.

The tenant has a base year rent of $30 per square foot. The base rent escalates at a fixed index of 3 percent per annum. The tenant is now in the second year of the lease. Accordingly, the second year rent is $30.90 per square foot.

The percentage rent payable is 11 percent, commencing above the threshold. The threshold is established by natural breakpoint. Dividing the current year rent of $30.90 per square foot by the 11 percent establishes the natural breakpoint for the year at $280.91 per square foot.

■ Chapter 4

Multiple-choice Questions

1. A   2. D   3. C   4. D   5. C   6. D   7. B   8. B   9. B   10. D

Application Questions

11. A

The property's total annual lease rental income is $375,000, the total annual other income is $2,000, and the total annual potential gross income is $377,000. The annual vacancy and collection loss is $18,850 and the annual effective gross income is $358,150.

Building Rentable Area Sq. Ft.	15,000	
multipled by:		
Average Rent per Sq. Ft.	$ 25	
equals:		
Lease Rental Income		$375,000
add:		
Other Income—Parking	1,200	
Other Income—Vending	800	
equals:		
Total Other Income		2,000
equals:		
Potential Gross Income		377,000
less:		
Vacancy & Collection @	5%	18,850
equals:		
Effective Gross Income		$358,150

12. D

The property's total annual fixed and variable expenses are $90,000, total annual replacement reserves expense is $3,750, and net operating income is $264,400. Vacancy and collection losses would not apply to these expenses.

Effective Gross Income			$358,150
less:			
Operating Expenses	Per Sq. Ft.	Total	
Fixed Variable	$6.00	$90,000	
Replacement Reserves	0.25	3,750	
equals:			
Total Operating Income			93,750
equals:			
Net Operating Income			$264,400

13. D

The purchase price for this building is $2,644,000.

Because the investor has estimated the amount of net operating income he will receive on his investment and the 10 percent rate of return on his investment, he can solve for the capital amount of the investment by the following calculation:

NOI ÷ rate of return = capital amount.

In this example:

$264,400 ÷ 10% = $2,644,000.

14. D

The lender's debt for this purchase is $1,983,000.

The purchase price has been established as $2,644,000. The lender has quoted the loan based upon a 75 percent loan-to-value ratio. This ratio expresses the relationship of borrowed funds as a percentage of the value of the property. The LTV is determined utilizing the following calculation:

$$\text{Purchase price} \times \text{LTV ratio} = \text{loan amount}.$$

In this example:

$$\$2,644,000 \times 75\% = \$1,983,000.$$

15. C

The pretax cash flow would be $96,215.

The net operating income was previously determined to be $264,400 (in question 12) and the purchase price has been established as $2,644,000. If the annual debt service is $168,185, the pretax cash flow would equate to $96,215, determined utilizing the following calculation:

Net Operating Income	$264,400
less:	
Total Mortgage Payments	168,185
equals:	
Pretax Cash Flow	$96,215

■ Chapter 5

Multiple-choice Questions

1. D   2. C   3. D   4. A   5. D   6. D   7. C   8. B   9. D   10. C

Application Questions

11. A

The net operating income is $110,000, the capitalized sales price is $1,571,430, and the profit to the developer is $771,430.

The developer has prepared a pro-forma profit and loss statement for the property, shown below. The developer has estimated his effective gross income and operating expenses. Subtracting one from the other results in a net operating income of $110,000. He expects to sell the rental property on the basis of a 7 percent capitalization rate, which is divided into net operating income. The resultant capitalized sales price is $1,572,430. The total development costs are estimated at $800,000. Deducting these costs from the sales proceeds results in a $771,430 profit to the developer.

Scenario	Sell as a Rental
Effective Gross Income	$ 190,000
less:	
Operating Expenses	80,000
equals:	
Net Operating Income	110,000
divided by:	
Cap Rate @	7%
equals:	
Sales Proceeds	1,571,430
less:	
Total Development Costs	800,000
equals:	
Profit to Developer	$ 771,430

12. C

The gross sales proceeds are $1,600,000 and the profit to the developer is $400,000.

The developer has prepared a pro-forma profit and loss statement for the condominium conversion property, shown below. The developer has estimated his gross sales proceeds at $1,600,000, based on 20 condominium units and an average sales price of $80,000.

The sales and marketing costs were budgeted at $10,000 per unit, which for the 20 units would equate to a total of $200,000. Subtracting these costs from the gross sales results in net sales proceeds of $1,400,000.

The total rental apartment development costs are $800,000. However, the conversion costs to condominium must also be added to obtain total development costs as a condominium. The conversion costs are estimated at $10,000 per unit or $200,000 in total. So the total development costs are $1,000,000. Subtracting these costs from the net sales proceeds results in a profit to the developer of $400,000.

Scenario	Sell as a Condo
Gross Sales Proceeds	$1,600,000
less:	
Sales and Marketing Costs	200,000
equals:	
Net Sales Proceeds	1,400,000
less:	
Total Development Costs	1,000,000
equals:	
Profit to Developer	$ 400,000

13. A

Development as a rental would provide the most profit.

As a rental, after all costs are considered, the profit to the developer is $771,430. As a condominium conversion, after all costs are considered, the profit to the developer is only $400,000. The rental apartment provides the most profit of the two alternative uses.

14. B

Development as a condominium conversion would now provide the most profit.

As a rental, after all costs are considered, the profit to the developer declines to $200,000. As a condominium conversion, after all costs are considered, the profit to the developer remains $400,000.

Scenario Alternative Use	A Sell as a Rental	B Sell as a Condomimium
REVENUES		
EGI/Gross Sales Proceeds	$ 190,000	$1,600,000
less:		
Operating Expenses/Marketing Costs	80,000	200,000
equals:		
NOI/Net Sales Proceeds	110,000	1,400,000
divided by:		
Cap Rate @	11%	N/A
equals:		
Sales Proceeds	1,000,000	1,400,000
less:		
COSTS		
Total Development Costs	800,000	1,000,000
equals:		
PROFIT		
Profit to Developer	$ 200,000	$ 400,000

15. D

All of the statements are true.

Given any income stream, as the capitalization rate increases, the capitalized value decreases.

WEB SITE DIRECTORY

Appraisal Foundation   *(www.appraisalfoundation.org)*
The Appraisal Foundation, a not-for-profit educational organization dedicated to the advancement of professional valuation, was established by the appraisal profession in the United States in 1987. Since its inception, the foundation has worked to foster professionalism in appraising by establishing, improving, and promoting the Uniform Standards of Professional Appraisal Practice (USPAP); establishing educational and experience qualification criteria for the licensing, certification, and recertification of appraisers; disseminating information on USPAP and the appraiser qualification criteria to the appraisal profession, state and federal government agencies, users of appraisal services, related industries and industry groups, and the general public; and sponsoring appropriate activities relating to standards, qualifications, and issues of importance to appraisers and users of appraisal services.

Appraisal Institute   *(www.appraisalinstitute.org)*
The Appraisal Institute is an international membership association of professional real estate appraisers with more than 18,000 members and 99 chapters throughout the United States, Canada, and abroad. Its mission is to support and advance its members as the choice for real estate solutions and uphold professional credentials, standards of professional practice, and ethics consistent with the public good. The Appraisal Institute is the acknowledged worldwide leader in residential and commercial real estate appraisal education, research, and publishing, and professional membership designation programs. Its extensive curriculum of courses and specialty seminars provides a well-rounded education in valuation methodology for both the novice and seasoned practitioner. The Appraisal Institute also houses the Lum Library, which provides support for the research needs of members as well as the profession at large.

Black's Guide   *(www.blacksguide.com)*
Black's Guide delivers actionable data to commercial real estate brokers, owners, developers, property managers, and tenants. Published throughout the year, 55 print directories contain information, statistics, and trends on more than 80,000 properties in 19 major metropolitan markets. With its companion Web site, *Black's Guide* provides free comprehensive and accurate data that

helps deal makers quickly find and compare properties and then locate the right people to contact. The *Black's Guide* Web site has the largest, most comprehensive and accurate free data on commercial properties. Free to registered users, *Black's Guide* is an incredibly useful research and marketing tool for commercial real estate brokers, owners, developers, and tenants. *Black's Guide* publishes more commercial free real estate data in more markets than any other publication or electronic service.

Building Owners & Managers Association   *(www.boma.org)*
BOMA International was founded in 1907 as the National Association of Building Owners and Managers. Today, BOMA International represents nearly 100 North American and 9 overseas affiliates. BOMA International is a primary source of information on office building development, leasing, building operating costs, energy consumption patterns, local and national building codes, legislation, occupancy statistics, and technological developments.

The organization publishes *BOMA.org* magazine, the official publication of BOMA International; research documents; and how-to guidebooks, including *Standard Method for Measuring Floor Area in Office Buildings*, recognized as an industry benchmark for over 75 years. BOMA presents The Office Building of the Year (TOBY) and Earth Awards, the most prestigious and coveted awards in the commercial real estate industry. The TOBY honors buildings demonstrating excellence in building management, operational efficiency, tenant retention, emergency planning, and community impact; the Earth Award honors environmentally friendly buildings.

CCIM Institute   *(www.ccim.com)*
Practitioners holding the CCIM designation are recognized as experts in commercial investment real estate and live up to their distinguished reputation as model business partners for commercial real estate users, owners, and investors. Only 7,500 commercial real estate practitioners nationwide hold the CCIM designation. This statistic reflects the caliber of the program and why it is the most coveted and respected designation in commercial investment real estate.

***Commercial Investment Real Estate* magazine**   *(www.ciremagazine.com)*
The online version of the magazine of the CCIM Institute. This member publication of the CCIM Institute reports on market trends and analysis, current developments in the field, and successful business strategies.

CoStar Group   *(www.costar.com)*
Marketed as the commercial real estate information leader, CoStar offers commercial real estate's premier database of property for sale listings, space for lease listings, and comparable sales listings. CoStar's proprietary databases are widely used by over 70,000 commercial real estate brokers, owners, lenders, and appraisers, offering the power to close more deals, generate more income, and save research time.

Counselors of Real Estate   *(www.cre.org)*
The Counselors of Real Estate (CRE) is a professional membership organization established exclusively for leading real property advisors. The purpose of the organization is to advance, enhance, and support these leaders by serving as a resource for information, creating opportunities for professional

development, facilitating networking, and providing the benefits of camaraderie. Members are awarded the CRE designation, bestowed by invitation only, in recognition of their achievements in real estate counseling.

Counselor of Real Estate Broker Managers   *(www.crb.com)*
The council confers the Certified Real Estate Brokerage Manager (CRB) designation, while continuously providing members with the educational, informational, and networking resources necessary to compete and succeed in the real estate marketplace.

Council of Residential Specialists   *(www.crs.com)*
The Certified Residential Specialist (CRS) is the highest designation awarded to sales associates in the residential sales field. The CRS designation recognizes professional accomplishments in both experience and education. Since 1977, the Council of Residential Specialists has been conferring the CRS designation on agents who meet its stringent requirements. Currently, there are more than 34,000 active CRS designees.

Emporis   *(www.emporis.com)*
Emporis leads the world today as the most comprehensive information provider on highrise buildings of 12 floors or more, with the ambition to cover the whole building market in the years to come. Emporis is already one of the world's most respected, widely utilized sources for research, ratings, and analysis on information concerning buildings. The firm publishes research results and commentary that reach millions of Web site users around the globe. Emporis rates and analyzes hundreds of domestic and international real estate markets covering approximately 135,000 buildings, 40,500 companies, 350,000 points of interest, and 8,000 cities within 206 countries. The Emporis Image Database publishes more than 80,000 new building photographs each year. The building data and services of Emporis help customers analyze the building industry. Independent ratings and research also contribute to efficiencies for firms operating in the architectural, construction, financial, insurance, engineering, and supply industries.

Institute of Real Estate Management   *(www.irem.org)*
The Institute of Real Estate Management (IREM) is an association of property and asset managers who have met strict criteria in the areas of education, experience, and ethics. Founded in 1933, IREM's mission is to educate real estate managers, certify their competence and professionalism, serve as an advocate on issues affecting the real estate management industry, and enhance its members' professional competence so they can better identify and meet the needs of those who use their services

International Council of Shopping Centers   *(www. icsc.org)*
Founded in 1957, the International Council of Shopping Centers (ICSC) is the global trade association of the shopping center industry. Its 54,000 members in the United States, Canada, and more than 80 other countries include shopping center owners, developers, managers, marketing specialists, investors, lenders, retailers, and other professionals, as well as academics and public officials. As the global industry trade association, ICSC links with more than 25 national and regional shopping center councils throughout the world.

The principle aims of ICSC are to advance the development of the shopping center industry and to establish the individual shopping center as a major institution in the community through promoting the role of shopping centers; establishing codes of fair business ethics and dealings with retailers and consumers and with government and public agencies; encouraging research into the architecture and design of shopping centers and into the development of improved management and maintenance methods; collecting and disseminating information among members pertaining to techniques of profitable operation, which can serve to improve the individual shopping center and the industry; studying economic, marketing, and promotional conditions affecting the shopping center industry; and promoting the prestige and standing of members as reputable specialists in the field of shopping center development and management.

investorwords.com *(www.investorwords.com)*
Promoted as the largest and most comprehensive financial glossary online or offline, it offers over 6,000 definitions and 20,000 links between related terms. The Web site has multiple search engines.

Korpacz Real Estate Investor Survey *(www.pwcreval.comsurveyhome.asp)*
The *Korpacz Real Estate Investor Survey*® is widely recognized as an authoritative source for capitalization and discount rates, cash-flow assumptions, and actual criteria of active investors, as well as property market information. Each quarterly issue of the *Survey* contains current, prior-quarter, and year-ago rates; cash-flow assumptions and other criteria used to analyze real estate investments; survey results with discussion and analysis vis-à-vis prior quarters for current and long-range perspectives of buyers' strategies; more than 40 tables, including yield comparisons, dividend comparisons, key value indicators by market, marketing time, institutional-grade versus noninstitutional-grade property rates, forecast periods and growth rates, and market characteristics; trends in real estate investment and valuation; economic news; plus separate quarterly reports covering the following markets: retail (three major sectors), office (two national and 14 specific), industrial (flexR&D and warehouse), multifamily, and net lease; and semiannual reports covering the following markets: hotel (four national; first and third quarter issues), development land (second and fourth quarters), and waste management markets (first and third quarter issues).

LoopNet *(www.loopnet.com)*
LoopNet, Inc., a leading information services provider to the commercial real estate industry, delivers a comprehensive suite of products and services to meet the national and local needs of commercial real estate firms, organizations, and professionals. LoopNet members can list, search, market, and finance commercial real estate properties over the Internet, reducing their marketing costs, expanding their reach, and accelerating the pace of transactions.

LoopNet operates the largest commercial real estate listing service online, with more than $240 billion of property listed for sale and 2.7 billion square feet of space for lease. With more than 1 million members, LoopNet attracts the largest community of commercial real estate professionals. LoopNet's market-leading LoopLink product powers the Web sites of more than 1,000 commercial real estate organizations and seamlessly integrates their Web sites with LoopNet's listing service (at *www.loopnet.com*).

LoopNet customers include virtually all of the top commercial real estate firms in the United States, including CB Richard Ellis, Century 21 Commercial, Coldwell Banker Commercial, Colliers International, The CORE

Network, Cushman & Wakefield, Grubb & Ellis, Lincoln Property Company, Marcus & Millichap, NAI Global, Prudential CRES, REMAX, RREEF, Sperry Van Ness, The Staubach Company, and Trammell Crow Company.

LoopLender, LoopNet's online financing service, provides direct access and fast loan approval to many of the industry's top lenders.

LoopNet also owns and operates BizBuySell, Inc., the largest and most heavily trafficked online exchange for businesses for sale in North America, with more business listings, users, and search activity than any other Web site. BizBuySell features over 30,000 businesses for sale listings that are searched by more than 400,000 monthly visitors, and has the largest database of sales comparables for recently sold businesses.

Marshall & Swift *(www.marshallswift.com)*
Marshall & Swift (M&S) is dedicated to providing the residential and commercial real estate industries with the most current building cost data and valuation software technologies available. M&S has the single most comprehensive building cost database in the marketplace. The M&S data has become the industry benchmark for preliminary budget feasibility and design alternative life-cycle costing; energy audits; estimating and bidding for new construction or partial loss and damage repair; evaluations for lending, assessing, insurance, and rate-setting purposes; real estate listing and market comparable tools; sinking funds and reserve estimates; and valuation.

Mortgage Bankers Association *(www.mortgagebankers.org)*
The Mortgage Bankers Association seeks to create an environment that enables its members to invest in communities and achieve their business objectives. The association creates this environment by developing innovative business tools, educating and training industry professionals, providing a gathering place for the sharing of ideas, acting as the industry's voice on legislative and regulatory issues, and developing open and fair standards and practices for the industry.

Municipal Code Corporation *(www.municode.com)*
Municipal Code Corporation (MCC) is the leader in the ordinance codification industry. MCC has over 50 years of experience publishing codes of ordinances, land use codes, charters, etc., for local governments. This includes original codification, recodifications, republications, and updating. MCC updates codes in print and electronic format on any schedule from biweekly to annual updates. The Web site contains the codes for more than 1,500 local governments in searchable online databases, and information about many other services and products including custom publishing and document management.

National Association of REALTORS®   *(www.realtor.org)*
The National Association Of REALTORS® is America's largest trade association, representing one million members, including NAR's institutes, societies, and councils involved in all aspects of the residential and commercial real
estate industries. NAR membership is composed of residential and commercial REALTORS®, who are brokers, salespeople, property managers, appraisers, counselors, and others engaged in all aspects of the real estate industry.
Members belong to one or more of some 1,600 local associationsboards and
54 state and territory associations of REALTORS®. They are pledged to a strict
code of ethics and standards of practice.

National Real Estate Investor   *(http:nreionline.com)*
National Real Estate Investor is the leading authority on commercial real estate
trends. The magazine's readers represent a cross-section of disciplines—brokerage, construction, ownerdevelopment, financeinvestment, property management, corporate real estate, and real estate services. No other publication
provides as much independent research on a variety of topics that pertain to
the office, industrial, retail, hotel, and multifamily markets as *National Real
Estate Investor.*

National Real Estate Investor Association   *(www.nationalreia.com)*
The National Real Estate Investors Association (NREIA) is a federation made
up of local associations or investment clubs throughout the United States.
The NREIA is an association of real estate professionals who know firsthand
the unique problems and challenges of real estate investing. The NREIA represents local investor associations, property owner associations, apartment
associations, and landlord associations on a national scale. Together NREIA
represents the interests of over 20,000 members across the United States and
is the largest broad-based organization dedicated to the individual investor.
The mission of the NREIA is to educate and support the leaders of real estate
associations through training, networking, motivation, and provision of benefits to their associations. The NREIA promotes a high standard of business
ethics and professionalism.

National Research Bureau   *(www.nrbonline.com)*
The National Research Bureau is a recognized leader in comprehensive shopping center intelligence offering "everything about retail property." It provides an extensive amount of information, reports, and services, some at no
cost. It is a subsidiary of CoStar Group, Inc.

Real Estate Buyer's Agent Council   *(www.rebc.net)*
Real Estate Buyer's Agent Council (REBAC) is the world's largest association
of real estate professionals focusing specifically on representing the real estate
buyer. There are more than 42,000 active members of the organization worldwide. The REBAC awards the Accredited Buyer's Representative (ABR) and
the Accredited Buyer's Representative Manager (ABRM) designations.

Real Estate Media Online Newsletters   *(www.remnewsletters.com)*
Real Estate Media Online Newsletters offers access to industry newsletters published by Real Estate Media. The newsletters are published weekly,
biweekly, or monthly and include the *Debt and Equity Journal, Industrial Property Journal, Multi-housing Forum, Net Lease Forum, TIC Monthly,* GlobeStreet

Week, and GSR Week. The Web site offers free trail issues of each publication and a searchable archive database.

REALTORS® Land Institute   *(www.rliland.com)*

The REALTORS® Land Institute is the only branch of the REALTOR® family focused on land brokerage transactions of five specialized types: (1)farms and ranches, (2) undeveloped tracts of land, (3) transitional and development land, (4) subdivision and wholesaling of lots, and (5) site selection and assemblage of land parcels.

RealtyRates.com   *(www.realtyrates.com)*

RealtyRates.com is a comprehensive resource of real estate investment and development news, trends, analytics, and market research that supports real estate professionals involved with more than 50 income-producing and sell-out property types throughout the United States. RealtyRates.com is the publisher of the award-winning Investor Survey, Developer Survey, and Market Survey, providing data essential to the appraisal, evaluation, disposition, and marketing of investment and development real estate nationwide.

Society of Industrial and Office REALTORS®   *(www.sior.com)*

The society certifies its members with the prestigious specialist, industrial, and office real estate (SIOR) designation, a professional symbol of the highest level of knowledge, production, and ethics in the commercial real estate industry. Designees specialize in industrial, office, sales manager, or advisory services categories.

Urban Land Institute   *(www.uli.org)*

The mission of the Urban Land Institute (ULI) is to provide responsible leadership in the use of land to enhance the total environment. Founded in 1936, the institute now has more than 25,000 members worldwide representing the entire spectrum of land use and real estate development disciplines, working in private enterprise and public service. As the preeminent, multidisciplinary real estate forum, ULI facilitates the open exchange of ideas, information, and experience among local, national, and international industry leaders and policy makers dedicated to creating better places.

The members of the Urban Land Institute are community builders, the people who develop and redevelop neighborhoods, business districts, and communities across the United States. ULI's practice program is interdisciplinary and practical, focusing on trends and the basics of many different parts of the industry including: resort and residential, retail and destination development, office and industrial development, transportation and parking, real estate finance, and capital markets. In local communities, ULI district councils bring together a variety of stakeholders to find solutions and build consensus around land use and development challenges.

GLOSSARY

absolute net lease A retail lease in which the tenant is responsible for all expenses relating to the premises as if the tenant were the owner. In addition to the pro-rata share of property real estate taxes, property insurance, and property common area maintenance (CAM), the tenant is also responsible for the pro-rata share of structuralroofsite repairs, reserves for replacements, capital items, and management. If there were only one tenant occupying a single-tenant building, then the one tenant would be responsible for all these costs.

accelerated cost recovery system (ACRS) The accelerated depreciation system adopted under the Economic Recovery Act of 1981.

accelerated depreciation A depreciation method of cost write-off in which the allowances made for depreciation of the wasting real estate asset are greater in the earlier years and decline in the subsequent years, based on a formula. Technically, the depreciation decelerates over time. The term *accelerated depreciation* refers to the accelerated, or faster, recovery of capital during the early years of an investment. Accelerated depreciation does not allow an owner to depreciate more than the price paid for the improvements. However, because it does allow the owner to take the depreciation charge sooner rather than later, it is more valuable to him.

ACRS The acronym for accelerated cost recovery system.

after-tax cash flow (ATCF) The portion of pretax cash flow that remains after all income tax liabilities have been deducted.

agency A relationship created when one person, the principal, delegates to another, the agent, the right to act on his behalf in business transactions and to exercise some degree of discretion while so acting. An agency gives rise to a fiduciary or statutory relationship and imposes on the agent, as a representative of the principal, certain duties, obligations, and a high standard of good faith and loyalty. An agency may be a *general agency*, as when a principal gives a property manager the power to manage a real estate project on behalf of the principal on a continuing basis, or it may be a *special agency*, such as the standard listing contract wherein the broker is employed only to find a ready, willing, and able buyer and is neither authorized to sell the property nor bind the principal to any contract for the sale of the property.

amortized loan A loan requiring periodic payments that include both interest and partial repayment of principal. As the loan amortizes, the loan balance declines. Because the total purchase price remains unchanged and the debt component is declining, the equity component is increasing in relation to the purchase price.

anchor tenant The retail store within a shopping center that attracts the most consumer traffic to the property. An anchor tenant has enough drawing power to stand alone and is effective in attracting visits from beyond the primary trade area.

appraisal The act or process of estimating value. It is an analysis, opinion, or conclusion relating to the nature, quality, value, or utility of specified interests in, or aspects of, identified real estate. As such, appraisal covers a variety of assignments including valuation, consulting, and appraisal review.

Appraisal Institute   The Appraisal Institute is an international membership association of professional real estate appraisers with more than 18,000 members and 99 chapters throughout the United States, Canada, and abroad. Its mission is to support and advance its members as the choice for real estate solutions, and uphold professional credentials, standards of professional practice, and ethics consistent with the public good.

appreciation   An increase in value due to the market forces of supply, demand, and inflationary trends. Because these market forces and trends are beyond the control of the investor, an increase in value due to appreciation is considered a passive form of increase in value. Appreciation occurs when there is excess demand for a property or a property type over and above the supply of the property or property type. When this market condition occurs, it is called *scarcity*.

ATCF   The acronym for after-tax cash flow.

base rent   For retail properties, it is the traditional and least complex method of setting the rent. It calls for the rent to be a fixed dollar amount per annum, payable monthly in advance. It may also be the basis for the calculation of additional or escalation rent. The primary disadvantage of a base rent–only lease is that it does not have an adjustment mechanism for inflation and, accordingly, represents an income stream with a decreasing purchasing power over time.

best and final offer   A *final* request from a seller of property, a real estate broker, or other authorized representative of the seller of a property for the *final* bid price and the terms of an offer relating to a property that has been presented for sale. Usually, there is an *initial call for offers*, followed by a *revised call for offers*, followed by a *best and final offer*. Offers usually are presented by the prospective purchaser via a letter of intent (LOI). Calls for offers are part of the offer-counteroffer process and a key component of negotiations for a property.

BOMA   The acronym for the Building Owners and Managers Association.

breakpoint   The sales threshold at which percentage rent payable commences. Determining what the breakpoint actually will be can be ascertained in various ways. It can be a natural breakpoint, which is determined by dividing a gross sales percentage into the base rent. Another variation would be a stepped-percentage lease whereby the percentage of gross sales applicable to the rental income decreases as gross sales increases.

broker   A person who for another and for compensation performs real estate services.

broker associate   A real estate classification used in some states to describe a person who is qualified to be issued a license as a broker but who still works for and is supervised by another broker and accordingly operates as a salesperson in the employ of another. Depending on the state, a broker associate may also be referred to as broker-salesperson, associate broker, or affiliate broker.

Building Owners and Managers Association (BOMA)   A primary source of information on office building development, leasing, building operating costs, energy consumption patterns, local and national building codes, legislation, occupancy statistics, and technological developments. BOMA publishes *Standard Method for Measuring Floor Area in Office Buildings*, recognized as an industry benchmark for over 75 years.

buyer's broker   The broker who works with a buyer. The buyer's broker is reffered to by various terms, including the *cooperating broker*, or the *selling broker*. The buyer's broker is either the agent of the buyer or the subagent of the seller.

buyer's market   Market conditions wherein buyers benefit from excess supply, relative to demand, and purchase their properties at a discount. In a buyer's market, prices are falling because demand is falling, relative to supply.

calls for offers   A request from a seller of property, a real estate broker, or other authorized representative of the seller of a property for bid price and the terms of an offer relating to a property that has been presented for sale. Usually, there is an *initial call for offers*, followed by a *revised call for offers*, followed by a *best and final offer*. Offers are usually presented by the prospective purchaser via a letter of intent (LOI). Calls for offers are part of the offer-counteroffer process and a key component of negotiations for a property.

CAM The acronym for common area maintenance.

capital The total amount of money from all sources available for a real estate acquisition. It is an amount of money available for investment.

capital assets Assets with two distinguishing characteristics: (1) they are used to produce income, and (2) they have a physical permanence. Real estate is a capital asset.

capital expenditure An investment to acquire or to improve real estate. The sum of money for investment may consist entirely of the investor's money, which is called *equity*. Alternatively, it may consist of a combination of equity and money borrowed from a lender, which is called *debt*.

capital markets Markets that deal in longer-term (greater than one year) mortgage obligations and equities.

capital market transaction A distinction made between the short-term and long-term equity (cash) and debt (including mortgage financing) markets. The main distinction is made between short-term markets for equity, debt, and financing that occur within money markets and long-term financing that occurs within capital markets.

capital recapture The return *of* equity from an investment as distinguished from the return *on* equity. Invested capital is usually recaptured through annual income and resale of the property at the conclusion of the investment.

capital stack Real estate jargon that describes the capital structure of a property. It describes the relative components, amounts, priority, and claims of traditional debt financing, mezzanine financing, and sources of equity that make up the capital structure of the property.

cash flow The income that remains each accounting period after all property-related revenues are netted against all property-related expenses, including deductions for mortgage debt service (financing), if appropriate.

CBD The acronym for central business district.

CCIM Institute An affiliate of the National Association of Realtors® (NAR). Practitioners holding the CCIM designation are recognized as experts in commercial investment real estate who work with commercial real estate users, owners, and investors. The CCIM designation is considered the most coveted and respected designation in commercial investment real estate.

CMBS loans Commercial real estate loans that are pooled together and transferred to a trust, which then issues securities based on the strength of the underlying mortgages. CMBS loans may offer borrowers more aggressive loans with higher loan-to-value ratios and lower debt-coverage ratios.

commercial real estate Any real estate that is required for the operation of a business enterprise or as a part of a business.

commercial real estate business Any business enterprise that provides the professional commercial real estate services to the buyers, sellers, and others who interact within the commercial real estate marketplace.

common area Part of the Urban Land Institute's established set of standards for retail building measurement. Common area is the total area within a retail property that is not designed for rental to tenants but that is available for common use by all tenants, their customers, and adjacent retailers. Common areas include parking areas, courtyards and plazas, sidewalks, landscaped areas, public restrooms, and truck and service facilities.

common area charges (CAM charges) The billing of a retail property's CAM expenses to tenants for recovery of the common area expenses.

common area maintenance expenses (CAM expenses) The operating expenses associated with maintaining a retail property's common areas.

community center A type of traditional shopping center that provides the convenience goods and personal services offered by a neighborhood center. Additionally, this type of center provides a wider range of soft lines (wearing apparel for men, women, and children) and hard lines (hardware and appliances). The community center makes merchandise available in a greater variety of sizes, styles, colors, and prices. Many centers are built around a junior department store, variety store, super–drugstore, or discount department store as the anchor tenant, in addition to a supermarket. Although a community center does not have a full-line department store, it may have a strong specialty store or stores. Its typical size is approximately 150,000 square feet of gross leasable area but, in practice, it may range from 100,000 to 300,000 or more square feet.

compensation Anything of value or a valuable consideration paid, promised, or expected to be paid or received.

competitive supply analysis A market analysis that identifies the supply of properties competitive with a subject property within a defined area. The analysis may also rank the competitive properties against a subject based on factors such as size, rental rates, operating expenses, net operating income, occupancy rates, location attributes, and amenities.

consulting The act or process of providing information, analysis of real estate data, and recommendations or conclusions on diversified problems in real estate, other than estimating value. Consulting assignments include land utilization studies, supply and demand studies, economic feasibility studies, highest and best use analyses, and marketability or investment considerations that relate to proposed or existing developments.

convenience center A type of traditional shopping center that provides for the sale of personal services and convenience goods similar to those of a neighborhood center. It contains a minimum of three stores with a total gross leasable area of up to 30,000 square feet. Instead of being anchored by a supermarket, a convenience center is usually anchored by some other type of personalconvenience service such as a minimarket.

correspondent lender Provides lending services on behalf of other lenders who desire to provide financing within a certain area but do not have a physical presence in that area. Also known as loan correspondents, they essentially negotiate a loan on behalf of another lender. Sources of financing for the correspondent lender include money center investment banking houses located in such markets as New York and Chicago, insurance companies, pension funds, and commercial banks. The correspondent lender originates loans on behalf of another lender through a process or system known as a correspondence system. Often, the correspondent will continue to service the loan for the lender and act as a collecting agent.

cost The amount of capital required to develop, build, or essentially create real estate. Cost concerns itself with land and improvements. Cost includes the expenditure for the four factors of production: land, labor, coordination, and capital.

cost-of-living adjusted rent (COLA rent) A popular method of rent escalation that is tied to changes in the consumer price index (CPI) or other specified index. In this method rent changes are tied to an outside price index and do not require internal justification.

Council of Real Estate Broker Managers An affiliate of the National Association of REALTORS®. The council confers the Certified Real Estate Brokerage Manager (CRB) designation, while continuously providing members with the educational, informational, and networking resources necessary to compete and succeed in the real estate marketplace.

Council of Residential Specialists An affiliate of the National Association of REALTORS®. The Certified Residential Specialist (CRS) is the highest designation awarded to sales associates in the residential sales field. The CRS designation recognizes professional accomplishments in both experience and education.

Counselors of Real Estate An affiliate of the National Association of REALTORS®. The Counselors of Real Estate (CRE) is a professional membership organization established exclusively for leading real property advisors. Members are awarded the CRE designation, bestowed by invitation only, in recognition of their achievements in real estate counseling.

cumulative attraction An increase in the total drawing power of a retail property. Cumulative attraction is created when complementary retail establishments locate next to each other so all the retailers can benefit from the increased number of customers drawn to the cluster of retail establishments. This market phenomenon encouraged the combination of complementary retail establishments into a clustered retail property. If the correct mix of retailers cluster together, they will tend to draw more total customer traffic as a whole than could be obtained individually. When this occurs the retailers are said to benefit from cumulative attraction.

DCR The acronym for debt-coverage ratio.

debt-coverage ratio (DCR) A basic yet important ratio that expresses the relationship of the annual net operating income to the annual debt service of the property. From a lender's perspective, the larger the DCR, the more of the property's operating income is available to pay annual debt service. Accordingly, DCRs are an important risk measure for lenders because the property is the primary source of income utilized for repayment of the loan. The formula for determining the debt-coverage ratio of a property is:

**Annual Operating Income ÷
Annual Debt Service = DCR**

demand The desire for goods and services.

depreciation An accounting concept that allows an investor to recover the cost of the real estate investment property. It provides an accounting deduction to the investor that allows for setting aside a sum each year that, together with the remaining salvage value of the improvements, at the end of the useful life of the real estate will allow the investor to purchase a replacement property.

depreciation allowance The amount of a noncash expense that is deducted from the property's income to write off the cost of the property. It is an expense only "on paper."

discount shopping center A specialty community shopping center that is anchored by a discount department store and is smaller than a regional mall. Discount shopping centers differ from other types of shopping centers because they are smaller than a regional mall, have a lower percentage of national or regional tenants, and have a higher percentage of local tenants. Discount shopping centers are generally oriented toward customers most comfortable making purchases in a discounted price range.

dual agent An agency relationship adopted by some states that has designated a category of service where an agent represents both the buyer and seller in a transaction as a dual agent.

economic obsolescence A loss in value that results from negative influences outside the site on which the property is located. These negative influences are caused by the market where the property is located and not the property itself. Economic obsolescence is usually beyond the control of the property owner and is usually not correctable.

effective demand Also referred to as *effective purchasing power*, it is the ability to purchase goods and services. Effective demand is the desire to buy combined with the ability to pay.

effective gross income The anticipated income from all operations of the real property after an allowance is made for vacancy and collection losses.

EGI The acronym for effective gross income.

equity The value of an ownership interest in property over and above all other claims against the property. These claims may be in the form of liens or mortgages. Equity may also be defined as the total value of a property less all other claims against the property.

equity buildup The change in equity that occurs over time. It is the increase in the equity investor's share of total property value. This increase results from gradual debt reduction through periodic repayment of principal on a mortgage loan, an increase in total property value, or both.

equity-debt ratio The ratio of the equity invested in a property to the amount of debt borrowed for that property. The equity-debt ratio is always described in relation to the total purchase price of the property, which may or may not be subject to adjustment for appreciation.

escalation rent For retail properties, it is an additional rent to be paid, over and above the base rent. Escalation rent is based on an escalation clause in a lease. Additional or escalation rent is based on increases in a predetermined index. These indexes are often referred to as cost-of-living adjustment indexes, or COLAs. Increases over and above the base rent occur when the cost-of-living index increases, usually annually.

exit Real estate jargon for exit strategy.

exit strategy Part of the jargon of real estate. An exit strategy concerns itself with the eventual sale or disposition of a real estate asset. It is an operating framework that addresses the investor's objective and purpose of the real estate investment by providing a viable scenario, or alternative scenarios, through which an orderly sale of the property will occur. An exit strategy concerns itself with reversion. An exit strategy is also called an exit.

fashion shopping center A specialty shopping center that contains a concentration of apparel shops, boutiques, and custom shops that carry special, high-quality merchandise. A fashion center includes a mixture of both smaller international boutiques and larger national, higher-quality fashion stores. Fashion centers are generally oriented toward customers most comfortable making purchases in an upper-price range.

FE The acronym for fixed expenses.

feasibility study A study of the cost-versus-benefit relationship of a real estate endeavor. It includes a marketability analysis. It analyzes whether a property will meet the objectives of a developer, lender, or investor. It is utilized to determine if a development is economically feasible and, if so, estimate the rate of return obtainable by that development. Feasibility studies are usually a prerequisite to any actual development or development funding.

festival center A specialty shopping center that contains stores that sell impulse goods, either exclusively or as a high percentage of their total merchandise mix. A large portion of its gross leasable area is devoted to restaurants and food vendors that offer ethnic authenticity and uniqueness. Frequently there is a blend of on-site food service and specialty food retailing. A festival center may also have a strong entertainment theme. Festival centers are generally oriented toward customers most comfortable making purchases in a mid-priced range.

fiduciary relationship A relationship of trust and confidence that results in a moral and legal obligation between a principal and the broker.

financial institution An organization in the business of holding cash and other assets on behalf of others. Examples of financial institutions include commercial banks, savings associations, credit unions, insurance companies, pension funds, and investment companies.

Financial Institutions Reform, Recovery, and Enforcement Act ("FIRREA") Act that restructured the savings and loan association regulatory system and was enacted in response to the savings and loan (S&L) crisis of the 1980s. The act provided regulatory guidelines for federally related transactions, which are any real estate–related financial transactions in which a federal financial institution is involved.

financial intermediaries Financial institutions that act as "middlemen" between depositors and borrowers.

FIRREA The acronym for Financial Institutions Reform, Recovery, and Enforcement Act.

fixed expenses (FE) Those recurring periodic expenditures that are usually unaffected by the level of occupancy and that would continue even if the property were totally vacant. Traditional examples of fixed operating expenses include real estate (property) taxes and property insurance.

flat rent A lease provision for fixed rental payments during the term of the lease. Flat rent is considered the traditional and least complex method of setting the rent. It calls for the rent to be a fixed dollar amount per annum, payable monthly in advance. The primary disadvantage of a flat lease is that it does not have an adjustment mechanism for inflation and, accordingly, represents an income stream with a decreasing purchasing power over time.

functional obsolescence A loss in value that results from deficiencies or overimprovements. These negative influences are caused by the property itself and not the market in which the property is located. Functional obsolescence may or may not be economically correctable or "curable."

GBA The acronym for gross building area.

GLA The acronym for gross leasable area.

government office building A building in which most of the office space is used or marketed for use by government.

gross building area (GBA) Part of the Urban Land Institute's established set of standards for retail building measurement. Gross building area is determined by computing the entire square footage contained within the exterior walls, including the building envelope. A retail property's gross building area is measured as the distance between the outer surfaces of the buildings exterior walls.

gross construction area Part of BOMA's standards of floor measurement for office buildings. Also referred to as gross building area or GBA, it is determined by computing the entire square footage within the floor's perimeter, excluding the building envelope. The gross construction area must be determined, even though it is not used in leasing, because it affects the cost of tenant installations.

gross leasable area (GLA) Part of the Urban Land Institute's established set of standards for retail building measurement. Gross leaseable area is the total floor area designed for a retail tenant's occupancy and exclusive use. This area includes any basement, mezzanines, or upper floors of the retailer's space. Gross leasable area is measured from the centerline of joint partitions that face outward toward the outside wall.

gross lease A retail lease in which the ownerlandlord pays the operating expenses. The ownerlandlord receives rent and is obligated to pay all or most of the operating expenses of the property from the rent received. Gross leases may incorporate a stop clause that would allow for an expense stop that sets a maximum limit on the amount of the operating expense to be paid by the landlord. Any amount above this maximum limit would then be the responsibility of the tenant.

hard money up Part of real estate jargon, it refers to good faith, binder, and other earnest money that has been advanced by a prospective purchaser of real property and deposited in an escrow account as part of the good and valuable consideration of a contemplated sales transaction. These funds are nonrefundable to the prospective purchaser.

highest and best use study A study that seeks the reasonably probable and legal use of either vacant land or an improved property that is physically possible, appropriately supported, financially feasible, and results in the highest value. Highest and best use studies incorporate feasibility analysis.

HVAC The acronym for heating, ventilation, and air-conditioning.

hypermarket A horizontally integrated community shopping center in which typical retail establishments, such as a supermarket, drugstore, apparel store, and general merchandise store, are operated by a single owner under one roof. Such centers have a centralized checkout for all goods and enter market areas offering a quasimonopoly position. Discount shopping centers are generally oriented toward customers most comfortable making bulk purchases in a discounted price range.

impulse goods Products that shoppers do not actively or consciously seek. They are purchased without a prior decision to shop for them.

information superhighway The network of rapidly evolving telecommunication systems that connect people all over the world to each other, and to businesses, information, and government agencies. This network is vital for businesses to remain competitive and, accordingly, these technologies are provided as amenities.

Institute of Real Estate Management (IREM) An affiliate of the National Association of REALTORS®. IREM offers the only comprehensive program exclusively developed for property and asset managers working with large portfolios of all property types. IREM confers the Certified Property Manager (CPM) designation, which is considered to be the industry's premier real estate management credential.

institutional-grade or institutional-quality real estate Usually the best real estate in class, quality, location, and income within any given market.

institutional investors These include large national pension funds, insurance companies, private real estate entities, and the advisors who provide acquisition services to those investors. They invest and manage the most "pristine" of real estate, which is usually the most marketable and demanded within any given market. Individual transaction sizes can range in the hundreds of millions of dollars and total portfolio assets managed can reach into the billions of dollars. Because institutional real estate is considered best in class, quality, location, and income, it is also considered to possess less risk than noninstitutional real estate.

intermediation A process in which "middlemen" accumulate, combine, and consolidate a number of smaller, individual equity accounts for the purpose of either lending or investing in real estate properties. Due to their size and vast deposit base, these intermediaries can provide financing or investment funds for larger, more complex, more management- and capital-intensive real estate properties.

investment analysis A process by which the attractiveness of an investment is determined by analyzing the costs and benefits utilizing time, the value of money, and the use of various ratios. Investment analysis incorporates the results of feasibility analysis and highest and best use analysis.

IREM The acronym for Institute of Real Estate Management.

letter of intent A preliminary written agreement summarizing the basis on which the buyer and seller plan to commit to a binding contract to acquire property. Usually the letter of intent is not binding.

leverage The effect that borrowed funds have on investment returns. Leverage may increase or decrease the investor's return that would otherwise be received on an all-cash basis.

liquidity The ability of an asset value to be converted into an equivalent cash amount. The long-term nature of commercial real estate investments is consistent with its illiquid conversion characteristics. Usually, as a property increases in size so does its complexity and value. These characteristics further impede the cash convertibility of real estate. Due to these factors, the total value of a real estate investment is usually not immediately convertible to cash without a loss in value. This characteristic of real estate makes it a nonliquid or illiquid asset

listing broker   A broker who represents a seller in a real estate transaction.

loan servicing   The collection of payments that include principal, interest, taxes, and insurance on a note from a borrower in accordance with the terms of the note. Servicing also includes accounting, bookkeeping, and preparation of insurance and tax records, loan payment follow-up, and delinquency follow-up and loan analysis. A servicing agreement is usually written and includes the obligations of both parties. Servicing fees vary widely and some lenders place a maximum on annual servicing income from one mortgage.

loan-to-value ratio (LTV ratio)   A basic yet important ratio that expresses the relationship of borrowed funds as a percentage of the value of the property. From a lender's perspective, the LTV is usually the lesser of the acquisition price or the appraised value of property. Accordingly, LTVs are an important risk measure for lenders because the property is usually pledged as security for the loan. The formula for determining the loan-to-value ratio is:

$$\text{Loan} \div \text{Value} = \text{LTV ratio}$$

LOI   The acronym for letter of intent.

loss factor   Part of BOMA's standards of floor measurement for office buildings. A loss factor is the difference between rentable and usable area. The rentable area less the useable area is equal to the loss factor in square feet. The useable area divided by the rentable area is equal to the loss factor percentage.

LTV   The acronym for loan-to-value ratio.

market   A gathering of people for the buying and selling of things.

market analysis   The study of real estate market conditions for a specific property type. Simply stated, market analysis is the study of real estate market conditions.

market share   The portion of effective demand that is captured by a particular property. Market share represents captured demand.

marketability study   An investigation of how a particular property will be absorbed, leased, or sold under current or anticipated market conditions. It includes a market study or analysis of the general class of property being studied. It examines the marketability of a given property or class of property, usually focusing on the market segment(s) in which the property is likely to generate demand. Marketability studies are used in determining the economic feasibility of alternative uses and the highest and best use of property.

MCRS   The acronym for modified accelerated cost recovery system.

medical office building   A building in which most of the office space is used or marketed for medical office activities.

mezzanine equity   Capital provided to "fill the gap" between the senior first mortgage loan and the owner's equity investment in a property acquisition. Because equity is not debt, the equity does not impact the loan-to-value ratio.

modified accelerated cost recovery system (MCRS)   The accelerated depreciation system adopted under the Tax Reform Act of 1986.

money markets   Those markets that deal in financial instruments with a maturity (when it comes due, or the time frame) of less than one year.

mortgage   A conveyance of an interest in real property that is given as security for the payment of the loan.

mortgage banker   An individual who can originate, close, and service a loan. Mortgage bankers can provide short-term, interim, and long-term financing. Mortgage bankers utilize their own funds or they may borrow funds from other commercial sources for the mortgage financing. Accordingly, mortgage bankers are not the ultimate lender in the transaction.

mortgage broker   An individual who brings a borrower of funds and a lender of funds together for the purpose of providing financing. Mortgage brokers are intermediaries.

mortgage brokerage fee   A fee charged by a broker for brokering a loan.

mortgage note   A written promise to pay back the money borrowed from the lender. It contains the specific terms and conditions, such as the length of the loan, the interest rate to be charged, and when the money is to be repaid. It is secured by a mortgage.

multiple-tenant building A building in which the space is occupied by more than one tenant.

NAR The acronym for the National Association of REALTORS®.

National Association of REALTORS® (NAR) America's largest trade association, representing approximately one million members—including NAR's institutes, societies, and councils—involved in all aspects of the residential and commercial real estate industries. NAR's membership is composed of residential and commercial REALTORS®, who are brokers, salespeople, property managers, appraisers, counselors, and others engaged in all aspects of the real estate industry.

National Real Estate Investors Association (NREIA) A federation made up of local associations or investment clubs throughout the United States. The NREIA is an association of real estate professionals, including local investor associations, property owner associations, apartment associations, and landlord associations, on a national scale. The NREIA represents the interests of over 20,000 members across the United States and is the largest broad-based organization dedicated to the individual investor.

negative leverage A condition that occurs when the interest rate charged by a lender for borrowed funds is greater than the rate of return that an investment is capable of generating on those borrowed funds. Accordingly, investors are incurring a loss on the borrowed funds.

neighborhood center A type of traditional shopping center that provides for the sale of convenience goods (food, drugs, and sundries) and personal services (laundry and dry cleaning, barbering, shoe repair, etc.) for the day-to-day living needs of the immediate neighborhood. It is built around a supermarket as the principal tenant, and typically contains a gross leasable area of about 50,000 square feet. In practice, it may range in size from 30,000 to over 100,000 square feet.

net lease A lease in which the tenant pays some or all of the operating expenses, in addition to rent requirements. Accordingly, the rent paid is "net" of expenses. When referring to a retail tenant's obligations for operating expenses, net leases are often referred to by how "net" the lease is. Specifically these types of lease may be single net, double net, triple net, or absolute net. The difference between these types of leases is what expenses the tenant will pay. A retail lease in which the tenant is responsible for its pro-rata share of property real estate taxes is referred to as a net lease or *single net lease*.

net-net lease Also referred to as a *double net lease;* a retail lease in which the tenant is responsible for its pro-rata share of property real estate taxes and property insurance.

net-net-net lease Also referred to as a *triple net lease;* a retail lease in which the tenant is responsible for its pro-rata share of property real estate taxes, property insurance, and property common area maintenance (CAM).

net operating income (NOI) The income that remains after all operating expenses are deducted from effective gross income but before mortgage debt service and depreciation are considered. It can be calculated before or after deducting replacement reserves, depending on what is considered customary for a property type or market area.

NOI The acronym for net operating income.

noninstitutional real estate All real estate assets other than institutional real estate assets. There is usually more risk associated with noninstitutional real estate.

nonstabilized property A property that is nonstabilized in one or more of the following areas: income, expenses, occupancy, and value.

NREIA The acronym for the National Real Estate Investors Association.

OE The acronym for operating expenses.

office building A building that contains office space. It is a building in which most of the space is used or marketed for office activities. The purpose of having the office space is to provide a place where a specific type of work activity can occur—professional- and business-related work activity.

office building class The sum total of a building's age, location, building material, building systems, amenities, lease rates and terms, occupancy, tenant profile, and management. Office buildings are "classified" according to their unique combination of these characteristics. These characteristics are simply summed up to provide an opinion of a building's class. Theses classes were established by the Urban

Land Institute and have become an internationally recognized benchmark for describing a building.

office nodes Clusters of suburban office buildings forming a separate and distinct suburban-downtown CBD within the particular suburb. These office nodes offer high-quality office space at a lower rental rate than comparable space within the historical CBD. Suburban office buildings tend to be developed in clusters or nodes, and this clustering has further evolved into the development of planned suburban business parks.

off-price and factory outlet shopping center Two different types of specialty shopping center concepts combined into one property. An off-price retailer functions as a discount store that sells brand-name merchandise at lower prices than can be found elsewhere. A factory outlet retailer is owned and operated by the manufacturer and sells goods directly to the public. Off-price and factory outlet shopping centers offer better-quality merchandise than discount stores and are generally oriented toward customers most comfortable making purchases in an upper price range.

operating expenses (OE) The recurring periodic expenditures necessary to maintain the property and continue production of revenues. There are three categories of operating expenses: (1) fixed expenses, (2) variable expenses, and (3) replacement allowances.

opportunity cost The theoretical cost associated with selecting one investment opportunity as compared to another. It is the theoretical cost associated with investment options foregone once another investment option or options have been selected.

origination fee A fee charged by a lender for making a loan.

parking area Part of the Urban Land Institute's established set of standards for retail building measurement. Parking area refers to the space devoted to car parking, including on-site roadways, aisles, stalls, islands, parking structures, and all other features incidental to parking. Parking areas are part of common area.

parking index Part of the Urban Land Institue's established set of standards for retail building measurement. Parking index refers to the number of car parking spaces made available per 1,000 square feet of GLA. Parking index is the standard comparison used to indicate the relationship between the number of parking spaces and the GLA.

percentage rent For retail properties, it is rental income received in accordance with the terms of a percentage clause in a lease. Rent, or a portion of it, represents a specified percentage of the volume of retail sales or retail profitability achieved by the tenant. Typically a retail store tenant will pay percentage rent based on a certain percentage of its retail sales volume. Accordingly, the obligation of the tenant to pay additional rent to the landlord only occurs when a predetermined percentage of gross sales is achieved. Percentage rent clauses in a lease usually consider a threshold level of sales that the tenant must reach prior to the commencement of percentage rent. This threshold level of sales is referred to a breakpoint. A breakpoint is the sales threshold at which percentage rent payable commences. Determining what the breakpoint actually will be can be ascertained in various ways. For example, it may be a natural breakpoint, which is determined by dividing a gross sales percentage into the base rent. Another variation would be a stepped percentage lease whereby the percentage of gross sales applicable to the rental income decreases as gross sales increases.

PGI The acronym for potential gross income.

pipeline Real estate jargon that is used to describe the future supply of a property type allocated by year of expected completion to the marketplace. Also referred to as *supply pipeline*.

positive leverage A condition that occurs when the rate of return that an investment generates is greater than the interest rate charged by a lender for borrowed funds that are utilized to acquire that investment. Accordingly, investors are generating a profit on the borrowed funds.

potential gross income The total income attributable to real property at full occupancy before vacancy and collection losses and operating expenses are deducted.

power center A type of super–community center. It contains at least four category-specific, off-price anchors of 20,000 or more square feet. These anchors typically emphasize hard goods, such as consumer electronics, sporting goods, office supplies, home furnishings, home improvement goods, bulk foods, drugs, health and beauty aids, toys, and personal computer hardwaresoftware. They tend to be narrowly focused but deeply merchandised "category killers" together with the more broadly merchandised, price-oriented warehouse club and discount department stores. Anchors in power centers typically occupy 85 percent or more of the total gross leasable area.

pretax cash flow (PTCF) The portion of net operating income that remains after mortgage debt service (financing) is paid but before income tax on property operations is deducted.

property enhancements Improvements and upgrades to the property and its operations that are implemented by the property owner. The goal of property enhancements is to cause an increase in property value.

price The amount of money that the real estate will sell for in the marketplace. It is the amount of money a purchaser of real estate is willing to pay for the property.

primary trade area (PTA) Part of a trade area surrounding a retail property. A primary trade area may be described in three ways: in terms of (1) travel time, (2) percentage of total customers, or (3) percentage of total sales. These three defined areas are estimated individually and then overlaid one upon another. The common area where they overlap is considered the property's PTA, so while there is a relationship between these three criteria, they may not result in the same areas.

principal The person who engages a broker to perform a service of real estate. The principal is the broker's employer. This client, who actually employs the broker to perform some real estate–related service, may be referred to as the broker's principal.

PTA The acronym for primary trade area.

PTCF The acronym for pretax cash flow.

rate of return on capital An amount measured in terms of an interest rate. Each year of the investment, it is expected to generate a measurable return at a certain rate of interest. However, because the income may fluctuate from one year to the next, so will the rate of interest. The rate of interest that the investment generates during the entire investment period is called a yield rate.

Real Estate Buyer's Agent Council (REBAC) An affiliate of the National Association of REALTORS®. The Real Estate Buyer's Agent Council is the world's largest association of real estate professionals focusing specifically on represent-

ing the real estate buyer. REBAC awards the Accredited Buyer's Representative (ABR) and the Accredited Buyer's Representative Manager (ABRM) designations.

real estate counseling Providing competent, disinterested, and unbiased advice, professional guidance, and sound judgment on diversified problems in the broad field of real estate involving any and all segments of the business, such as merchandising, leasing, management, planning, financing, appraising, court testimony, and other similar services. Counseling may involve the utilization of any or all of these services.

real estate investment banker An individual or business that can provide the services of a loan underwriter, provide sources of capital, and act as a real estate broker for individual clients or businesses. Known within the industry as I-bankers, they may act as an intermediary between a lender and a borrower, with similarities to the mortgage brokerage business. They may act as a real estate broker, with similarities to the real estate brokerage business. They may provide valuation services, with similarities to the appraisal business. They may provide advisory services to clients, with similarities to real estate counseling business. Ideally, investment bankers will strive to provide most, if not all, of these services during the same transaction or engagement thereby offering comprehensive transaction services. I-bankers can provide real estate sales, real estate markets, capital markets, and related support services, and are subject to appropriate state laws, including license law.

real estate market A gathering of individuals who are in contact with one another to buy and sell real property rights for money and other assets. A real estate market may also be described in terms of individuals, groups, or firms that are in contact with one another to conduct real estate transactions. Market participants often use the terms *real estate market*, *the market for real estate*, and *the market* interchangeably.

REALTORS® Land Institute An affiliate of the National Association of REALTORS®. The REALTORS® Land Institute is the only branch of the REALTOR® family focused on land brokerage transactions of five specialized types: (1) farms and ranches, (2) undeveloped tracts of land, (3) transitional and development land, (4) subdivision and wholesaling of lots, and (5) site selection and assemblage of land parcels.

regional center A type of traditional shopping center that provides general merchandise, apparel, furniture, and home furnishings in depth and variety, as well as a range of services and recreational facilities. It is built around one or two full-line department stores of generally not less than 50,000 square feet. Its typical size is approximately 500,000 square feet of gross leasable area. In practice, it may range from 250,000 to more than 900,000 square feet. The regional center provides services typical of a business district yet not as extensive as those of the super-regional center.

rentable area Part of BOMA's standards of floor measurement for office buildings. It is a generally accepted formula that a proportionate share of core space is added to the usable space of each tenant on the floor. The public elevators and stair space are usually excluded in making these calculations. In buildings where the heating, ventilating, and air-conditioning (HVAC) system is located in the basement or on the roof, the rentable area is identical with the useable area. However, in some office buildings, the HVAC may occupy one or more floors between the basement and the roof. The space is not rentable but its gross construction area is apportioned to the rentable office floors serviced by the HVAC equipment and is considered part of their rentable space.

replacement reserves (RR) Amortized periodic expenditures of major property components that have a useful life of more than a year but are wearing away each year. All building components wear out over time. The period of time that a building component is expected to wear out is called its estimated useful life. A replacement reserve accounts for those building components that wear out faster than others. These building components include the building, everything that is contained within and attached to the building, and any site improvements. However, land does not depreciate or wear out and, accordingly, the allocated cost of land is excluded from a replacement reserve. Replacement reserves are also known as replacement allowances, reserves for replacements, and reserves.

Resolution Trust Corporation (RTC) A corporation formed by Congress in 1989 to replace the Federal Savings and Loan Insurance Corporation and respond to the insolvencies of about 750 savings and loan associations. As receiver, it sold assets of failed S&Ls and paid insured depositors. In 1995 its duties, including insurance of deposits in thrift institutions, were transferred to the Savings Association Insurance Fund.

retail building A building that contains retail space. The purpose of having the retail space is to provide a place where a specific type of business activity can occur—retail sales and related business activities.

retailing Any business involving the sale of goods, commodities, and products in small quantities directly to consumers.

return of capital The return of the capital invested in real estate. The return of capital originates from two sources: a property's income and a property's reversion. The income component of the return of capital consists of the income stream created by the investment. The reversion component of the return of capital consists of the net proceeds from the sale of the investment at the conclusion of the investor's holding period.

return on capital Additional received money for the use of an investor's capital until it is returned.

reversion A lump-sum payment that an investor receives at the conclusion of an investment.

risk The probability that foreseen events will not occur.

RR The acronym for replacement reserves.

RTC The acronym for Resolution Trust Corporation.

sales associate A person who performs real estate services for compensation but who does so under the direction, control, or management of a licensed real estate broker. The sales associate is employed, either directly or indirectly, by a licensed broker. The sales associate can carry out only those responsibilities assigned to him by the supervising broker. Depending on the state, a sales associate may also be referred to as salesperson or associate licensee.

scarcity The present or anticipated undersupply of a property or property type relative to the demand for it. Scarcity usually leads an increase in value called appreciation.

secondary mortgage market The market in which existing mortgages and mortgage-backed securities are bought and sold.

secondary trade area (STA) The area immediately surrounding the primary trade area. Secondary trade areas are always viewed by their relative location to the adjoining PTA. A secondary trade area may be described in three ways: in terms of (1) travel time, (2) percentage of total customers, or (3) percentage of total sales. These three defined areas are estimated individually and then overlaid one upon another. The common area where they overlap is considered the property's STA, so while there is a relationship between these three criteria, they may not result in the same areas.

seller's market Market conditions wherein sellers of property benefit from excess demand, relative to supply, and sell their properties at a premium. In a seller's market, prices are rising because supply is becoming scarce, relative to demand.

selling broker The broker who works with a buyer. The selling broker is referred to by various terms including the *cooperating broker* or the *buyer's broker*. The selling broker is either the agent of the buyer or the subagent of the seller.

shopping center A clustering of retailers within one property. This retail property is designed and developed to be owned, leased, and managed as a one entity. If the shopping center is to be successful, it must address the type of retailers that best serve its trade area, as well as the size and location of the property. Because shopping centers are expected to have increased drawing power, they must also provide for increased on-site parking, pedestrian-friendly walkways, and building flexibility relating to the types and sizes of stores.

shop tenants Local area tenants that occupy space within a retail property.

single-tenanted building A building in which the space is occupied by one tenant.

smart building A term used to describe buildings that offer the very latest systems available for fully integrated broadband communications service, high-speed Internet access, and data network service. These buildings also offer state-of-the-art security systems. Office building entrances, elevators, and parking garages are access controlled with a card key or fingerprint reader. Security cameras monitor property entrances, common areas, elevators, garages, and restricted areas. The building's heating, ventilation, and air-conditioning systems employ the latest technologies and are geared to ensure complete tenant comfort and reliability. Smart buildings offer flexibility of use to accommodate future market and tenant preferences.

Society of Industrial and Office Realtors An affiliate of the National Association of Realtors®. The society certifies its members with the prestigious specialist, industrial and office real estate (SIOR) designation, a professional symbol of the highest level of knowledge, production, and ethics in the commercial real estate industry. Designees specialize in industrial, office, sales manager, or advisory services categories.

soft money up Real estate jargon referring to good faith, binder, and other earnest money that has been advanced by a prospective purchaser of real property and deposited in an escrow account as part of the good and valuable consideration of a contemplated sales transaction. Until such time as these funds are nonrefundable to the prospective purchaser, they are considered soft.

specialty goods Products that a shopper will examine more carefully and make a greater effort to purchase.

specialty shopping center A shopping center that is characterized by a lack of a traditional anchor tenant. The role of the anchor will be filled by another type of tenant or by a group of tenants that when clustered together will function as an anchor tenant.

STA The acronym for secondary trade area.

stabilized property A property that has the characteristics of stabilized income, stabilized expenses, stabilized occupancy, and stabilized value.

standards of floor measurement A set of standards for office building measurement established by the Building Owners and Managers Association (BOMA). These measurement standards are used in most areas nationally and measure office buildings in terms of gross construction area, usable area, and rentable area.

step-up rent An additional increment of rent to be paid at specific dates during the lease. This lease provision has the benefit of its simplicity.

stop clause A provision in a lease that calls for the tenant to pay a fair share of increases in some or all of the building operating expenses. Operating expenses are established, fixed, and "stopped" by a stop clause in the base year of tenant occupancy. In subsequent years to the base year, any increases in operating expenses are allocated in proportion or pro rata to the tenants on the basis of their rentable space.

straight-line depreciation A depreciation method in which the depreciable part of the real estate asset, estimated at cost or some other basis, is written off in equal annual amounts over the estimated useful life of the asset.

super-regional center A type of traditional shopping center that offers extensive variety in general merchandise, apparel, furniture, and home furnishings, as well as a variety of services and recreational facilities. It is built around three or more full-line department stores generally not less than 75,000 square feet each. The typical size of a super-regional center is about 1,000,000 square feet of gross leasable area. In practice, the size ranges from approximately 500,000 to more than 1,500,000 square feet.

supply The amount of a type of real estate available for sale or lease at various prices in a given market at a given time. Accordingly, supply is type, location, and time sensitive.

take-out buyer A buyer's commitment to acquire a property contingent upon an event such as completion of construction or stabilization at a future date.

take-out commitment A lender's commitment to provide financing when a building or other improvement on real estate is completed.

tax shelter An investment feature of real estate that provides relief from income taxes or allows the investor to claim deductions from taxable income.

teaser letter Real estate jargon for an introductory marketing letter that briefly introduces a property for sale to prospective buyers, provides the property's benefits, and invites the reader to request additional information.

total floor space Part of the Urban Land Institute's established set of standards for retail building measurement. Total floor area comprises all areas held by the center owner and any areas that are independently managed or owned but that are physically a part of the shopping center. It includes GLA and all other enclosed space in the shopping center, as well as outparcels.

trade area The geographical area that surrounds a retail property. Trade areas are further separated into primary or secondary trade areas.

transaction agent A designated category of service where the broker represents neither the buyer nor the seller in a transaction, rather treating both as customers. In some cases there is only one broker involved. Transaction agency is actually a nonagency relationship.

ULI The acronym for the Urban Land Institute.

uncertainty The probability that unforeseen events will occur.

underwrite A process of analysis of commercial real estate. From a sales transaction perspective, underwriting refers to the preparation of a summary or detailed report, called an offering memorandum, relating to the prospective sale of the property. From a financing perspective, underwriting refers to the preparation of a report, called an underwriting memorandum, relating to such uses as the prospective financing of the property in connection with a proposed loan, an infusion of equity capital, or a capital restructuring.

upside down Real estate jargon for a capital structure of a property whereby the debt component exceeds the property market value or property sales price.

Urban Land Institute Organization that provides responsible leadership in the use of land to enhance the total environment. Founded in 1936, the institute now has more than 25,000 members worldwide representing the entire spectrum of land use and real estate development disciplines, working in private enterprise and public service. As the preeminent multidisciplinary real estate forum, ULI facilitates the open exchange of ideas, information, and experience among local, national, and international industry leaders and policymakers dedicated to creating better places.

ULI's practice program is interdisciplinary and practical, focusing on trends and the basics of many different parts of the industry, including resort and residential, retail and destination development, office and industrial development, transportation and parking, real estate finance, and capital markets. In local communities, ULI district councils bring together a variety of stakeholders to find solutions and build consensus around land use and development challenges.

useable area Part of BOMA's standards of floor measurement for office buildings. On a multilevel floor, usable area is gross construction area minus core space. Core space includes the square footage used for such areas as lobbies, public corridors, stairways, bathrooms, elevators, electrical and janitorial closets, fan rooms, and mechanical system rooms for generators and HVAC. On a floor occupied by a single tenant, corridors and bathrooms are considered part of the usable area. GBA less core space is equal to useable area.

V&C The acronym for vacancy and collection loss.

vacancy and collection loss (V&C) An allowance for reductions in potential gross income attributable to vacancies, nonpayment of rents, and releasing of space.

value The worth of real estate as measured by its monetary equivalent within the real estate market. To a real estate investor, the value today represents the present worth of the anticipated future benefits associated with that real estate.

variable expense (VE) Those recurring periodic expenditures that usually vary in relation to the level of occupancy and may decline or discontinue if the property were totally vacant. Traditional examples of variable expenses include management fees, administrative charges, payroll, advertising and promotion, telephone, utilities (including water, sewer, and electric), trash removal, repairs and maintenance, general supplies, pool maintenance, landscape maintenance, and pest control, among others.

VE The acronym for variable expense.

INDEX